# VOLUNTEER

## A TRAVELLER'S GUIDE TO MAKING
## A DIFFERENCE AROUND THE WORLD

D0107871

# CONTENTS

# AUTHORS

## Charlotte Hindle
**Coordinating Author, International Volunteering: an Overview, Choosing Your Volunteer Experience, The Practicalities, Coming Home**

 Charlotte has written numerous newspaper and travel articles on volunteering and organised debates and talks on the subject. She has worked on Lonely Planet's *The Career Break Book*, *The Travel Writing Book* and *The Gap Year Book*, updating the volunteering and conservation material for the latter.

## Rachel Collinson
**Do-it-Yourself Volunteer Placements**

 While at university, during career breaks and in life in general, Rachel has spent many an hour volunteering. This includes working in a home for street children in Ecuador and visiting foreign nationals imprisoned for drug trafficking.

## Nate Cavalieri
**Organised Volunteer Programmes**

 Nate has volunteered at the Pop Wuj School in Guatemala, with the American Red Cross in the Gulf Coast and across Europe, Central and North America.

## Korina Miller
**Structured & Self-Funding Volunteer Programmes, Religious Organisations and Start Your Own Charitable Project**

 Korina has volunteered in rural Uttar Pradesh and with remote tribal communities in Jharkhand. She also worked with minorities in southwest China on a sustainable tourism development project; ran an Asian arts charity in Vancouver, worked as a children's writing coach for a Canadian charity and managed an intercultural arts charity in London.

## Mike Richard
**All information for American volunteers**

 Mike has worked and played in Honolulu, studied Japanese in Hakodate, taught English in Shanghai and served as a TEFL Volunteer with the United States Peace Corps in Romania.

## Sarah Wintle
**Tying Up Loose Ends, all information for Australian volunteers**

 Sarah worked in conservation while serving a year-long youth ambassador role in Laos as part of the Australian Volunteers for International Development.

# EXPERT ADVISORS

### Katherine Tubb

 Katherine founded an international volunteer agency that places individual volunteers into development NGOs in Africa, Latin America and Asia. She has also volunteered with VSO in Nepal, and has a masters in development studies from the London School of Economics.

### Dr Kate Simpson

 Dr Kate Simpson has spent years researching and working in the international volunteering industry. She has written extensively about gap years and international volunteering and has completed a PhD on these subjects at Newcastle University. Currently, she works as Commercial & Operations Director with Wasafiri Consulting, which works to improve governance, build productive markets and create stronger more resilient communities across Africa.

### Paul Goodyer

 CEO of Nomad Travel Stores and Travel Clinics (www.nomadtravel. co.uk), Paul has been travelling since he was 17. He and his wife set up a charitable project called Karmi Farm in the the foothills of the Himalayas, which operates as a medical clinic for the local hill farmers of Darjeeling and Sikkim province. Paul advised on the 'What To Take' and 'Health & Hygiene' sections of this book.

### Anthony Lunch

 Anthony taught in The Gambia as a volunteer with VSO in the 1960s. He went on to hold senior positions in corporate finance and international trade development before being appointed to the VSO Executive Council for seven years. In 2001, after becoming deeply involved with the village of Sermathang durng travels in Nepal, he set up MondoChallenge (www.mondochallenge. org), which focuses on career breakers and older volunteers.

### Matt Phillips

 Matt spent countless hours researching volunteering organisations around the globe for this book. When he's not managing Lonely Planet's sub-Saharan Africa content as a Destination Editor in London, he's writing about everything from epic adventures to responsible travel in Africa, Asia, Europe and the Americas.

# 01

International
Volunteering:
an Overview

'Time is money'. How often have you heard that said? Perhaps it came to mind as you spent yet another late night in the office trying to meet a deadline; or perhaps you work in a profession where your time is billed in blocks of 15 minutes. Maybe you've just retired, having worked hard for years in return for an annual salary. Unless you're a professional parent, the chances are you're used to being paid for the work you do. And, whatever your circumstances, you probably consider your time a precious commodity.

So, why give your time for free? Or, as is the case with the majority of international volunteering opportunities, why pay for the privilege of working for nothing? This chapter offers a broad cross-section of answers to these questions.

'Think globally, act locally' was a phrase coined in 1972 by René Dubos, an adviser to the UN Conference on the Human Environment. Although the phrase initially referred to looking after our environment, it touched a global nerve and came to mean acting locally in any worthwhile capacity. Then, 12 years later, Bob Geldof and Midge Ure formed Band Aid and challenged the world not only to 'think' globally but 'act' globally as well, and raised money for famine relief in Ethiopia. Whatever you think of this campaign (and subsequent ones such as Make Poverty History), the actions of Geldof and Ure ignited high-level debate about world inequality. The ongoing efforts of many ensure that such imbalances are kept in the global media spotlight.

Buying coloured wristbands and donating money via text message from the comfort of your lounge room to send abroad is one thing. Actually giving up your time and going to another part of the world to contribute your knowledge, skills or labour is quite another. But this is exactly what an increasing number of people around the globe are choosing to do with their holidays, during gap years, on career breaks, or upon retirement.

However, the more popular international volunteering becomes, the more difficult it is to pinpoint where to go, what to do and which organisation you want to volunteer with. For starters, the sheer number of volunteering opportunities today can be overwhelming. Then there's the problem that not all volunteering is good volunteering. There are plenty of volunteer organisations that are not meeting or responding to local needs, not working in proper partnership with host communities and certainly not working towards sustainable solutions. And, let's face it, no-one wants to become that volunteer who has just built a bridge where no bridge was needed.

Volunteering abroad should be the best thing you've ever done, but the onus is on you to act responsibly, do the research and find a volunteer programme that works both for you and for the host community. This book aims to equip you with all the tools to do just that.

One volunteer, Linda Walsh, who worked with street children in Rio de Janeiro for Task Brasil (p210), urges:

*Go and volunteer. Love the experience, even when there are times when you feel unappreciated, tired, fed up or lost with the language. No matter what, if you throw yourself whole-heartedly into it you will love it and it will do more for you than you could ever imagine.*

As Clodagh O'Brien, who volunteered in Borneo with the Orangutan Foundation UK (p220), succinctly puts it:

*Every insect bite, cut, argument and awful bus journey was well worth it.*

## WHY VOLUNTEER?

This is a good question and one you need to think very carefully about from the outset. The most common reason to volunteer is the desire to 'give something back'. Vikki Cole, who volunteered on an environmental project in Borneo, explains:

*Without sounding clichéd, I really wanted to be able to look back on my life and to have done something of substance that didn't directly benefit just me.*

Jacqueline Hill, who volunteered with VSO (p175) building management capacity with local NGOs in Bangladesh, had similar feelings:

*It had been a long-term dream. I had a vague plan that I'd spend the first 20 years of my career earning for myself and the next 20 giving something back.*

Wanting to help others, wishing to do good and hoping to make a difference are all important reasons to volunteer. But nine times out of ten, these may not be enough to make you to feel that your time was well spent. But, as you can imagine, there are plenty more reasons to go. Mike Laird, who travelled with a project funded by the Scientific Exploration Society (p173) to work on scientific, archaeological and community-aid projects in Bolivia, lists a well-balanced mix of altruistic and personal motivations for volunteering:

*To see the delight on people's faces when they realise they now have a clean and safe water supply or better school facilities. To know that they will benefit from these for years to come. The personal benefits are almost too many to mention: being exposed to new cultures; seeing new places and sharing in great experiences; making new and lasting friendships and discovering a bit more about myself. That apart, I also got fitter, lost weight and felt terrific when I came home.*

Mike picks up on a key point for travellers – volunteering is an excellent way to get under the skin of a country and come to grips with a different culture. The cultural-exchange element of international volunteering is a key part of what both you and your hosts will get out of the whole experience. Plus, you can build volunteering into almost any segment of your travels, whether you decide to arrange it formally or just turn up and find a placement yourself (see p256).

The educational aspect of volunteering is equally crucial. In almost every placement you'll have the opportunity to learn a foreign language or to brush up on one. And many of the new skills you'll acquire or develop can be used back home in your profession. Recognising that transferable skills can be gained while volunteering, the global management consulting group Accenture was one of the first companies to sign up to VSO's corporate volunteering for business scheme. The Accenture spokesperson Gib Bulloch elaborated:

# IS INTERNATIONAL VOLUNTEERING THE NEW COLONIALISM?

The question of whether volunteering is the new colonialism gets asked a lot, and the short answers are: 'yes', 'no', 'sometimes' and 'maybe'. International volunteering is part of a long tradition of people from the West setting off to help or change the countries of the Global South (aka the developing world) and have adventures while they do it. Where once these people were missionaries and soldiers, colonialists and explorers, teachers and entrepreneurs – now they are international volunteers.

If volunteers travel in the belief that they have little to learn and a lot to give, then they do risk being little more than 'New Age colonialists'. No-one becomes an international volunteer for purely altruistic reasons: they also do it because it is exciting, because they might learn something, because they want to meet new people who live differently and because, just maybe, they might have something to offer. By acknowledging why you volunteer, you are telling your hosts that they are people you can learn from and with, not that they should be the grateful recipients of your altruism. You ask them to be your teachers, instead of forcing them to be your students.

So, whether international volunteering is the new colonialism or not is, in large part, down to the attitudes of you, the volunteer, and the organisation you go with. If you don't want to be a 21st-century colonialist, rule out organisations that suggest you'll be 'saving the world' or give a patronising image of the developing world. Then question yourself. Be open about why you want to be an international volunteer and what you have to learn from those you visit. Avoiding being patronising will take some effort and research, and will require getting rid of many of the usual preconceptions about the developing world.

**Dr Kate Simpson**

*Volunteering with VSO allows staff to hone their leadership and communication skills. Often working in environments where they need to coach or influence people, they also develop key listening and understanding skills. Plus, volunteering abroad means that staff can add 'overseas work experience' to their CV – so crucial these days if you want to progress within an organisation.*

Ben Keedwell, who volunteered in Kathmandu developing a visitor and community centre in a national park, agrees and goes even further:

*International volunteering helps to increase understanding of development issues, consolidate practical skills, and gain first-hand experience of working in the field. Volunteers can develop self-confidence, focus their career objectives and show adaptability, self-motivation and dedication. These benefits can kick-start a career and may be more valuable than undergraduate (or even postgraduate) education.*

Many people have found that international volunteering has helped their career or given them the necessary experience to change careers. For instance, Ann Noon wanted to switch from working in tourism to the charity sector. She volunteered as a press and marketing manager for a project in Peru, and says:

*If I'd not gone to Peru, I almost certainly wouldn't have got my job with Sightsavers International, a charity that works to combat blindness in developing countries. I am convinced that I did the right thing, even though it all seemed like a leap into the unknown at the time.*

Similarly, Amanda Allen-Toland, who volunteered to work as a youth ambassador as part of the Australian Volunteers for International Development (AVID, p155 & p164) programme with the Thailand Business Coalition on AIDS in Bangkok, could not have predicted the positive impact her volunteering experience would have on her career. She moved on to work as a programme manager for the Asia-Pacific Business Coalition on HIV/AIDS in Melbourne, Australia. She explains:

*It's paid dividends for me. I'm in an area I want to be in with a higher level of responsibility, excellent pay and job satisfaction. It's the icing on the cake. My experience working with TBCA and living in Thailand was so fantastic that even if my next role had been making fruit shakes, I'd do it all over again.*

## KINDS OF INTERNATIONAL VOLUNTEERING

There are thousands of volunteer opportunities around the world and a number of different approaches to getting involved. The rest of this chapter offers an overview of what's out there. Detailed listings of recommended volunteer organisations are provided in Chapters 5 to 8, according to what they offer. If you're after something completely different, read Chapter 10 on how to set up your own grassroots charity.

# AREAS OF WORK

What tasks you perform as an international volunteer depends both on what you want to do, and on what is needed by the community or environment where you're going.

Within this framework you've got a number of broad choices, shown in the diagram on p13. The first choice is whether you want to work with people (usually called 'development volunteering') or with the environment and animals (referred to as 'conservation and wildlife volunteering').

Once you've made that basic choice, decide whether you consider yourself a skilled or unskilled volunteer. This is not as straightforward as it sounds. Skilled volunteers are often people such as teachers, accountants, civil engineers or nurses who work in their professions abroad. However, everyone has skills to offer: a parent might be skilled in conflict resolution, or a university graduate in acting and drama. In the final analysis, being skilled or unskilled will not necessarily dictate what area you work in, but it will impact on the level of responsibility you're given.

Whatever you decide, it's wise to be prepared for your role to change or develop. You might apply to do something, then find that something rather different is required of you once you reach your placement.

# DEVELOPMENT VOLUNTEERING

There are nine main areas within the development volunteering sector:

**Emergency and relief** An option for highly skilled and experienced volunteers only, this is where doctors, nurses, midwives, psychologists and so on, respond to humanitarian crises, conflicts, wars and natural diasters abroad (see p179). Some volunteers are on 72-hour standby to go anywhere in the world. Many of the organisations working in this sector have longer-term volunteer opportunities for skilled non-medical staff, such as logisticians or administrators.

**Working with children** Typically, work in this area might include volunteering as a sports coach, working in an orphanage or with street children. A clean criminal record is paramount in this area as all organisations featured in this book require them. Rachel Oxberry arranged her own placements (for information on how to do this, see Chapter 8) in two orphanages in Ecuador and remembers:

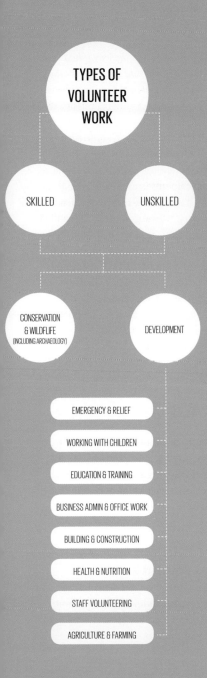

## TYPES OF VOLUNTEER WORK

- SKILLED
- UNSKILLED

- CONSERVATION & WILDLIFE (INCLUDING ARCHAEOLOGY)
- DEVELOPMENT

- EMERGENCY & RELIEF
- WORKING WITH CHILDREN
- EDUCATION & TRAINING
- BUSINESS ADMIN & OFFICE WORK
- BUILDING & CONSTRUCTION
- HEALTH & NUTRITION
- STAFF VOLUNTEERING
- AGRICULTURE & FARMING

*I worked in a home looking after 20 children who were either abandoned or orphaned. I thought I was going there to help out generally and teach English but I actually took on the role of 'mother' too, trying to teach routine and discipline as well as doing the cleaning and laundry. I also coached sports, taught drawing and played games with the kids. I volunteered in an orphanage for children with special needs as well. I looked after babies under the age of one, preparing their food, feeding them, changing nappies and doing baby massage.*

**Education and training** Most volunteer placements in this category are teaching English (with or without qualifications, though criminal background checks are required) in preschools and primary or secondary schools, although teaching adults is also common. Depending on your talents or qualifications, however, you could end up teaching almost anything. Sarah Turton volunteered in Ghana and taught English along with art and photography. This is how she describes her time there:

*Sometimes I had over 40 students crammed into a classroom designed for much less. Some of them would stroll in half an hour before the end of class or not turn up for weeks at a time and then expect to pick up where they left off. This was the way it had to be for students where farming and helping sell came first, and I had to develop a flexible teaching style. It was very tough at first and exhausted me but I loved every single second of my time there.*

**Business administration and office work** Depending on your experience, you might work for a local Non-Governmental Organisation (NGO) writing fundraising proposals, managing a project or volunteering in their marketing, PR or finance departments. The aim of these placements is usually to train local people in the skills you possess so that they can become self-sufficient (such work is referred to as capacity-building).

**Building and construction** Good old-fashioned manual labour often plays a big part in volunteering overseas. You are usually sent as part of a team to help build schools, community centres, houses, bridges, dams or latrines. There is also a need for skilled volunteers in this area to work as civil or structural engineers and construction or site supervisors. Emma Campbell went to Ecuador and quite literally volunteered with her bare hands:

*We built a house on the coast of Ecuador, near a national park, so that future volunteers could base themselves there. We had no power tools so everything was done by hand! We were supported by a very friendly and hard-working bunch of locals that the charity were paying.*

**Health and nutrition** Health professionals are required in this area, but you don't have to be a fully trained nurse, doctor, speech therapist, nutritionist or physiotherapist to contribute. Non-medical volunteers can often help in other areas, like the promotion of health and hygiene issues in a local community. Kate Sturgeon volunteered with Médecins Sans Frontières (MSF, Doctors Without Borders, p181) in Zimbabwe and explains:

*I was the project nurse for an HIV/anti-retroviral programme working alongside the Ministry of Health to provide free anti-retroviral drugs in one of the first HIV/opportunistic infections clinics in the country. I ran follow-up clinics, seeing all patients who had started on these drugs either weekly, monthly or quarterly to monitor their progress and any side effects.*

**Community development** This covers a wide variety of community and social programmes. You might help women's groups set up income-generating schemes (eg selling handicrafts), work with a local village on empowerment issues or help establish a system for disposing of rubbish in a village or region.

**Staff volunteering** Some volunteer organisations, particularly those aimed at the youth market, need in-country volunteer staff to help manage and run their overseas programmes. You might be a medic on an expedition, an interpreter at a field base or a project manager working with a group of 17- to 24-year-olds. Michelle Hawkins volunteered with Raleigh International (p151) in Ghana, Costa Rica and Nicaragua and describes the roles she filled:

> *On the first expedition I was a public relations officer in Ghana. On the second I was project manager on a construction site in an Indian village in the rainforest. My role was to ensure that everything happened on time and under budget. I was also responsible for motivating the Venturers, briefing each one to be a 'Day Leader' and then assessing and reviewing what they had done well and what could be improved.*

**Agriculture and farming** This is almost exclusively for skilled volunteers. Communities often need horticulturalists, foresters, agronomists and agriculturists.

One further option, if you have extensive travel plans and only want to spend a day or two doing something for others, is to consider a visit to a prisoner. If there is an organisation in your country that arranges prison visits abroad, get in touch with them. In the UK, you could contact the charity Prisoners Abroad (www.prisonersabroad.org.uk), which supports British prisoners overseas; it does not organise visits but can offer advice and British Embassy contact details. Their Chief Executive, Pauline Crowe, reminds us:

> *Visiting a British prisoner detained overseas can be a really positive experience if you approach it with the right motivation and sensitivity. It's important for people detained in faraway places to know they are not forgotten. In some places it can be reasonably easy to arrange a visit, particularly in South America and Southeast Asia. Contact the local British consulate and they will advise on what is possible, may know who wants a visit, and give you information about how to arrange it, and what you can take in.*

# CONSERVATION & WILDLIFE VOLUNTEERING

The words 'conservation' and 'wildlife' sum up most of the options for volunteering in this area. The majority of opportunities involve short-term stints working on long-term projects alongside scientists or other experts. Sometimes you're based in one location but often you join an expedition through a particular region.

## Conservation Volunteering

Volunteering in conservation could involve clearing or constructing trails in African national parks, studying flora and fauna in a cloud-forest reserve in Ecuador, or monitoring climate change in the Arctic. There are wide-ranging options available.

Karen Hedges went to the Madagascar with SEED Madagascar (p168) and worked on a variety of projects:

*We planted trees with various communities and held workshops for the local people to teach them the importance of replanting in a country that has lost so much of its natural habitat. We also did a forest survey to measure how quickly the forests in St Luce were diminishing through local use.*

Archaeology and palaeontology also come under the conservation banner and are two fields that rely heavily on international volunteers (see the blue box opposite).

Robert Driver travelled to Central America with Gapforce (p157) and worked in the jungle:

*Our project involved the clearing and three-dimensional mapping of the most prominent ancient Mayan ruined city in all of northern Belize, called Kakantulix. The area of jungle around it had been subject to logging by the local community, who were reliant on the trees as a source of income. We had to clear the site of low-level vegetation and then map each ruin to gain an accurate image of what the site once looked like. The maps were forwarded to the Institute of Archaeology and Wildtracks (our project partner) and the area has since received protected status, is attracting sustainable tourism and is, in turn, generating an income for the local community.*

# ARCHAEOLOGY

If you fancy yourself as the next Indiana Jones or Lara Croft, archaeology is probably not for you – volunteers are more likely to be digging out fire pits than unearthing buried treasure. You don't have to be a scientist or historian to take part, but you do need to be patient and committed. Real-life archaeology can be painstakingly slow and laborious, and you must log and record every find, no matter how insignificant.

This said, archaeology does have its glamorous side and there are opportunities to excavate burial chambers, temples and ancient shipwrecks.

Volunteers typically cover all their own expenses and camp or stay on site or in local guesthouses. You can work for just a few weeks or for a whole season and there are usually a few free days a week to do some exploring. However, you should be prepared for back-breaking, dusty days spent hunched over in the sun – bring a wide-brimmed hat and a big tube of sun screen!

**The Council for British Archaeology** (http://new.archaeologyuk.org), the **Archaeological Institute of America** (www.archaeological.org) and the website www.archaeologyfieldwork.com all publish global fieldwork opportunities on their websites. Some of the mainstream volunteering organisations also place volunteers on archaeological digs (see Scientific Exploration Society, p173; Condordia, p228).

If you fancy helping out on a marine excavation, the **Nautical Archaeology Society** (☎+44(0)23-9281 8419; www.nauticalarchaeologysociety.org; Portsmouth, UK) offers specialist courses in Foreshore and Underwater Archaeology for aspiring marine archaeologists who have a PADI Open Water or equivalent diving certification.

## Wildlife Volunteering

If you choose to work with animals you might do anything from helping monitor sea turtle populations in Costa Rica to analysing the migration of grey whales in Canada to working in a home for neglected or orphaned wild animals in Namibia.

Samantha Elson has participated in five programmes in Sri Lanka, Azores, the Altai Republic, Namibia and Peru with Biosphere Expeditions (p216). She describes her broad range of experiences:

*I've worked with extremely enthusiastic scientists and have always felt part of the team. Volunteers are not just given the donkey work. It is really rewarding and I have learnt so much. I have no zoological training but have had the chance to do everything from photographing whale flukes for identification, measuring snow-leopard footprints in the snow, to releasing a cheetah from a humane trap.*

Elaine Massie and Richard Lawson (see p90 for their Top Ten Tips from Two Volunteers) have undertaken more than a dozen projects with Earthwatch (p211) and recount one of their best moments from the sea turtle programme in Costa Rica:

## SHARON'S STORY

There was rarely a dull moment during my six months in Tibet – apart from the winter evenings. I ended up being interviewed by a TV crew about why I had come to teach Tibetan children; I was taken out to dinner by the local police, who took it in turns to stand up and make speeches thanking me for coming to do voluntary work, and who also serenaded me in turn (I then had to sing a song for them). I was propositioned by a man dressed as a monk; I visited various reincarnated holy men and had an important empowerment from one; I visited a nomadic family in their tent and bravely ate a home-made sausage which was dripping with blood. I visited a 'sky burial' site and saw some tufts of hair and bits of bone; I saw a frozen lake against a backdrop of black and snow-white mountains and a turquoise dawn sky. I saw the biggest plains in the world; I sat on the grasslands in summer and marvelled at the beauty of enormous flower-filled meadows surrounded by velvet hills that reminded me strangely of Ireland. I met the sweetest children in the world, who bring themselves and each other up, wash their own clothes in freezing water, walk from the classroom to your flat so that they can hold your hand and make the average Western child look like a spoilt, demanding brat.

My advice to people reading this book is: '*Go for it!*'

**Sharon Baxter**

*With a population on the verge of extinction every hatchling counts, so volunteers check each nest, count the number of hatchlings and put them in a bucket. They are then walked along the beach, released and allowed to crawl to the ocean escorted by volunteers, to ensure that none are eaten by crabs on the way. This is a wonderful job. Picking the wiggly hatchlings out of the sand at the nest site and seeing them scamper down the beach into the ocean is brilliant. Elaine wished the first couple of hatchlings, 'Goodbye, good luck and be careful,' not realising that she'd be releasing hundreds of hatchlings. Then it seemed unlucky not to wish them all the same. So, almost a thousand were wished, 'Goodbye, good luck and be careful,' as they were safely seen to the ocean. Turtle hatchlings may well be the cutest baby animal ever and deserve all the protection and luck they can get.*

### Marine Conservation

Marine conservation straddles both the conservation and wildlife camps. Tasks for volunteers may include underwater surveys of coral reefs in the Philippines, diving with whale sharks in Honduras or helping with dolphin conservation in Florida.

# PACKAGE PLACEMENT OR DO IT YOURSELF?

Once you know what you might want to do and where you might want to go, there are two things you need to consider: what sort of volunteering experience you want, and how to find the right volunteer opportunity for you. All the organisations offering opportunities are different and it is crucial to find one that best suits you.

Local charities or NGOs in search of volunteers often don't have the time or resources to recruit directly (although some volunteer placements are organised this way). Instead, the most common practice is that they work with partners in Europe, the USA, Canada, Australia and New Zealand who match the right placement with the right volunteer. Throughout this process the emphasis should always be on meeting the needs of the host programme abroad, rather than on your individual requirements as a volunteer. (To avoid signing up with an organisation that does not operate this way, see p30 for a discussion of ethical volunteering.)

In these cases, partners can be limited companies, not-for-profit organisations or registered charities, although the latter often recruit and run their own volunteer programmes. Regardless of their status, all three are normally referred to as 'sending agencies'. Within this framework there are three main types of experiences that you can choose from: organised programmes, structured and self-funding programmes, and do-it-yourself placements.

## ORGANISED VOLUNTEER PROGRAMMES

This category is comprised of organisations that offer all-inclusive, highly organised volunteer experiences. Almost everything is arranged for you: your volunteer placement; international flights; board and lodging; travel insurance; visas; orientation courses; in-country support and transport. Volunteers can work on either development or conservation and wildlife projects. They often work in teams, but individual placements are also common. The cost of volunteering through one of these organisations can seem high, although their 'all-inclusive' nature means that everything is covered in the cost (bar pocket money).

Organisations that recruit skilled volunteers like VSO (p175), AVI (p164), or Volunteer Service Abroad (p165) also fall into this bracket due to the organised nature of their placements. This is also the case for organisations providing emergency and relief services like MSF (p181) or International Federation of the Red Cross and Red Crescent Societies (IFRC, p179). However, this is where any similarities with other organisations in this category end. For more information see the relevant sections in Chapter 5.

Organised volunteer programmes can be divided into two types:

**Options for the under 30s** Organised volunteer programmes catering specifically to the youth market, including gap-year students.

**Volunteering plus** These are organised volunteer programmes that offer a 'sandwich' or combined volunteering experience, combining a volunteer placement with other travel-related experiences. For instance, you could learn a language for one month, volunteer for one month, then undertake some adventurous group travel for a further month or two.

## STRUCTURED & SELF-FUNDING VOLUNTEER PROGRAMMES

Some charities and sending agencies offer a structured volunteer programme but might require you to find your own accommodation or book your own flights. Basically, not everything is organised for you, and this is reflected in the fee. There is support from your agency but much less hand-holding than with an organised volunteer programme – both in your home country prior to departure and once you're abroad.

In terms of independence, the next rung on the ladder is self-funding volunteering programmes. An agency will match you with an overseas placement but you're pretty much on your own from then on. You pay all your own costs, organise all the practical details (eg flights, visas and accommodation) and receive very little additional support.

For a detailed look at structured and self-funding volunteer programmes, see Chapter 6.

## A NOTE ON RELIGIOUS ORGANISATIONS

Religious organisations can operate both organised volunteer programmes and structured and self-funding volunteer programmes. The main difference is that much of the work is faith based. And, as you'd expect, religious organisations mostly conduct development rather than conservation and wildlife programmes.

For details of volunteering with religious organisations, see Chapter 7.

## DO-IT-YOURSELF VOLUNTEER PLACEMENTS

If you don't fancy any of these options, you can cut out the middle man and tee up a volunteer placement directly with a grassroots NGO or locally run programme. There are two main ways of doing this: you can either organise a placement using one of the many online databases of worldwide volunteering opportunities, or arrange a volunteer placement once you arrive in a country.

For details on do-it-yourself volunteer placements, see Chapter 8.

## WHO CAN GO?

Almost anyone can volunteer: if you're aged between 18 and 75 you should be able to find a placement. New Zealand's largest provider of overseas volunteers, Volunteer Service Abroad (p165), has an upper age limit of 75 years, for instance. If you're over 75, talk to your sending agency (and your travel insurance company) and you might be able to come to some arrangement. Catherine Raynor, former Press Officer for VSO, remembers:

*We had a volunteer working as an engineer in Mongolia and he had his 70th birthday while there. He became something of a local celebrity because the standard life expectancy there is significantly lower. Various parties were held for him around Mongolia and he was even paraded through the town where he worked.*

Interestingly, volunteering has been part of the international scene for long enough to allow some people to use it as a kind of lifelong education. In such cases, people usually find that what they learnt and what they had to offer were very different at different stages of their life.

Among southern hemisphere types, volunteering is still particularly on the rise among the over 60s. In Australia for instance, a government study found that Australians are world leaders in volunteering within their local communities once they are retired. And a similar survey in New Zealand, conducted in 2012, revealed that Kiwis are incredibly active in this sector, with almost 40 percent of people over the age of 65 working as volunteers. On the international front, Australians and New Zealanders have also taken to incorporating self-funding volunteering stints, such as assisting with a whale conservation project, into their travel itineraries and a record number of volunteer places are being offered on skilled volunteer programmes like Australian Volunteers for International Development (AVID, currently managed by two organisations: Scope Global, p155, and AVI, p164).

Volunteering attracts people from all round the world. Whether you go abroad alone or with a group of compatriots, you will meet and mix with volunteers of all nationalities and creeds. International volunteering is also drawing an increasingly diverse spectrum of candidates from within individual countries. In North America, for example, since the inception of the Peace Corps (p178) by President John F Kennedy in the 1960s, volunteering overseas has often been stereotyped as a vehicle for relatively well-off – and generally white – twentysomethings to go out and 'save the world' by digging wells, working with farmers to increase food supply and teaching English in the developing world. However, recent world events have made volunteering an attractive option to Americans, for example, of African, Asian and Hispanic descent, of both liberal and conservative political stripes, and from a variety of faiths and backgrounds. Many more people have come to appreciate the benefits of international volunteering – including the forming of rewarding relationships, the gaining of linguistic and technical skills and the creativity and cultural awareness that flow from the experience.

In addition, there is a growing number of organisations that cater for volunteers with a disability. See the listings in Chapters 5 to 8 to find out which organisations can cater for volunteers with a disability.

# FINDING THE TIME

A volunteer placement can last from a day to two years or more. This means that volunteering can be fitted into your life at any time. If you're in full-time employment and want to spend a week of your annual leave volunteering, you can.

Robin Glegg, who has been on three wildlife projects with Biosphere Expeditions (p216), explains:

*Although you can sign up for longer, I signed up for one 12-day slot. As some of the locations are fairly remote, this gives you two days' travelling time if you are taking a two-week break from work. Twelve days can be a little short in the field, but it is a practical time frame and a reasonable commitment for most working people.*

However, many people want to volunteer for longer and choose to do it at a stage of their lives when they have more time. This means that your first encounter with volunteering might come in the year between school and higher education, or between university and before starting full-time employment. David Grassham, who helped upgrade facilities in a village school in India, says:

*I had just finished university and wanted to have a year doing something completely different from the norm, and something that I may not have time to do once I eventually do start working.*

Of course, plenty of people in the workforce take extended breaks or have gaps when changing jobs or careers. Jackie Bowles, for instance, worked with children and adolescents in Rio de Janeiro through Task Brasil (p210):

*I was dissatisfied with my job and really wanted to change my career. I didn't have any family responsibilities so I felt this was the perfect time to volunteer.*

Kate Sturgeon, who volunteered in Zimbabwe, says:

*I had three years of nursing on an HIV/infectious diseases unit at the Royal Free Hospital in London and I'd completed a Tropical Nursing Diploma and Advanced Diploma in Infectious Diseases. I felt I had enough experience to confidently work abroad. I then negotiated a career break and the hospital held my post open for me.*

When you, the employee, decide you want to take a career break, that's great, but all too frequently it's your employer that makes the decision. This is what happened to Peter Bennett, who taught English in Sudan for seven months with the Sudan Volunteer Programme (p209):

*The bank I was working for made significant redundancies. As a senior manager I had been involved in deciding who we could do without – only to discover on the day that my name was on the list too.*

If you find yourself in this situation, it could be the perfect springboard into volunteering. What better way to spend your redundancy cheque?

In recent years, international volunteering has become increasingly popular with retirees, who have a lifetime of skills to offer, as well as savings, maturity and a bit more time. In particular, North Americans with a few more years under their belts – and a few more dollars in their bank accounts – are applying for international volunteer placements in greater numbers than ever before. Some of these folk witnessed, or participated in, the early years of the Peace Corps and are eagerly (re)living their volunteer dream in retirement. Others have never found the time to venture abroad amid career and family responsibilities and are taking advantage of their new-found personal freedom to work overseas. Oliver Walker is 63 and volunteered teaching English in Sri Lanka. He feels:

*… there is a need for older volunteers who have seen a lot of life. They have time on their hands and are often young at heart, looking for adventure and a worthwhile experience. Volunteering is so rewarding.*

Deborah Jordan and David Spinney were both retired head teachers when they went to Ethiopia to work in education with VSO (p175). Julie Jones, a grandmother, went to Kenya to work in an orphan outreach programme:

*My family and friends were great with support and encouragement. My nine-year-old granddaughter thought it was 'cool' to have a granny doing something unusual. What I did at Omwabini cannot be described as 'work'. Together with other volunteers, I visited far-flung communities, went out with a mobile clinic and spent time in a primary school where most of the children had lost at least one parent to AIDS.*

## TIMING

Some things to take into consideration before deciding when to volunteer include the climate, the timing of your volunteer project, and, if you plan to combine volunteering with a holiday.

It may seem obvious, but some volunteer projects run only at certain times of the year. If you want to help protect baby sea turtles, like Elaine Massie and Richard Lawson (see p90), then you must volunteer during the nesting season.

If you plan to volunteer as part of an extended period of travel then it can fit almost anywhere in your itinerary. However, most gappers and career-breakers volunteer at the start as it's a good way to meet people to travel with afterward.

## USEFUL WEBSITES

Most volunteer organisations (see Chapters 5 to 8) have helpful websites, but here is a list of more general websites:

• **Australian Council for International Development (ACFID)** (www.acfid.asn.au) Broad-based volunteering information for Australians.

• **Council for International Development (CID)** (www.cid.org.nz) A New Zealand site representing the non-government aid and development sector.

• **Development Gateway** (www.developmentgateway.org) Has learning tools and references, along with the ability to search for volunteer postings.

• **International Association for Volunteer Effort** (www.iave.org) Links to national volunteer organisations.

• **InterVol** (www.intervol.org.uk) Offering free registration, this site has lots of information on international volunteering.

• **OneWorld UK** (www.oneworld.net) News, views, campaigns and information from an international network of people interested in global justice.

• **Online Volunteering Service** (www.onlinevolunteering.org) The UN site connecting development organisations and volunteers over the internet.

• **Relief Web** (www.reliefweb.int) A favourite of UN staff, development consultants and globetrotting volunteers.

• **Volunteering Australia** (www.volunteeringaustralia.org) The site of Australia's governing body on volunteering, with links to not-for-profit organisations.

• **Volunteering New Zealand** (www.volunteeringnz.org.nz) The New Zealand volunteering world's resource centre.

# 02

## Choosing Your Volunteer Experience

## ARRANGING A WORTHWHILE PLACEMENT

The majority of volunteer placements are organised through an intermediary called a 'sending agency' (see p19 and Chapters 5 to 7 for more details). This means that it's crucial to choose an agency that operates in a way you feel comfortable with and that does its best to place volunteers on projects that are genuinely sustainable and responding to local needs. Even if you choose not to go through a sending agency, but contact an NGO or programme directly, you still need to take the same things into consideration.

There are hundreds of sending agencies based all over the world. And it's all too easy to make the wrong choice. Ian Flood was a 48-year-old mechanical engineer with 16 years' experience with Rolls-Royce when he did a language course in Ecuador. His school organised for him to volunteer in a day centre for street children. His experience turned out to be a disappointing one:

> *The organisation that fixed my placement was not willing to look at my background and skills (even though they had my CV) and match what I had to offer to the volunteer programme. Instead, I felt like I was given 'any old' placement and it was only when I turned up that the people there really asked about my history and tried to use my skills and experience. By this stage it was too late. Any 18-year-old with good Spanish could have worked very usefully in the day centre. I felt my skills were underutilised.*

On the other hand, when Jackie Bowles was looking for her placement with street children in Rio de Janeiro she was choosy right from the start:

*I looked at several different projects but chose Task Brasil, as they have such a well-established volunteer programme. Some others I had researched were in great need of volunteers, but didn't really have the network to support them. In other words, I felt that a volunteer could build up relationships with the children and then suddenly leave the children on their own. With Task Brasil there is a healthy balance between the volunteers that help and the educator, so the children don't suffer when the volunteers leave. I volunteered for five months then returned for a further three months on a part-time basis because I missed it so much!*

The key message here is that all organisations are different and work to varying standards. Many are excellent but some, like Ian Flood's, will dish out 'any old' placement with little consideration for you or your host programme. It's crucial to do your homework and check the credentials of any organisation you're considering volunteering with. Good credentials are what attracted Kate Sturgeon to Médecins Sans Frontières (MSF, Doctors Without Borders, p181). She remembers:

*I primarily chose MSF because it's got such a good reputation. I liked its charter – that it is independent and not affiliated with any religion, culture or government and that it receives most of its money from donations. I liked the fact that they work where the most vulnerable people are and that they're often the first NGO in and the last out.*

As well as checking out credentials, you need to feel that you share the philosophy and ethos that drives the sending agency you ultimately choose. This is what initially attracted Deborah Jordan and David Spinney to work with Voluntary Service Overseas (VSO, p175):

*We knew about VSO and how it works in partnership with governments and NGOs in developing countries. We looked forward to living in a local community at a similar level to our colleagues, and working with them to achieve shared targets. We liked their approach of 'sharing skills' rather than giving out money or things. Their approach was not that of the 'do-gooder' with poor people overseas, but a much more professional commitment to working with skilled individuals in their context to bring about sustainable change.*

But there are many other factors that may influence your choice of agency or programme. Emma Campbell who volunteered in South America says:

*I searched under 'responsible travel' on the Web. I was looking for a company that was carbon neutral and that included Spanish lessons. I also wanted to be part of a group with mixed ages and backgrounds.*

As volunteering can often seem expensive (see p38), the cost of a particular programme or placement is also a deciding factor. Ann Noon who volunteered in Peru says:

*I spent a long time looking for the right project, as I wasn't keen on the idea of paying a lot of money, particularly as I am suspicious about what proportion of the (often substantial) fees organisations charge actually trickles down to the host project.*

Sarah Turton, who volunteered at an art project in Ghana, was also influenced by price as well as her interests and the environment in which she would be placed:

*I searched the internet long and hard. I was influenced by cost and what was on offer. My main interest was Africa and art but I was also keen to go somewhere very remote and not be surrounded by Westerners and live as the Ghanaians live.*

And, weighing in with the final word, Robert Driver who volunteered in the jungles of Belize, chose to volunteer with Trekforce (now Gapforce, p157) for two different reasons:

*They are a registered charity and, for me, this had two benefits. Firstly, being a charity they would have a real focus on preserving the environment as opposed to being partly focused on profits. Secondly, it meant I could fundraise to contribute towards the cost of going on the expedition. The number of people who took an interest in what I was doing and supported it was really encouraging.*

All in all, there's a lot to be taken into account. This chapter examines many of the issues raised here in more depth and looks at other key deciding factors in choosing a sending agency or liaising directly with a local NGO or charity.

# ETHICAL VOLUNTEERING

The ethics of international volunteering are complex, particularly with development work. On the surface it sounds like a match made in fairy tales: you help local people to help themselves; you benefit; they benefit and you all live happily ever after.

Of course, the reality may not be quite so 'charming'. The more you find out about international volunteering, the more aware you become of some key ethical issues. When this happens you start to ask yourself more questions and, hopefully, ask more questions of the organisations you are researching. This is a healthy process, as getting answers to some key questions is exactly what is required to ensure that everyone benefits for the long term from your volunteering experience.

Below are some basic questions you might have swirling around in your head. Responses follow, although they are often more 'grey' than 'black' or 'white' (reflecting the complexity of some of the issues involved).

Team building, literally. A group from the British Exploring Society hard at work.

Photo: © British Exploring Society

**How do I know if the host community or country will really benefit from my volunteering?**

That's a crucial question. There should only ever be one reason for a volunteer programme to exist, and that is to meet the needs of a local community. Just as importantly, all volunteer programmes should do this in a sustainable way.

For instance, there's little point in a one-off placement where you're parachuted into a school, orphanage or community centre to work for a month or two and then leave. What happens to the work you were doing? How is it continued? Has your departure created a vacuum that no-one can fill? Has your work been more of a hindrance than a help?

Of course, there are exceptions to this rule. Perhaps you had a specific aim to achieve and you trained a local person to take over from you. That would be useful and classified as a sustainable volunteer project. However, you are more likely to find sustainable projects with sending agencies that have a long-term relationship with their partner programmes.

So, the bottom line is this: if you volunteer on a well run programme (whether you apply through a sending agency or go direct) you will make a contribution that should be of benefit to those you wish to help.

**If I only have a short amount of time to give, will I be able to make a difference?**

This is a tricky one and is discussed in more detail on p36. The answer very much depends on the aims and objectives of your project. The shorter the time you have, the more specific your project needs to be. For instance, volunteers with the faith-based charity Habitat for Humanity (p238) go overseas for one or two weeks and help build a house for a low-income family in great need of shelter. At the end of their week or two they have achieved something tangible and worthwhile.

**Am I actually doing more good by volunteering than just donating my money?**

The two short answers to this question are 'yes' and 'no'. All organisations working overseas need money to implement their programmes. But sending yourself, as opposed to sending your money, means you are making a very special contribution.

How valuable your contribution is depends on the effectiveness of the volunteer programme and feeds into the response given to the first question in this section. To some extent it also depends on what work you are doing. If you are passing on your skills to local people so they can do your job when

# THE ETHICAL VOLUNTEERING GUIDE

### Get the Most, Give the Most

To get the most out of international volunteering you need to put effort into choosing who you go with and what you do. These seven questions are designed to help you learn as much as possible about the quality and value of the projects or placements an organisation offers BEFORE you sign up.

### What work will I be doing?

An organisation with a good volunteer programme should be able to tell you what you will be doing, including how many hours a day, how many days a week and what sort of work it will be. For example, if an organisation offers a placement in a school, this may or may not be teaching. Likewise, a placement may involve 50 hours a week or just four. The greatest source of dissatisfaction for volunteers is usually not doing what they planned (and paid) to do.

### Does the organisation work with a local partner organisation?

If a volunteer programme is to be of value to a local community it should work in collaboration with, rather than be imposed on, that community. Good programmes should therefore work with a local partner organisation. Find out who that partner is and how the relationship works. Is someone from the local organisation involved in the day-to-day management of your project? What sort of local consultation took place to build the project? Why is the project of value?

### Does the organisation make any financial contributions to its volunteer programmes? If so, exactly how much is this?

Volunteer programmes need funds as well as labour; indeed, in much of the world, unskilled labour is often one thing of which there is little shortage. So ask where your pennies are going, and be persistent about getting a clear figure, not a percentage of profits. Also, be aware that payments for your food and lodging often do not assist your volunteer programme.

### Does the organisation have policies on ecotourism and ethical tourism?

If you really want to make a valuable contribution to the community you work with, then you have a responsibility to ensure that the organisation with which you travel has proper ecological and ethical policies. Look for organisations that have a long-term commitment to a community, employ local staff and have some mechanism for local consultation and decision making. Otherwise, how will you know that the clinic you built is really needed, or that an adult literacy programme is more relevant than a new bridge? Are there funds to maintain the project you have worked on?

## What time frame is the volunteer programme run on?

A well-structured volunteer programme should have a clear time frame, and organisations should know from one year to the next whether a programme will continue. One-off programmes, and especially placements, can be problematic. If you are acting as a teaching assistant for a month, what happens the rest of the school year? Are other volunteers sent or is the placement simply ended? It may also be very disruptive for children to have a constantly changing staff. Establishing the level of commitment an organisation has to a given project or placement is vital in establishing the quality, and therefore value, of that volunteer programme.

## Can the organisation give exact contact details for your chosen programme?

Organisations tend to work in one of two ways. The better ones build a relationship with a host organisation, identify local needs, arrange placements and projects and then fill vacancies. Others wait for travellers to sign up and pay up, and then find relevant placements. A good organisation can let you know several months before you travel where you will be going and what exactly you will be doing. If it cannot (or will not) give you these details be very wary – hastily arranged programmes can be disorganised, leaving volunteers and local hosts with unclear expectations.

## What support and training will you receive?

Organisations offer vastly different levels of training and support. Look for an organisation that offers not only pre-departure training but also in-country training and support. Learning about both the practicalities of your volunteer job and the culture of where you are travelling to will help you get and give the most. Local support is also important, but ask if 'local' means just across the road or several hours away by bus. Make sure there is somebody in the country with direct responsibility for you. All projects require problem solving at some point and you will need someone on hand to help you with this.

Dr Kate Simpson

you leave, if you are training the trainer or helping to build international understanding through cultural exchange then, obviously, this is invaluable work and much more important than money.

In addition, many sending agencies donate a proportion of the fees they charge to the overseas project you're working with. For a more detailed discussion of this, check out question three in the Ethical Volunteering Guide written by Dr Kate Simpson, on p32.

**Will my volunteering take a paid job away from a local person?**
It is crucial that it doesn't, and you need to ask this question of your sending agency or local organisation (if you are finding your own placement) before you sign up. Again, there's no chance of this if your volunteer agency is reputable and well run but, there is if it isn't.

**Some sending agencies place thousands of volunteers annually, while others place relatively few. Is this an indication of how good they are?**
Not at all. In fact, in the world of international volunteering small is often beautiful. Instead of looking at the number of volunteers, find out how many partner programmes an organisation works with abroad. The relationship between a sending agency and its partners is key. There needs to be mutual trust, frequent correspondence and visits, and long-term commitment if the relationship is to thrive.

So, beware the agencies that appear to offer every international volunteering option under the sun. You can't work with everyone everywhere. In fact, an abundance of choice usually means that host programme partnerships are weak, that not all projects are properly vetted and that quality control is poor.

In addition, check out how an organisation matches its placements to its volunteers, particularly if you plan to work in development. Some organisations spend hours interviewing volunteers, talking through the possibilities and really searching for the perfect match, while others either do this by telephone, or not at all (you simply apply online).

**Is there a difference between volunteering with a registered charity, a not-for-profit organisation and a limited company?**
Volunteer programmes are run by all three types of organisation. In the Listings section of Chapters 5 to 8 the status of organisations is given. However, it is questionable whether these distinctions make any real difference to your

volunteer experience or the worth of a volunteer programme. Having said that, registered charities are normally regulated by national bodies and, from an ethical point of view, have an extra layer of responsibility to act in a genuinely charitable way. Of course, nothing is black and white. From time to time, charities are criticised for how they use their money, while certain limited companies within this sector choose to operate like not-for-profit organisations. Some sending agencies are set up as limited companies because decision making can sometimes be easier and quicker (no board of trustees to involve). Certainly, no-one wants to find out that a limited company is making vast profits from international volunteering.

The bottom line is this: all types of organisation should be transparent about how they spend your money.

### As standards vary so much, are there any best-practice guidelines that organisations sign up to?

Interestingly, there is no governing body that regulates this growing, and sometimes profitable, sector. However, **Comhlámh** (info@comhlamh.org; www.comhlamh.org; Dublin, Ireland) – the Irish Association of Development Workers – has put together a Volunteer Charter and a Sending Agencies Code of Good Practice. It is hoped that both documents will be adopted by similar organisations in Scotland, England and Wales. There is clearly a need for such self-regulation. Volunteers from outside the UK and Ireland should check whether organisations in their countries of origin follow similar regulatory guidelines.

At this stage, you might be thinking this is all getting rather too difficult. Take heart, it isn't. If you are asking the right questions of yourself, you'll ask the right questions of everybody else. And in this instance, 'everybody else' includes returned volunteers. It is particularly important to talk to volunteers who have recently returned from a placement with the sending agency or local NGO that you're thinking of volunteering with. This is one of the best ways of finding out what a project is really like on the ground.

Of course, you also need to ask questions of your sending agency or local NGO as well. To help you pick an ethical international volunteering organisation, seven key questions to ask are given in the box on p32. They were put together by Dr Kate Simpson after spending over six years researching and working in the international volunteering sector. As well as studying for a PhD at Newcastle University in the UK, she has written extensively about gap years and international volunteering.

# HOW LONG?

In the world of international volunteering there are short-term, medium-term and long-term placements. However, there's no real consensus on the length of time each category refers to. For the purposes of this book, short-term volunteering comprises one week to two months, medium-term is more than two months but less than 12, and long-term is one year or more. Outside these time frames, some volunteering organisations will let you volunteer for less than a week (sometimes just a day or two) and, at the other end of the spectrum, some skills-based or faith-based charities expect a volunteering commitment of two years or more.

How long you volunteer for depends on how much time you have. Elaine Massie and Richard Lawson have volunteered on a variety of wildlife projects lasting from two to 14 days. They explain:

*The length of the projects suits us very well, as we both work and so need to be able to fit the volunteering into our annual holidays.*

Volunteering for such short amounts of time can work, particularly with conservation or wildlife projects where the financial contribution that volunteers make to sustainable research projects overseas is invaluable. (See the following section and Chapters 5 and 6 for more details on this.)

However, as a general rule of thumb, the shorter the volunteer placement, the more specific the project needs to be. Also, it is the accepted view that the longer the volunteer placement, the better it is for both you and the host programme. This makes sense if you think about your volunteer placement as a new job (which, to all intents and purposes, it is). How useful are you in the first few months of starting a new job? Doesn't it take time to learn the ropes, to get to know everyone and to become familiar with new systems? Sarah Turton, who spent one month teaching in Ghana, confesses:

*One month – that was too short. It takes a long time to adjust to somewhere that is so different to your own culture and I felt that I had just started to fit in properly and make good friends when I had to go home again.*

This view is endorsed by Julie Jones, who worked on an orphan outreach programme in Kenya:

*I came home after only four weeks and felt that I was leaving prematurely. I had only just got into the swing of things and felt there was more I could do.*

Poonam Sattee volunteered for a year in Guatemala, where she worked with street children. She says:

*Just under a year – it worked out perfectly. This provides stability for the children and the volunteers are also able to get the most out of their time there.*

Some skills-based and faith-based volunteer organisations require volunteers to sign up for a minimum of two years. Deborah Jordan and David Spinney went to Ethiopia with VSO (p175), where they worked in education. For them to achieve the goals of their project, they found that two years was not sufficient:

*We volunteered for a two-year placement and we were happy to do so. We recognised that it does take time to integrate into a new community and a different way of life and to earn the confidence and respect of new colleagues. We extended our contract by six months to enable us to complete the second phase (second academic year) of the programme and ensure a smooth handover to another volunteer and local colleagues.*

This is not to say that only long-term volunteering is a valuable use of your time, money and limited resources. Nevertheless, the length of your volunteer placement will usually have a direct impact on how much you can achieve.

It is important to understand this link because it will help manage your expectations. Bottom line: you won't be able to do a great deal in a short amount of time and this can be frustrating. However, as was the case with Deborah Jordan and David Spinney, you can often extend a volunteer placement (visa regulations allowing).

You can also do the converse: curtail your placement. Ann Noon, who volunteered in Peru, describes finishing her placement early:

*I volunteered for a year but returned home after 10 months – partly for financial reasons (too many pisco sours) and partly because I had problems with the tenants in my flat that needed resolving.*

Obviously, breaking your volunteer commitment in this way should not be done lightly. Just as with a regular contract job, you have agreed to volunteer for a certain period of time and you should fulfil that obligation. However, being away from home for longish periods of time does come with its own set of potential problems. To minimise these (such as problems with tenants), see Chapter 4 Tying up Loose Ends.

## COSTS

It often comes as a surprise to would-be volunteers that giving up their time isn't enough. In the majority of cases, you also need to pay to volunteer. There are a number of reasons for this:

• There are significant administrative costs involved in maintaining a well-managed volunteer programme and in finding you a volunteer placement. As such, it is normal for a fee to be charged (note: charities call this fee 'fundraising').
• The host programme incurs costs by using volunteers. Volunteers have to be looked after, possibly trained and certainly supervised. Then there's the question of who is going to pay for board and lodging, in-country transport and any other ancilliary costs.
• Hosting volunteers is often a way for local projects to earn an additional source of income. In many cases, a proportion of your fee (whether charged by a sending agency or a local NGO) will go towards helping fund the project you're working on.

The cost of volunteering varies considerably. It usually depends on the volunteering experience you want and how long you're going for. If you want an all-inclusive, bells-and-whistles organised volunteer programme, you might pay between £3250 and £4500 (US$4000 to US$5500; A$5275 to A$7250; NZ$5600 to NZ$7725) for a three-month placement. However, almost everything is paid upfront and all you'll have to take with you is spending money. For more detailed information on the costs of organised and structured volunteer programmes, see Chapters 5 to 7.

At the other extreme, you may sign up with a charity, NGO or sending agency that charges you a placement fee but then expects you to be completely self-funding. In the UK or US, if this is the case, you might be charged £1000 (US$1200) in fees and have to pay all other costs, such as international flights, accommodation and food.

In Australia and New Zealand, a prospective volunteer may be asked to pay between A$300 and A$500 (NZ$320 and NZ$530) in partially refundable fees, or as a deposit to reserve a place on a programme. Incidentally, these self-funding volunteer programme fees cannot be claimed as a tax deduction in Australia because they are not an expense incurred while earning assessable income. Check with the Australian Taxation Office's Volunteers and Tax guide for more details (www.ato.gov.au/nonprofit). For more details on self-funding volunteer placements, see Chapters 6 and 7.

There is some good news for your wallet if you're a US or Canadian citizen: certain programme fees paid to charitable and religious sending organisations based in the Americas may be income tax deductible. Most of these organisations will advertise this fact on their websites.

Of course, you may think all this sounds much too expensive and decide to cut out the intermediaries and find your own placement. If you find one while you're travelling you'll have to pay only what the local NGO or charity charges (if anything). If you tee up a placement before you travel, you'll incur the small cost of registering with an online database of volunteer opportunities and all the

A pair of volunteers tending to crops at the Centre for Alternative Technology

Photo: © Centre for Alternative Technology

travel- and living-related costs of volunteering. Although this is the cheapest option, it does come with far more risks. For a discussion of the pros and cons, see Chapter 8. For a detailed breakdown of how to budget for a self-funding volunteer placement, see p66.

Organisations running conservation and wildlife projects usually offer only organised or structured volunteer programmes and, more often than not, conservation and wildlife volunteering is more expensive than development volunteering. This is because many projects are expensive to run, take place in remote, inaccessible parts of the world and require lots of expensive equipment. It's also because volunteer fees are one of the main ways that a sustainable research project is funded.

Whatever you pay your sending agency, it is important to understand where your money is going and who pays for what. Ask for a breakdown of costs if one isn't readily available; in many cases, you will find one on the organisation's website.

Having said all this, some volunteers don't pay anything. In fact, not only are their costs covered but they are also paid a monthly stipend. (In most regions accepting international volunteers, stipends are in the range of US$125 to US$1250 – enough to cover meals, local transportation, phone and internet usage, and other in-country incidental expenses.) This is the case with many of the skilled volunteer placements with organisations like VSO (p175), Médecins Sans Frontières (Doctors Without Borders, p181) or the Peace Corps (p178), to name but a few.

The Australian Government's Australian initiative Volunteers for International Development (AVID), which is delivered by Scope Global (p155) and AVI (p164), also includes monthly allowances intended to cover the costs associated with living a modest life while undertaking an assignment. Airfares and travel insurance are also included. With the AVID programme a variable establishment allowance is provided to cover visas and settling-in costs (like purchasing a local SIM card, or a kettle for that matter). A resettlement allowance is a welcome contribution to costs associated with returning to Australia. Volunteers in this programme are effectively tax exempt for the duration of their overseas assignment because they are not earning assessable income.

## LOCAL CULTURE

It is widely recognised that cultural exchange is one of the great benefits of international volunteering. However, living 24/7 in a foreign culture for several months or years has its challenges. Depending on where you go and what you do, you may encounter racism, sexism or homophobia. Female volunteers working in male-dominated societies have to overcome very specific gender issues and it is sometimes hard to be understanding of these and sensitive in dealing with them.

You may also have to deal with local people reacting to you based upon your government's foreign policies. International volunteers from the USA, for example, often face unique challenges. The word 'American' may trigger intense reactions in many parts of the world, both positive and negative. Prepare yourself for this eventuality, and try to keep a low profile in public places. Loud exclamations in your native English while striding through the marketplace, for instance, may make you a target for opportunistic pickpockets.

Australian, New Zealand and Canadian volunteers are generally well received, particularly in the Asia-Pacific region, as governments from these three nations have made concerted efforts to build stability and prosperity in the region through their respective aid agencies. However, it's important to consider that certain political decisions and alliances the Australian Government has forged in the recent past may not have a loyal fan base in parts of the Middle East and Asia.

In addition to political concerns, volunteers also have to come to terms with stereotypical notions local people might have about their nationality or culture. Perceptions about volunteers from the USA might be mixed, for instance. As the homeland of Hollywood, Google, and more global cultural icons than you can shake a KFC drumstick at, many people believe they have a pretty good grasp of what an American is. On the one hand, folks from the US are generally considered outgoing, optimistic and independent; on the other, Americans may be characterised as as rich, brash or arrogant.

On a more general note, like any traveller in a foreign culture you may be viewed as something of a novelty and become the focus of a lot of attention. Unlike a traveller however you can't just move on should it become overwhelming. This is exactly what Sarah Turton initially found in Ghana. She confides:

*The first weekend in Ghana I spent in the village. I wanted to settle in. It was very strange as I didn't know what I was supposed to do. No-one was particularly responsible for me and I had this sense of apprehension about stepping out on my own. I mean, I stuck out like a very, very sore thumb. It has confirmed to me that I would HATE to be famous. I never realised how much I valued fitting in and being 'one of the crowd'. I didn't feel confident going out alone and I got so pestered. I was the only* obruni *(white person) for miles around.*

To begin with, Jacqueline Hill, who volunteered in Bangladesh also felt a bit lost and stressed in her new environment:

*I did my own shopping in the market, gradually working out what all the strange-looking vegetables were. I found cooking for myself difficult, as shopping was quite stressful. I generated a lot of attention, could not recognise much of what was on offer and had to haggle for everything.*

And then, of course, there's the language barrier. Some sending agencies or local NGOs insist you speak the language of the country before you are accepted onto a programme. This is particularly the case in Latin America. If you think about it, this requirement makes perfect sense: as a volunteer you are ten times more useful if you can communicate with everyone.

Fundamental to choosing where to volunteer is thinking carefully about the culture and language of the country you wish to live in.

## LIVING CONDITIONS

What will the accommodation and food be like? How will you entertain yourself when you're not volunteering? These are important questions and it is wise to research the answers before you go abroad. Many volunteer organisations find accommodation for you, but if you are a self-funding volunteer it will be up to you to find your own accommodation.

Helen Tirebuck, Operations Manager at Challenges Worldwide (p176), says:

*The country in which you are placed influences where you will stay. But, on the whole, our volunteers live with local hosts. This might be a young family who is interested in hosting a foreigner or it might be a colleague from the volunteer's host organisation who has a spare room. Living with a local host means there is instant support and local knowledge for the volunteer on their arrival in country. There is also no better way to integrate into a culture and learn about a new environment than from the locals themselves.*

Homestays are common for international volunteers and have their advantages. However, not everyone wants to live as part of someone else's family for a sustained period of time and sometimes privacy can be an issue. Obviously, homestay experiences can also vary enormously, as Ian Flood found out when he volunteered in Bolivia:

*I stayed with a large, very well-off family who employed four maids and lived in a big house. The father was a medical professor at the local university. I had a top-floor room with a large terrace, my own bathroom and great views over the city. This was an exception and subsequent families were less well off, but I still had my own room and good meals. I did not cook or wash up and they also did my laundry once a week.*

Living in a shared house with other volunteers is another popular option. Kate Sturgeon, who volunteered in Zimbabwe with MSF (p181), says:

*I lived in a house with five other people. We had a big garden and a small swimming pool, so it was very nice. We had a lady who cooked our dinner during the week and did our washing and cleaning so we were terribly spoilt.*

Sharon Baxter lived in a shared flat when she volunteered in Tibet and tells a less luxurious story:

*Inside the school compound there was a flat reserved for the English teachers. It had an indoor 'long drop' toilet. There were electric lights but no running water. As the flat was on the first floor it was hard work getting water, as it had to be carried up the stairs in aluminium buckets. Due to the altitude, any physical exertion made you breathless. The cooker in the flat regularly broke down, and I learnt how to purchase and replace the wire element. I washed my clothes by hand in a basin on the table. Clothes tended to dry very quickly even when the weather was cold, as the air is extremely dry.*

Sharing your accommodation with a few flatmates is one thing, but sharing your kitchen with a totally different species is another, as Jacqueline Hill discovered when she volunteered in Bangladesh:

*I had a fridge but it only had a small freezer compartment which needed constant defrosting. The ants got into everything, especially as they were able to chew through plastic. The smaller cockroaches also managed to get into the fridge. Cooking was difficult, particularly in the 40-degree heat and 98 per cent humidity of summer, and my diet became mainly mangoes. I did not get brave enough to buy live chickens but had a cooked meal every day at the office. I ate lots and lots and lots of rice, but on the whole a good, balanced diet of fish, meat and vegetables.*

Where you live and how you adapt to domestic arrangements are important parts of your volunteer experience. As well as flats, rooms and houses (either shared or not), you will also find volunteers living in guesthouses, hostels and cheap hotels.

Who you live with is also a consideration. Sometimes it is refreshing to have the company of other volunteers, especially in the evenings. But, as Kate Sturgeon points out, it can be stressful:

*There were six of us in the house and it was an intense way to live. If the team is good and the dynamics are healthy, it becomes your family and you make excellent friends. Trying to get privacy was not always easy but the hardest aspect for me was everyone knowing what you were doing all the time in or out of work.*

Living on your own or with a friend or partner may be the best arrangement for some – see p52 for more details on volunteering with others. Volunteering on a conservation and wildlife project is often another kettle of fish. Vikki Cole volunteered in the jungles of Borneo and this is how she describes her living conditions:

*Mud. That pretty much sums up the part of the jungle we were living in. It was knee-deep clay mud, which also got deeper and gloopier the more it rained and the more we walked in it. Every day we washed in a little waterfall 200 metres below us, which sounds beautiful except for the leeches which, trust me, get everywhere. We also used this to wash our clothes in biodegradable soap. Our meals, which consisted every day of noodles or rice, were cooked by live-in locals who were camped with us. We slept in hammocks, which is a very interesting experience indeed. Trying to get into them while up to your knees in mud is definitely an acquired skill and was very funny after a few mess-mug-fulls of the rice wine that was passed around the camp at night! The jungle is definitely not the place for the squeamish: every bug and insect was on steroids and had tattoos. And everything bites or stings. But the wildlife and scenery is breathtaking.*

Don't be put off by Vikki's experiences: it doesn't always have to be like that. Compared to Vikki, Robin Glegg, who volunteered with Biosphere Expeditions (p216), was positively pampered on one of his wildlife expeditions in the Altai (Siberia):

*Accommodation consisted of tents. The toilet facilities were known as 'long drop'. Yes, a deep hole in the ground, surrounded by a toilet tent. But the meals were superb considering we were well away from civilisation; plenty of soups and stews with loads of vegetables and fruit. Having been in the field every day until 5 or 6pm, we would bowl into the large mess tent and be greeted by an evening meal prepared by a hired cook and helpers. We really were fed like kings. Washing ourselves was interesting. There were two or three shower tents, where the water was supposed to be heated by solar showers. However, the helpers started to boil water before we returned from the field, so that a warmish shower actually became a reality.*

Finally, there's the issue of what you do with yourself when you're not volunteering. How do you spend your evenings?

Sometimes you're so shattered you just crawl thankfully into bed. Otherwise, volunteers make their own entertainment (this is where living with, or nearby, other volunteers can help). Of course, if you are working in a city or large town you'll have the usual night-time attractions (as long as you can afford them). Linda Walsh, who volunteered in Brazil, says:

*Entertainment whilst living in Rio was endless. The volunteers were all really friendly and we had a very active social scene outside work.*

Jacqueline Hill's experience in Bangladesh was different but rather closer to what a lot of international volunteers find themselves doing when they are not working:

*Entertainment consisted mainly of reading (I got through the entire VSO library and had books sent from home), writing an online diary, writing emails, letters and visiting local friends. I listened to the BBC World Service a lot and talking books. There really wasn't much else a single female could do.*

Kerry Davies, who volunteered in Cambodia with VSO, agrees:

*Evenings were quiet and the Cambodian people would often lock up their houses at 8pm. I spent my evenings reading books, watching DVDs bought locally and I also studied with the Open University, although I had to go to the capital, Phnom Penh, for an internet connection.*

On the other hand, as many conservation and wildlife projects are group-based, the team spirit often continues long into the night. Clodagh O'Brien's experience in Borneo is typical:

*We had a wonderful time. Many of the guys who worked at the reserve played guitar so we sang together most nights, had bonfires, learned poi and, when the tropical rain set in, watched a DVD or two. Put it this way, I was rarely bored.*

Robin Glegg, remembers this about his last trip to Namibia:

*After helping to clear the dishes (helpers were on hand to wash them) we all gathered around the campfire telling tales and generally discussing where the cheetahs were hiding and recapping the day's activities. We generally went to bed on the wrong side of midnight, with some of the group staying up until the last embers of the campfire had died.*

## THE WORKING WEEK

As Dr Kate Simpson advises in her Ethical Volunteering Guide on p32, try to obtain a rough estimate of how many hours a week you will work before you go overseas. Also try to clarify what happens work-wise on weekends.

On most volunteer programmes you are expected to work full-time five days a week, with weekends off. Sometimes, though, you may work a six-day week. At times, the hours might be longer. Rachel Oxberry, who worked in an orphanage in Ecuador, says:

*I generally worked six days a week from 7.30am to 9.00pm. Every so often I took a weekend off.*

Sometimes you may need to work shifts. Jackie Bowles, who also worked in an orphanage, but in Brazil, says:

*Volunteers had various timetables according to what suited the children and the educators. Your shift could either be 9am to 5pm with weekends off, or 7am to 7pm with every second day off.*

Or your time might be a little more flexible, as with Peter Bennett, who was a volunteer teacher in Sudan:

*At the university we were contracted to teach for 15 hours a week. In theory, we were expected to use the same time again for lesson planning and preparation. In addition, our host organisation expected us to get involved with other local voluntary initiatives. Time off was strongly discouraged and hard to negotiate.*

Some volunteers, of course, don't wish to work full-time and opportunities do exist within well-managed volunteer programmes for part-time work. Jackie Bowles even did this after a period of full-time volunteering. She explains:

*I volunteered for five months, then returned for a further three months on a part-time basis as I missed it so much!*

What you want to avoid at all costs is any misunderstanding about the hours you'll be expected to work. There is nothing more discouraging than thinking you'll be volunteering full-time then finding that you're only needed for a couple of hours a day or less. Sometimes, this can happen mid-placement rather than at the start. Sharon Baxter, who taught in Tibet, comments:

*When I first arrived we taught 15 classes a week. That was nice and easy and even with preparation and marking meant we still had plenty of free time. However, about half way through the six months, the school employed a Tibetan English teacher and cut our classes to only nine per week. There wasn't really enough to do after that and at times I felt a bit redundant.*

If you are volunteering on a short-term or medium-term basis, the issue of holidays or extra time off might not be relevant. Poonam Sattee, who worked with street children in Guatemala, admits:

*I was told I could have time off but I chose not to take it as I genuinely enjoyed my work and wanted to be there. I also knew I would be having a long holiday at the end of my time volunteering and so was prepared to wait.*

Even on short-term or medium-term assignments, you can usually negotiate time off with your host organisation or you'll be given a certain amount of leave commensurate with the time you have worked. Whatever your arrangements for free time are, it is important to have a responsible and professional attitude towards arranging it.

Photo: © British Exploring Society

Working (and sleeping) in the wilds of the
Himalayas with the British Exploring Society

However, if you are volunteering long term you will expect (and need) proper and pre-arranged vacation times. Many charities or sending agencies that arrange these types of placements have standard terms. For instance, Kerry Davies, who volunteered for two years in Cambodia, had to choose between two options:

*I had the choice of either the VSO holidays (four weeks plus all the public holidays – totalling 25 days) or UNICEF holidays (30 days plus seven UNICEF standard public holidays). I chose the latter as it was more flexible and I was working with other UNICEF staff.*

Depending on how long you volunteer for, weekends off and holidays are an important part of your volunteer experience. Many international volunteers choose to travel at weekends to see more of the country in which they are living and many manage to visit neighbouring countries too. Oliver Walker taught in Sri Lanka and explains:

*At the weekends I stayed at a guest house in Kandy which is owned by the charity's representative. I became friendly with another volunteer and we travelled around the country together on Saturdays and Sundays.*

VOLUNTEER

# HEALTH, SAFETY & IN-COUNTRY SUPPORT

Volunteering in a foreign country miles away from home is not without its risks. If there's a medical or security emergency you need to know that the organisation you're volunteering with has up-to-date plans and procedures for dealing with the situation.

Before you travel overseas it is important that you feel fully briefed and prepared. In some cases there will be further briefings or training once you arrive in the country. For instance, Andrew Sansom, who volunteered with Biosphere Expeditions (p216) on wildlife projects in Slovakia and Sri Lanka, remembers:

*At the start of the expedition, our leader took us through the Risk Register, which related to everything from wild animals to heatstroke. She then pointed out that we had already survived the biggest risk of all: Sri Lankan drivers.*

When Robert Driver volunteered in Belize with Gapforce (p157), he says:

*We had intensive jungle training and an acclimatisation period, so when we went to the jungle for the first time we felt confident we could live there for eight weeks. Medics were also on the project site at all times.*

One of the key ways to ensure that volunteers remain safe and well overseas is through in-country support. This means that your sending agency either has one or more local staff members whose job it is to help you and advise you, as well as deal with any emergencies. When choosing a volunteer organisation it is always wise to ask about in-country support and find out how 'local' the local support really is. Are they talking about a person just down the road or someone a hundred miles away looking after dozens of volunteers?

Rachel Guise, who volunteered in health and sanitation, sustainable livelihoods and conservation with SEED Madagascar (p168), says:

*The charity ensured there was always a night guard at our campsite and there was always a local guide on site with us. We could go into town by ourselves if we chose, but the guides were always happy to come with us and offered advice and assistance. There were also other representatives of the charity in Madagascar who were easy to contact.*

So much for predictable risks; however, what happens if the country you're volunteering in becomes politically unstable? In this case, not only do you need good in-country support, but well-planned security procedures. Sue Towler, ex-Transform Programme Manager at the charity Tearfund (p249), had a difficult security issue to handle in early 2006 but the organisation was well prepared to assist staff in the field:

# LONG-TERM VOLUNTEERING WITH YOUR PARTNER

We volunteered with VSO for two years in Ethiopia. We worked for the Ministry of Education, setting up a postgraduate qualification for teacher educators. We researched and wrote the Higher Diploma Programme with support and advice from colleagues in colleges and universities.

Because we had spent a year travelling through India prior to doing VSO, I think we had already recognised and adjusted to some of the challenges of living and travelling together in sometimes difficult circumstances.

For us, there were far more advantages than disadvantages to being a couple. It was reassuring to have one aspect of our lives familiar as we set off into the unknown and we were able to be mutually supportive. There were difficult and distressing times but we found that when one of us was 'down' the other was able to be 'up' and so we got through these periods. Sharing our problems helped us find solutions to them and we were able to be supportive of others, too. It added a new dimension to our relationship as we had different experiences to share.

The only disadvantage related to the fact that we were doing the same job. This meant that we were together almost ALL the time! We did have some professional disagreements, which inevitably spilled over into our personal lives. However, most of the time we worked together creatively and by the second year we had identified distinct roles for ourselves within the project. In our opinion, the ideal form of volunteering with a partner would be to have different jobs in the same place.

As an aside, we knew some couples where only one member had a placement while the other was an 'accompanying partner'. It was often difficult for the partner to find a role for themselves in a context where there were limited social opportunities.

**Deborah Jordan & David Spinney**

*We had a Transform team in Bangalore, India, for four months, working with Tearfund's partner, Oasis. As with all teams, we had conducted a thorough risk assessment before departure and considered it safe for the team to travel. But a month into their stay, a leading Indian actor died, triggering major riots in the city. As news of the unrest reached us, the team was immediately advised to return to its accommodation on the outskirts of the city and to remain there until further notice. Events were unfolding quickly so we had a decision to make: was it safe for the team to stay or should we evacuate? We were particularly concerned when we learned that the unrest had prompted the British consulate in the city to close. We were in twice-daily phone contact with the team and our partner, Oasis, as well as in regular contact with Tearfund's Security Adviser and the Foreign and Commonwealth Office. Thankfully, the situation soon calmed and the consulate reopened, enabling us to avoid initiating our evacuation plan.*

First-class support and emergency planning was also a feature of Jacqueline Hill's volunteer placement in Bangladesh:

*Hmmm. Going to a Muslim country at the beginning of the Iraq war does not make for a restful placement. VSO were great at contacting us every day during the most difficult times to update us on the security situation and to explain their escalation procedure, ranging from recalling us all back to Dhaka through to full-scale evacuation. I'm happy to say we never got anywhere near that level, but we did stay indoors on Fridays for a few months, as that is the main day for prayers and things could get heated as people came out of the mosques. Apart from those exceptional circumstances, safety and security issues in Bangladesh were a feature of our in-country training.*

Tried and tested procedures are also essential for medical emergencies. Michelle Hawkins, who volunteered as a staff member for Raleigh International (p151), was a project manager with the Bri Bri Indian community in a village in the Talamancan Indian Reserve of Costa Rica. She remembers:

*Health and safety were paramount, as the village was only accessible by canoe and had no roads, electricity or phones. The nearest hospital was five hours away by river. I ran 'casualty-evacuation' drills to ensure we all knew what to do in the event of someone falling off the suspension bridge or getting bitten by a snake. End result: everyone fine.*

Health, safety and in-country support are important elements of keeping safe when you volunteer. Smaller organisations, though, may have fewer resources: your pre-departure briefing may come in the form of a handbook and your emergency support may simply be a telephone number in your home country. Even this is likely to be more than you get if you arrange a placement yourself with a local charity or NGO, and this is something you should take into consideration. See p98 for the Top Ten Safety Tips for Female Volunteers and p92 for details on health and hygiene while volunteering.

## WHO TO GO WITH

You can volunteer on your own, with a friend or family member, or on team-based projects with people you either do or do not know. Sometimes the choice is down to you but sometimes it is up to your sending agency. Some organisations prefer to place you either on your own or in pairs.

Rachel Oxberry volunteered in Ecuador on her own and is a strong advocate of going solo:

> *I went alone which I feel helped me get the most out of my experience. I had to immerse myself fully in the culture and language and work out how to deal with very challenging situations. I was often out of my comfort zone which made me much stronger as a person.*

Poonam Sattee, who volunteered in Guatemala, agrees:

> *I went by myself and that worked out fine. Initially, until I made friends, it was an isolating experience, but after the first two months I felt very settled. The pros of going by yourself are that you are much more independent and your Spanish will really take off. It helps you take more initiative and I think you are more likely to make local friends as opposed to relying on your group or partner. The cons: the initial stages of settling in can be quite tough, but apart from this my experience worked out well.*

If you choose to volunteer alone, you will usually make friends pretty quickly when you arrive at your placement. But if your placement is an isolated one then your options may be limited. This is what Sharon Baxter experienced when she taught in Tibet:

*I got a bit depressed and lonely towards the end. I spent the last two months on my own and by that time the weather was very cold and it got dark early. There didn't seem to be as many people around as in the summer. The children studied in the classrooms from 7pm until bedtime, so most nights I didn't see another human being after 7pm. Sitting on your own in a freezing flat with no radio or TV does eventually get a bit wearing. Very few people spoke any English and even though I made a few friends who could speak some English, it is difficult to get really close when there are language difficulties. By the end I was desperate to have an easy conversation with someone, without having to talk in pidgin English.*

The thought of volunteering with a friend can give you more confidence, particularly before you leave home and just after you arrive. But in some cases, it can mean that making other friends is not as easy as it would be if you were on your own. In Linda Walsh's experience it didn't make much difference to her stay in Brazil:

*I went with a friend but we did different work. There were obvious advantages in this – we supported each other, especially when we were living out at the farm with no-one else around. When we were back in Rio with lots of other volunteers it didn't really make any difference as we worked different hours and had different friends. Overall, it was good to have a friend along, but not necessary.*

Volunteering with a partner is a popular option for long-term volunteers and has it own set of advantages and disadvantages (see the box on p50 written by Deborah Jordan and David Spinney on volunteering with your partner). Sometimes you can volunteer with children, too. It's still uncommon but is a growing trend. Jo Morgan volunteered teaching in the Indian Himalayas with her seven-year-old son, Liam. She admits:

*On the first day he was embarrassed about the colour of his white skin and I began to wonder why I'd put him through this. But by the second day he'd made friends with his classmates, was 'one of the gang' and started to realise that children all over the world are basically the same and have similar needs and desires. He learned that some children have only one set of clothes, eat only rice and can't afford to be fussy. One of his friends had a birthday yet it was unmarked – no presents, cards or a party. Liam was initially incredulous but is now beginning to understand that these things are not to be taken for granted.*

Of course, you may decide to set off on your own but join a team-based volunteer project in the field. These are more common on conservation and wildlife programmes than on development programmes. On many group-based volunteer programmes where everyone arrives and departs at the same time, you can ask to be put in touch with other team members prior to travelling overseas. This can help the team to bond, although evidence suggests that some groups need little help with this. On Robin Glegg's expedition to the Altai (Siberia) with Biosphere Expeditions (p216) he remembers:

*I went by myself and knew nobody who was going. There was slight trepidation at spending 12 days in the very close company of 12 or so individuals from various countries whom I'd never met. In reality it was a great way to meet a diverse group of people from different walks of life. We all jelled incredibly well and some close friendships were made. This certainly heightened the enjoyment of the expedition. When I did the Oman expedition it was a reunion with six of the 12 from the Altai trip.*

But sometimes you're not so lucky. David Grassham volunteered in the Indian Himalaya and says with regret:

*Unfortunately, our group did eventually split. Three girls tended to spend time only with each other, which was a shame. Even through I did get on with everyone, if you volunteer with a group it is possible that you may not like some of the other members. In our group, one particular person did seem to be disliked by quite a few others.*

## MEET THE ORGANISATION

As part of your research, try to meet representatives from the various charities or sending agencies that have volunteer programmes you're interested in. Many of these organisations hold regular information or briefing evenings, which are publicised on their websites, and many also attend travel shows.

## SUMMARY OF QUESTIONS

To recap, here are some key questions to ask all the organisations you may be interested in volunteering with. It pays to do your research and make an informed choice:

• **Organisation** What are your aims and objectives? Are you a charity, not-for-profit organisation or limited company? When were you established? What are your policies on ecotourism and ethical tourism and how are they implemented?

• **Selection process** What are your selection criteria and processes? Will the interview be in person? What is the average age of volunteers? Do you rightly ensure that those working with children or vulnerable adults have clean criminal background checks?

• **The programmes** Do you work with local partner programmes? If so, how many partner programmes do you currently work with? How many of these partner programmes have you worked with for more than three years? How do I know I'll be working on a worthwhile, sustainable project that is needed by a local community? How will the work be continued after I leave? How many volunteers do you place annually? What job will I be doing and can you give me a brief job description? How do I know that my volunteering won't take a paid job away from a local person? What is the time frame of the volunteer project I'll be working on? What hours will I work? Will I need to speak the local language? What will the accommodation be like? Can I volunteer with another person? Can I talk to some returned volunteers?

• **Costs** What exactly is included in the costs? Do you make a financial contribution to your volunteer programmes and, if so, exactly how much is this? Can I see a breakdown of where my money goes? Do you help with fundraising? (Only ask this if you're volunteering with a charity.)

• **Pre-departure** What briefings, training and/or cultural orientation sessions are there?

• **Health and safety** What health and safety and emergency procedures do you have in place? Are there staff members on site or do you have local representatives? If so, how far will they be from where I am volunteering? What medical care is available?

• **Debriefing** Is there any support and debriefing procedure when I get home? How can I stay in touch with the organisation?

## DO YOU HAVE WHAT IT TAKES?

So, what qualities or skills make a good volunteer? Let's ask the experts – those that have 'been there, done that' and have heaps of advice and learning to pass on.

Poonam Sattee, who volunteered in Guatemala with street kids, suggests these are the qualities you need:

*A good sense of humour. Lots of patience. An open mind – particularly to new ways of working, cultural norms, values and traditions. An ability to speak the language – if you are learning the language as you go along, it can be frustrating for you and the people you work with if you spend more time trying to understand what has been said than getting stuck into work. Also important are enthusiasm, initiative and dependability (the more you show the more responsibility you will be given).*

Patience is a quality that comes up time and time again. Jacqueline Hill, who volunteered in Bangladesh, had to find plenty of patience, along with some other key qualities:

*Flexibility and adaptability are key. These are the qualities that I developed hugely while I was away. Also important are appropriate self-confidence, the ability to work with others and not only accept, but make the most of, differences in approaches and ways of working. You need to build relationships too, often without the help of a common language. I found I had to 'switch off' quite a lot to generate the patience needed to get everyday things done. Everything took so much longer and was so much more complicated and difficult than at home – particularly anything to do with officialdom. Another thing I learned in Bangladesh was to ask for help. The ability to listen and think are much more important than telling other people what to do or rushing in and doing things.*

Keeping an open mind was important for Poonam Sattee and was also key for Kerry Davies, who volunteered in Cambodia:

*A good volunteer should approach their placement with an open mind. Cambodian logic is not generally the same as that of UK people. It is important to remember that your colleagues are all highly intelligent and have survived many atrocities in their life. They don't need anyone patronising them or thinking they are superior because they have had the luxury of an education. Cambodians have a great sense of humour and a smile speaks a thousand words. It takes a long time to fit in and gain their trust, but when you do the rewards are well worth the wait.*

A New Zealander, John Gordon, worked as an agricultural tutor in Bougainville for the Volunteer Service Abroad (VSA, p165). He agrees that patience and respect are important:

*You sow seeds, plant cuttings and graft on new ideas but whether they 'take' or not is part of someone else's future.*

Sandra Sinclair was also with VSA and worked as a midwife in Bougainville. She says a bit of realism is necessary:

*You do have to accept that, as a foreign health professional, you can't change the world or do anything quickly. But I made small changes which I am confident are continuing.*

Respect and understanding for the local people you work alongside are also crucial qualities, in Phil Sydor's eyes. He volunteered in Zambia, where he helped build a teaching centre and says it's important:

*Not to assume you know it all! We worked with the local people, not as managers to tell them what to do, but as labourers. They had appointed a site manager and we made sure we deferred to her and asked her what we should be doing. The local people were surprised at this.*

The ability to relate to all sorts of different people is what Elaine Massie and Richard Lawson believe is important. They have volunteered many times on short-term environmental projects and say:

*You have to be able to get on with all sorts of people. Earthwatch volunteers range from 16 to 80 years of age and you may have this wide age range in your group. Also, you generally live in close quarters with everyone and there is often very little opportunity for you to have your 'own space'.*

But for a comprehensive summary of what qualities you need to have as a volunteer on conservation and wildlife projects, let's turn to the words of Robin Glegg (a veteran of three expeditions):

*You need to be open-minded, team-spirited and tolerant but enquiring. Do not expect to be 'nannied' and be prepared for some tough times, such as adverse weather, hard physical activity or basic living conditions. Be prepared to mix with people you have never met before and be prepared to experience a very different lifestyle to the one at home. Remember that the more you*

# THE ILLS AND CURES OF LONG-TERM VOLUNTEERING

**Homesickness**

Some of you will feel this common condition of travelling overseas, some of you won't. One thing I have witnessed on many occasions with homesickness, especially with younger long-term volunteers, is that their placement seems like an eternity when they first get overseas. The temptation to go home is very high.

• **Cure** Keep time in perspective. Sure, 'there's no place like home'… but home is always there. The time you have will go very quickly! Try to join social groups for support outside of work. One thing I always recommend is contacting your embassy for advice about these. Also, introduce familiar activities into your daily routine. Joining a local health club (if there is one) is good because it gives you an element of familiarity in your daily life which can be helpful.

**Communication Shock**

Volunteering is all about different cultures, both personally and professionally. There are elements of a culture that you may not be able to explain or understand – this is where communication comes in. Language barriers and a different way of communicating could be potential obstacles to your happiness. Don't isolate yourself from your surroundings and misinterpret the behaviour of colleagues and friends.

• **Cure** Allow yourself time to get used to your new environment. Give people the benefit of the doubt until you are accustomed to your surroundings. Be proactive in communicating – ask for information and assistance and for people to translate.

**Privacy & Independence**

Your host organisation may feel responsible for your welfare and may want to 'look after' you in a way you are not used to back home. This is especially relevant to volunteers who are provided with accommodation. For instance, your hosts may be concerned about you going out unaccompanied late at night. In addition, you may have little privacy, with people entering your bedroom without permission.

• **Cure** Again, proactive, patient communication can help resolve these situations, as can understanding of different points of view and ways of life.

**Your Host Organisation**

You may find certain elements of your workplace very frustrating. The structure of the organisation may have apparent failures (from your perspective). Some of the problems that volunteers have mentioned to me are: poor management; misspent funds; overstaffing; time-wasting; lack of transparency; and poor strategic planning.

• **Cure** What is different may not necessarily be bad. If it clearly is, your role is to SLOWLY suggest ways that the organisation can improve. Don't suggest a radical change on day three (I know people who have done this), save this till week seven!

## Your Role

How you want to help and what is needed may not be the same things. A great deal of your time may be devoted to fundraising, for instance, as a way of improving the capacity of your host organisation. You may be given a lot of office work instead of field work, which could conflict with your objectives. Initially you may not be given huge responsibilities and may not feel you are achieving what you set out to do.

• **Cure 1** In the first six weeks you should not rely on the fact that you are committing your time (and money) to guarantee your integration and acceptance into your host organisation. Work closely with your host organisation in negotiating a role for yourself that both you and they are happy with. Build trust.

• **Cure 2** 'Doing by learning' not 'learning by doing' is a good mantra here. Don't expect to change the world in your first six weeks. And when you do start 'doing', see your achievements for what they are. I have worked with volunteers who achieve a lot in their placement, even after the initial settling-in period, but still insist that they aren't doing enough. Write down your achievements, however small, and think carefully about the time you have and what you should realistically expect to achieve.

## General Cures...

• **The six-week rule** The first six weeks of overseas volunteering is a critical stage in adapting to new surroundings. When you are living and working in a new country as a long-term volunteer, you will have to adapt to a very different environment.

• **Slow down** You probably will not operate as fast as you would in your home country when volunteering. This is fine! Take small steps to achieve what you want from your volunteering experience.

• **Knowledge is power** Research the country you are volunteering in and the organisation you are volunteering with before leaving your home country. Also, it can be positive to establish communication with your colleagues in your host organisation before you depart. Expose yourself to as much information as possible about the country you are going to, such as images, documentaries, films and books, and try and talk to people who have been there.

**Katherine Tubb**

*put in, the more you get out of these expeditions. Oh yes, I nearly forgot, do not necessarily expect to see lots of wildlife. The tragedy is that in many parts of the world, much of the wildlife has been poached, driven away or become extinct. Many Biosphere expeditions have been set up in order just to ascertain the presence of a species. Do not build up your hopes and you will not be disappointed.*

Robin makes an extremely valuable point here. Part of 'having what it takes' to be an international volunteer, whether you work in development or conservation and wildlife, is to have realistic expectations of your placement. Nine times out of ten if a placement doesn't work out the reason is that the expectations of the volunteer didn't match the reality of the experience.

There are things you can do to ensure that you approach your placement in the right spirit of respect and tolerance. Research your chosen destination and leave cultural norms and expectations behind. Be mindful of how your arrival on the scene might impact on the locals you're working with. Successful volunteers are like sponges soaking up as much as possible about the circumstances they find themselves in and taking their cues from how the local people interact. For instance, casual clothing may be the norm in your country of origin but if you're working for an NGO or government agency in Laos, you'll be expected to wear modest traditional dress. If you're receiving a monthly allowance from your government, you may find yourself earning more than the locals you're working alongside, so be discreet. And remember that volunteers are subject to the laws of the local country. In Western democracies it's acceptable to be an anti-royalist, but in Thailand, speak out against the monarchy and not only do you cause great offence you could also become familiar with the interior of a local police station.

# MORE INFORMATION

## PUBLICATIONS

• *Volunteer Work Overseas for Australians and New Zealanders* by Peter Hodge (Global Exchange, 2010). Tells how to find and prepare for a volunteer position from childcare to plumbing, with workplace issues to ponder and accounts from returned volunteers.

# USEFUL WEBSITES

• **British Overseas NGOs for Development (BOND)** (www.bond.org.uk) A network of voluntary organisations that promotes the exchange of experience, ideas and information among its members both in the UK and internationally.

• **Center for Responsible Travel (CREST)** (www.responsibletravel.org) The website of this research institution is packed with quick tips on responsible travelling and has useful publications for download.

• **Comhlámh** (www.comhlamh.org) A membership organisation that supports returned development workers and campaigns on global development issues. It is the Irish equivalent of BOND, NIDOS and WCIA (listed here).

• **The Telegraph Adventure Travel Show** (www.adventureshow.co.uk) A chance to make contact with some of the UK's international voluntary organisations.

• **Destinations: The Holiday & Travel Show** (www.destinationsshow.com) One opportunity to meet some of the UK's international voluntary organisations.

• **Network of International Development Organisations in Scotland (NIDOS)** (www.nidos.org.uk) A network of over 100 organisations that aims to strengthen Scotland's contribution to reducing inequality and poverty worldwide.

• **ServiceLeader.org** (www.serviceleader.org) General articles on issues faced by North American volunteers, with links and information focusing on international service positions.

• **Welsh Centre for International Affairs (WCIA)** (www.wcia.org.uk) This site is the Welsh equivalent of BOND, NIDOS and Comhlámh.

• **World Service Enquiry** (www.wse.org.uk) Lots of information on international volunteering and working in development, including one-to-one advice.

# 03

## The Practicalities

This is where the fun really begins. You've done your research, you have an idea of what you'd like to do, where you might like to go and you've set aside the time. All you have to do now is make it happen…

## APPLICATION & SELECTION

Most international volunteers apply to sending agencies eight to 12 months before they wish to volunteer. This time frame works well for three reasons: it gives you and your organisation enough time to find the right volunteer project; it allows you sufficient time to save the money; and it means you've got months in which to organise your life at home so you can go abroad (see Chapter 4 for more details on this).

If you are not as organised as this or have decided to volunteer at the last minute, don't worry. Most sending agencies will still work with you to find a placement with only a month or two's notice. However, places on the most popular conservation and wildlife expeditions can fill up a year in advance, and many of the organisations placing skilled volunteers need at least four months' notice.

In Australia and New Zealand, some sending agencies specialise in short-term placements and place volunteers without a great deal of experience or tertiary qualifications. Placements such as these are usually for self-funding volunteers. Long-term placements, however, mostly require a commitment of at least a full year and people must have a minimum of a couple of years' experience in their area of expertise in order to meet the specific needs of the host organisation. Such programmes generally attract volunteers in their mid-twenties up. The application process is fairly rigorous and isn't unlike applying for a job, with specific selection criteria needing to be addressed, written references provided and the possibly of a phone interview. Personal qualities and attributes like cultural awareness, self-assurance, flexibility and good communication and interpersonal skills are viewed as equally important as professional experience, since these placements require living and working in a developing country.

The majority of sending agencies ask you to download an application form from their website. This usually asks for your personal details, including your education, qualifications, skills, medical history and any criminal convictions. It may also ask you a few questions, like: 'Why do you want to volunteer overseas?' 'What experiences have you had that show you are adaptable?' 'What are your strengths and weaknesses?' Usually, you then post this off with your CV, two references (one personal and one professional) and two passport-sized photos.

Some organisations prefer you to apply by sending in your CV with a covering letter. If this is the case, make sure that your covering letter tells the organisation why you want to volunteer and what you can offer. Eoghan Mackie, CEO of Challenges Worldwide (p176) tells us what he is looking for in a covering letter and at interview:

*Each particular host organisation has its own culture which we will assess the applicant against. The applicant must also have the relevant professional experience our host partner is looking for. However, there are generic qualities that a person must show in their application (and later at interview) before we will seriously consider them for selection as a CWW volunteer. These include independence, adaptability, flexibility, communication skills, determination and a sense of humour. Perhaps the most important quality of all is the ability to be objective.*

After you have sent in your application, you wait for the organisation to contact you. They will usually do this by phone to either arrange a personal interview or ask you to attend one of their selection or assessment days. These events are fascinating and usually involve problem-solving tasks and programmes designed to test how you work in a team. Jacqueline Hill, who volunteered in Bangladesh, remembers her assessment day with VSO:

*It was well organised and a lot of fun. The day consisted of some group exercises and an individual interview. The interview goes into more depth, particularly about personal circumstances, than an ordinary job interview, but it was sensitively handled and we could see the reasons why it was important to make sure we were ready for the huge commitment we were signing up to. My advice to anyone going for the assessment day? Be yourself and enjoy it.*

Sometimes the selection process takes place over a weekend, as it does if you apply to become a Raleigh International staff member. Duncan Purvis, associate trainer at Raleigh International (p151), explains:

*Successful applicants will be invited to attend a Staff Assessment Weekend. This is an intensive programme designed to recreate programme life and gives you a taste of what staff roles entail, as well as allowing us to assess your suitability. Depending upon your performance during the weekend, we will either offer you a post on a programme which makes best use of your particular skills and qualifications or suggest further action for you to take in order to reapply in the future.*

If you are the type of volunteer the organisation is looking for, UK and USA organisations will request a deposit from you (naturally this applies only to fee-based programmes). This could be anything from £50 to £500 in the UK or US$75 to US$750 in the US, and is usually non-refundable. Australasian organisations generally don't require a deposit. You will also need to read the organisation's terms and conditions document and sign it (very standard stuff). Some organisations also ask you to fill out a detailed medical history questionnaire and, if it highlights any potential problems, to visit a health expert nominated by them.

Over the subsequent weeks or months the organisation will work with you to find a suitable placement. As this is dependent on local demand, it is good to remain flexible about where you go (there may not be a demand for your skills in your country of first choice). Programme fees, or 'fundraising targets' as they're also called (see the next section for more), must usually be paid in instalments, with the final payment made three to six weeks before departure.

Of course, every organisation has a slightly different process. Conservation and wildlife programmes often have less stringent selection processes, because working with animals or the environment is quite different to working closely with local people in a development capacity. And if you arrange your own placement directly, some, none, or all of this process may occur.

# RAISING THE MONEY

Whether you volunteer through a sending agency in your own country or fix up a placement directly, costs will be involved. Even if you go with one of the organisations that covers your costs and pays you a stipend (eg VSO, Médecins Sans Frontières, AVI), you will still want extra money for weekends away, holidays and possibly independent travel after your placement has ended.

However much your volunteer placement costs, it is a good idea to start saving (or fundraising) as soon as you can. It can take volunteers up to a year to get the money together.

## PAYING VS FUNDRAISING

If you volunteer with a charity, the money you pay for your placement is always referred to as the money you need to 'fundraise'. Effectively it is payment (you won't be able to go if you don't meet your fundraising target). However, charities don't like to call it that because the nature of how you saved the money is supposed to be different. One motivation for approaching the money issue in this way is that self-promotion is important to charities. It makes sense for them to encourage you to use their name to run special events to raise funds and to collect donations from friends, family and members of the public. In addition, for younger volunteers, in particular, fundraising is supposed to be part of your overall experience and integral to the self-development aspect of your volunteering experience.

Of course, if you're an older volunteer, or don't have time to fundraise and just want to pay out of your own pocket, this is allowed, though slightly frowned upon.

## YOUR BUDGET

Regardless of what is (and is not) included in the overall fee or donation you pay your sending agency, it is a useful exercise to work out a detailed budget of all likely costs. Bear in mind while you're doing this that fluctuating exchange rates can affect that all-important account balance. It also pays to do some investigation into the cost of living at your destination. You may be surprised to learn, for instance, that Angola's capital, Luanda, was found to be the second most expensive city in the world in a 2016 worldwide cost-of-living survey. Kinshasa and N'Djamena, the respective captials of the Democratic Republic of Congo and Chad, also cracked the top 10, beating out London, Paris, New

York and San Francisco. You can break your budget into three main cost areas: pre-departure; in-country; and coming home.

### Pre-departure Costs

Costs that apply here may include:

• **Placement fee/donation** If you have arranged your placement directly with a grassroots NGO there may not be a fee (although you may be asked for a donation towards the project). Otherwise you may pay anything from £850 to £4000 (US$1000 to US$5000), depending on how long you're going for, where you're going, what you're doing and what is included in this cost. In Australia or New Zealand fees might range from A$750 to A$7250 (NZ$800 to NZ$7700). For more detailed information on the cost of specific volunteer programmes, see Chapters 5 to 8.

• **Interviews and briefing events** Remember to budget for expenses (eg travel, accommodation) related to face-to-face interviews with your sending agency and also any follow-up briefing or training events.

• **Research material** You may want to buy a couple of maps, guidebooks or language-learning apps.

• **Putting your life on hold** This is a big one, with potentially significant costs. For instance, will you need to put your personal belongings into storage? Will you continue to pay rent? And what about the cost of redirecting your mail?

• **International flights** Regardless of where you're going, flights will be a big part of your pre-departure budget. For more information on airline tickets and travel, see p75.

• **Visas** For a discussion about whether you should obtain a tourist visa or a volunteering visa, see p80. Most tourist visas range in price between £25 (US$30) and £75 (US$90). Tourist visas for Asia and Africa are often quoted in US dollars and start from around US$30 and US$50 respectively

• **Travel insurance** This could cost anything from around £400 in the UK to over US$500 in the USA for 12-month worldwide cover. You could certainly obtain travel insurance for less but you don't want to skimp when you're an international volunteer. Read the section on travel insurance on p81.

• **Immunisations and medication** In the UK most vaccines cost between £30 to £65 per dose, with some vaccinations requiring two or three shots. Doses in the the USA range from US$20 to US$150. In Australia, a standard consultation at a travel clinic will cost around A$65 plus any required vaccines, which range from as little as A$30 to as high as A$315 for a rabies or A$360 for two doses of the Japanese B encephalitis vaccine. Add in cost of malaria prophylactics, which can be up to £100 (US$130; A$150) per month, and a trip to the travel clinic could easily set you back a hefty sum. See p89 for more information on health-related matters.

• **Medical kit** A decent medical kit in the USA or UK will cost between £30 to £50 (US$50 to US$80). In Australia it's a similar investment – between A$60 to A$100 (excluding antimalarials). See p93 for suggestions on what your medical kit might contain.

• **Equipment** The majority of volunteer organisations send you a kit list prior to departure (see p84 for our suggestions and ideas from returned volunteers on what to pack). What you spend on equipment depends on where you are going and what you are doing. The kit you need for marine conservation, for instance, can sometimes be more costly than for other projects. On a musical note, if you don't have one already you might want to invest in an MP3 player or put your music on a smartphone.

• **Travel to airport** Something to add into your budget spreadsheet.

### In-Country Costs

These costs may be more difficult to judge, as you're estimating from afar. However, the organisation you're volunteering with will be able to give you guidance; you can obtain an indication of costs from many guidebooks, too. It is also crucial to talk to returned volunteers.

Here are the main spending areas that you will need to consider:

• **Travel to and from airport and placement** It's important to think about this from a safety perspective. In some cases a representative from your organisation will pick you up or drop you off, but you may have to pay for this. Otherwise, you'll need money for public transport or a taxi.

• **Living expenses** This includes accommodation, food and drink, laundry and entertainment expenses, and spending money. How much you should budget for depends on the cost of living in the country and whether you are city based or in more rural surroundings. To a certain extent it also depends on your own standards and what you can afford. For reasons of cultural sensitivity though, regardless of what they can afford, volunteers rarely splurge on their accommodation. Rachel Oxberry volunteered in Ecuador and lived simply:

*I had my own room which was very basic with just a bed. I had a cold shower with hot water about once a week. My meals were pretty simple and I either hand washed or took my laundry to a laundromat in town. I rarely left the* *home at night: I tended to read and go to bed. I was spending approximately US$40 a week.*

• **Keeping in touch** This is not a costly business these days, unless you use your mobile phone unwisely (presuming you do get network coverage). For a discussion of all the options for keeping in touch, see p104.

• **Travel at weekends** Chances are you'll want to see a bit of the country you're in, get away for a short while to relieve any job-related stress or pop over the border to renew your visa. Weekend breaks are often a volunteer's lifeline, so you need to budget for them.

• **Post-volunteer travel** Many international volunteers take the opportunity of being abroad to travel after their placement. You could choose to travel home slowly overland (as far as possible) or spend more time exploring the region where you are based. Whatever you choose, you may like to allow for this eventuality in your budgeting.

• **Sundry expenses** You may want to buy a few presents for the folks back home or the people you have met while volunteering, or get some souvenirs for yourself. There are a hundred other reasons why you may need a little extra money floating around in your budget.

• **Departure tax** Sometimes this is included in the cost of your ticket, sometimes it isn't. If it's not, don't forget to keep sufficient local currency so you can pay for it at the airport.

### Coming Home

Coming home can be a costly business, too. If you don't have a job to return to, you may need enough money to cover several months of living expenses while you look for one. Of course, it all depends on your circumstances. Will you be able to stay with friends or family while you find work, or will you move straight back into your house and have to cover the mortgage? Will you need to find several months' rent plus a deposit on a flat or house? Realistically, it is a good idea to budget for between £2500 to £5000 (US$3000 to US$6000) as a decent coming-home fund. For more information on coming home, see Chapter 9.

# SAVING

If you are not volunteering for a charity, you won't have the opportunity to fundraise officially (although, of course, friends and family may still want to help you on your way, because you are planning to work for a good cause for free).

Many volunteers work hard for the privilege of volunteering. Maggie Wild has been a volunteer leader for around 18 months on a variety of international projects. She says:

*I worked for three years in a graduate job and saved from the moment I started with this in mind. Half of my wage every month went into a savings account and this has been my safety net for the past two years.*

Sixty-nine-year-old David Daniels, who has undertaken two expeditions with the Scientific Exploration Society (p173) to the Amazon and Mongolia, funded his trip in the following way:

*I'm spending the kids' inheritance.*

Emma Campbell, who volunteered in Ecuador, explains:

*I used my redundancy money and I sold loads of my stuff on eBay.*

If you do start early, there are heaps of ways you can save or raise money in everyday life. For instance, you could get a second job, sell your car or items you can do without, use public transport instead of taxis, eat out less often, cancel the cleaner or jog around the park rather than pay for an expensive gym membership.

## FUNDRAISING

If there's one thing that almost all volunteers say about fundraising, it's that it takes up lots of time. With this in mind, it's a good idea to focus on events or schemes that will give you the maximum return (although this can be hard to judge at the outset).

When fundraising, most volunteers start with friends and family. At the time we spoke to him, Michael Tuckwell was fundraising to volunteer with Task Brasil (p210) in Brazil. He explains:

*I have a lifetime of connections and a full address book. I am also riding in the Bristol Biggest Bike Ride and have written to 78 people asking them to sponsor me for Task Brasil. To date, I have received £1200 from friends and family, some of whom have been extremely generous.*

Vikki Cole, who volunteered in Borneo, was also blessed with good personal contacts:

*Fundraising is the best part. I began bullying people I knew to donate directly to the website I set up. My sister and I (she came with me) also held a Valentine's ball and curry nights. Needless to say, more men came to the curry nights than the ball. Writing to large corporations to ask for donations is tough and you have to prepare for a lot of rejections. But walking door-to-door on a high street can yield some great raffle prize donations.*

Talking of big events that will bring the money in, this is Judith Stephen's experience of running two fundraising events:

*We did: 1) a quiz night plus supper – this raised £1500 after deducting our expenses; and 2) a concert plus supper – this raised nearly £1000 after expenses. The venue for both was a local church crypt with good kitchen facilities, so making a two-course supper for 75 each time was manageable. We charged £25 per ticket for each event and managed to create a nice dinner of mince-based casserole, couscous and salad followed by strawberries and cream for less than £1.50 per head (including a free glass of wine). As with most things, the planning was crucial. We had a team of about eight friends managing specific tasks like serving the wine, keeping a tally of quiz scores etc. With the quiz questions you need to be careful – the questions must not be so hard that people feel stupid. Both events went very smoothly but required a lot of work.*

If you are fundraising for a charity, the organisation itself will give you help and pointers. Mark Jacobs, managing director of SEED Madagascar (p168), explains:

*Fundraising resources include a full fundraising manual, fundraising documentation such as sponsorship forms, events to join in with and resources such as collection boxes, raffle tickets, posters and Christmas cards.*

In Australia, trivia nights are a great way to gather people in the interests of a good cause. Also, in a country known for its love of sport, it's no coincidence that events such as 24-hour marathons and cycling odysseys (only the fit need apply) are popular ways of convincing your nearest and dearest to empty their pockets of loose change to get you volunteering overseas.

Some organisations offer general advice on volunteer programme fundraising, others like British Exploring Society (p143) give active support to this endeavor. There is also an entire website devoted to fundraising ideas, resources and links – click over to www.fund-raising.com. The website for JustGiving (www.justgiving.com) is a great social platform to spread the word about your project, and it also seemlessly takes care of collecting the actual funds. As the UK's *Sunday Times* was quoted as saying:

*JustGiving has rewritten the fundraising rulebook.*

## PREPARATION

Many of the larger sending agencies run pre-departure briefing and training events. Subjects covered usually include: managing your expectations; cultural awareness and integration; what life could be like on your placement; and what to do if something goes wrong. In the case of Maggie Wild, a volunteer leader, training sessions were tailored to her role:

### CREATIVE FUNDRAISING

I used my old sixth form to do a lot of fundraising. One of my ideas proved really successful. Having gone to an all-girls' school, I approached three of the male teachers and asked them if they were willing to get their legs waxed for charity. After three weeks' of persuasion they agreed. I hyped the event, produced 'wanted' posters of the teachers around the school and ran an assembly saying that it would be up to the school which teachers got their legs done. I then charged people to vote for the teacher they most wanted to see get their legs waxed. I ran the voting over one week. The results showed a tie between two particular teachers so I ran the event again, just between the two. Again, I charged for people to vote. After the voting was over, I charged people to come and see the event, sold popcorn, drinks etc, and if people wanted to wax the teacher's legs themselves, I charged them per wax strip. It was a simple event and with lots of friends I managed to raise £600.

**Poonam Sattee**

*As a leader, my training was different to that of the other volunteers. I took the following courses: Residential Leadership Training; International Leader Training; First Aid at Work; and Wilderness First Aid.*

Even though this is specialist training, it is wise to consider what courses you could do independently to equip yourself for your placement. It is certainly a good idea to think about a first-aid and travel-safety course (for more information on both, see p92 and p99).

If you have a placement teaching English, you may want to obtain a teaching certificate. There are two main training systems: TEFL (Teacher of English as a Foreign Language) is most popular in Europe; and TESOL (Teachers of English to Speakers of Other Languages) is the main system in the USA. Before Sharon Baxter volunteered to teach in Tibet she says:

*I took a TEFL course, and also tried to learn some Tibetan. But the latter was not easy, as different dialects are spoken in different regions.*

Most volunteers follow Sharon's lead by preparing for their time overseas by learning the local language or reviving their dormant language skills. Poonam Sattee, who volunteered in Guatemala, says:

*I really immersed myself in the language before I left – I spoke Spanish to everyone I could find. I found out as much as I could about Guatemala so it wouldn't be such a culture shock when I arrived. And I did research on the issues surrounding street children there.*

Jacqueline Hill, who volunteered in Bangladesh, also tried to find out as much as possible about where she was going:

*I attended the VSO training agreed with my placement adviser. I talked to friends and relatives from Pakistan and Bangladesh, and I read the* Lonely Planet *guidebook . I was also able to talk to returned volunteers, as I was provided with a list. I had already travelled in Pakistan, so mistakenly thought I was prepared for the living conditions.*

Talking to returned volunteers is very important. Also, if you are volunteering on a team-based project, your organisation will usually circulate contact details for everyone prior to departure. This means you can do a little preparation together, forward information of interest and pass on any tips. If you want to take this one step further, Karen Hedges, who volunteered in Madagascar, remembers:

> *I read some books on Madagascar and helped in the charity office for a few days before I went, to help understand more about the organisation I was going to work for.*

Volunteers who expect their placement to be physically challenging also address this prior to departure. Ann Noon, who volunteered in Peru, advises:

> *I tried to do more sport in the run-up to leaving, to be better equipped to deal with living at altitude.*

In the months before you leave, your sending agency will also be in regular contact, forwarding you information packs, detailed handbooks and generally keeping you informed about what's happening, what you should be doing and when you need to do it by.

## USEFUL DOCUMENTS

Your sending agency will let you know of any documentation you may need to take with you. However, these few bits of paper might also be helpful.

• **International driving permit** These need to be taken in addition to your normal driving licence and are valid for one year only. In the UK, you can apply for one through the **AA** (www.theaa.com), **RAC** (www.rac.co.uk) or some post offices. In the US, **AAA** (www.aaa.com) and **NAC** (☎+1 800 622 2136; www.thenac.com) are the only entities federally authorised to distribute permits; AAA's online application form is the most convenient way to get one. In Canada, **CAA** (www.caa.ca) is the way to go. In Australia, members of the **Australian Automobile Association** (www.aaa.asn.au) can issue these.

• **Itinerary print-out** Of course, you're likely to want to take this for your own purposes anyway, but in addition you may be required to show it as evidence of onward travel at border crossings or airports.

• **Criminal record clearance** If you are working with children or vulnerable adults, your sending agency or organisation will probably arrange for one of these as part of their eligibility criteria. If they don't, it is something you should arrange as it is law in many countries. All the organisations included in this book insist on this check, even if it is not required in the nations they are working, before allowing volunteers to supervise children. In the UK, the **Disclosure & Barring Service** (DBS) runs these checks, though they can't be organised by you – access is only available to registered employers. In the States, either your local police department or the FBI's **Criminal Justice Information Services** (CJIS) (www.fbi.gov/services/cjis/identity-history-summary-checks) can supply you with a document indicating you have no criminal record. Canadians must visit their local police station for fingerprinting and a criminal record check application. Australians should contact the Criminal Records Section of their relevant state or territory police department.

• **Curriculum vitae** Your CV may be required by your host organisation, especially if your work history is impressive.

• **Birth certificate** There's no harm in taking a photocopy of this along with you.

• **Passport photos** A few wide-eyed shots may be handy when applying for tourist visas.

• **Photo ID** Always useful to have on you. A driving licence should fit the bill.

# AIRLINE TICKETS

If you are a self-funding volunteer or going through a sending agency that requires you arrange your own flights, here's a quick reminder of how to get the best deals.

## SEASONAL LIMITS

Think carefully about your departure date, because the price of your ticket will depend on this. Try to avoid departing during school and major national holidays, as all airline fares are at their peak during these times.

## WHEN TO PURCHASE

Ideally, you should start looking for bargain fares eight to 12 months in advance of your departure date. You may get cheap tickets at the last minute but this is rare, even if seats are still available. Unfortunately, many of the best deals will require you to pay in full soon after booking. And special or bargain fares often don't allow changes or carry heavy change penalties (which are rarely covered by your travel insurance).

## MAXIMUM TIME LIMITS

If you are volunteering for more than a year, it is likely you won't be able to use the return portion of your ticket. This is because it is virtually impossible to find a ticket that allows you to be away for more than 12 months. It may still be cheaper for you to buy a return (rather than a single fare) and simply not use the return flight. However, before you go down this route, do some research on the web to see how much it'll cost to buy a ticket home from your placement.

## CANCELLATION PENALTIES

These vary considerably but cancelling your ticket once it's booked may mean you lose the entire value of your ticket. (Most travel insurance policies protect against unavoidable cancellation fees but only if the reason for cancelling is one covered by the particular policy you took out.)

## REFUND POLICY

Sometimes volunteers want to extend their placements when in the field. If you do this and don't use a certain portion or sector of your airline ticket, it is unlikely you'll get a refund. Most airline tickets are sold on a 'non-refundable if part used' basis. And don't rely on what you're told about refund value by overseas travel agents or airline office staff – staff in Nairobi, for example, don't know all the rules of a discounted ticket sold by an agent in another country. If you are entitled to a refund, this can usually be arranged only through the booking agency where your ticket was purchased (and it may take several months). This isn't terribly useful if you're volunteering in the middle of Africa somewhere.

## CHANGE PENALTIES

There are three main types of changes: name changes, date changes and route changes. It's very rare that a name change will be permitted. There are usually restrictions on changing your departure date from your home country. However, if volunteering is only a part of a much longer trip, the dates of onward flights can often be changed (subject to seat availability). Although in many cases date changes are free, quite hefty fees can be levied depending on the rules of the ticket (and the policies of the booking agency and the airline(s) concerned). In some cases, tickets will allow no date changes at all. Route changes may be possible but usually attract a fee, and where they are permitted there is likely to be a stipulation as to how many route changes you're allowed (often only one).

## STOPOVER LIMITS

Most fares restrict the number of stopovers permitted. Again, this is mostly relevant for volunteers who intend to travel independently before or after a placement.

## TYPES OF TICKETS

You could write an entire book on the many types of airline tickets (probably not a very interesting one). But there are four main categories of ticket that international volunteers might want to buy: discount return, open-jaw or one-way tickets, and air passes.

### Discount Return Tickets

If you plan to fly in and out of one country, all you need is a normal return ticket. However, if you want to see a little more of the world, either on the way out or the way back, then you can usually add in some stopovers – often at no extra cost.

### Open-Jaw Tickets

With these tickets you fly into one destination and out of another. Again, this is a great option if you want to volunteer and also do a bit of travelling. You can fly straight to your volunteer project and afterwards do some good old-fashioned overland travel before flying home from another airport, whether in another city or even country.

### One-Way Tickets

These might be an option if you are volunteering for more than one year. Proportionally, a one-way long-haul ticket is expensive – almost always costing a lot more than half the price of a return. In fact, they are sometimes even more expensive than a return. If you only want a one-way ticket, check in case a return is cheaper. If it is, buy the return and simply don't use the homeward leg.

One drawback of one-way tickets is that you often have to show how you're going to get out of a country before you can get in (immigration officials may want to see an onward ticket). Often, if you can prove that you've got sufficient funds for your stay and enough to purchase an exit ticket (whether by air, land or sea), you should be fine.

### Air Passes

To explore a large country in depth (eg Brazil, India or Malaysia), ask a travel agent about air passes. These offer you a certain quota of flights within a single country. The flights are worked out either using a points system, a total mileage limit or a number of flights within one region. Air passes are often very good value, so long as journeys involving plane changes are not counted as separate flights.

For the international volunteer, these passes can be a cheap way of seeing more of the country on weekends. However, there are two drawbacks: they are usually valid for 30 days only (which means you have to do most of your travel in the first few weekends after your arrival) and you usually have to buy them in advance of getting to the country.

## BUYING YOUR TICKETS

### Buying from Airlines

For short-haul flights buying from airlines is almost always the best plan. For long-haul flights it's almost always the worst plan.

### Buying from Specialist Travel Agents

A good specialist travel agent will be familiar with all routes that airlines fly and will have up-to-the-minute information on discounted fares around the world.

Specialist travel agencies in the UK and Ireland include:
- **Flight Centre** (☎+44 (0)800 587 0058; www.flightcentre.co.uk)
- **Trailfinders** (☎+44 (0)207 3681200; www.trailfinders.com)
- **Travel Mood** (☎+353 (01)960 9536; www.travelmood.ie)

North American volunteers should try:
- **Liberty Travel** (☎+1 888 271 1584; www.libertytravel.com)
- **Travelosophy** (☎+1 800 332 2687; www.itravelosophy.com)

In Australasia, try:
- **Flight Centre Australia** (☎133 133; www.flightcentre.com.au) or **New Zealand** (☎+64 0800 24 3544; www.flightcentre.co.nz)
- **Student Flights**, Australia (☎1800 046 462; www.studentflights.com.au)
- **STA Australia** (☎+134 782; www.statravel.com.au) or **New Zealand** (☎+64 0800 474 400; www.statravel.co.nz)

## Buying Online

If you are doing nothing more complicated than flying in and out of the same country you can find some good bargains online.

Here are some of the main UK online travel providers:
- **ebookers** (www.ebookers.com)
- **Expedia** (www.expedia.co.uk)
- **Kayak** (www.kayak.co.uk)
- **Opodo** (www.opodo.co.uk)
- **Travelocity** (www.travelocity.co.uk)

There are several solid online options in Canada and the USA:
- **Airtreks** (www.airtreks.com)
- **Cheaptickets** (www.cheaptickets.com)
- **Hotwire** (www.hotwire.com)
- **Kayak.com** (www.kayak.com)
- **Orbitz** (www.orbitz.com)

In Australasia, try:
- **Travel.com.au** (www.travel.com.au)
- **Zuji** (www.zuji.com.au)

## Not Booking Your Own Ticket

If you are volunteering on an organised programme, you will be sent details of your flights, accompanied by any other information you need.

Sometimes, an organisation will book flights on your behalf but require that you pay for them. This often happens on a group-based project where team members fly out together. This can be a good arrangement, because it often means the organisation has block-booked seats at a discounted group rate (sometimes up to 20 per cent off) and the savings are passed on to you.

# PASSPORTS, VISAS & TRAVEL INSURANCE

## PASSPORTS

There are other things to bear in mind as you're dusting off your passport:
- **Expiry dates** Check your passport's expiry date – it has a habit of sneaking up on you. Also, make sure that your current passport is valid for at least six

months after you get home from volunteering, as some countries are suspicious of passports that are approaching their use-by date.

• **Blank pages** If you do a lot of travelling, you may run out of blank pages in your current passport. Many immigration officials around the world refuse to issue visas, entry or exit stamps on anything other than crisp, clean, unsullied pages. If you have few of these left, apply for a new passport. You can do this at any time during the life of your current passport.

• **Volunteering in the USA** There are specific passport requirements for entering the USA without a visa under the Visa Waiver Programme (VWP). For information see www.travel.state.gov.

## Visas

As you know, a visa is a stamp or document in your passport that says you may enter a country and stay there for a specific amount of time. Countries usually have five or six main categories of visa and one of them may be a volunteer visa. However, even if a volunteer visa does exist for the country you're going to, it is rare that you will need to obtain one to volunteer there.

You must get advice on this matter from your sending agency or local grassroots NGO but, nine times out of ten, you will be asked to obtain a standard tourist visa. There are a few reasons for this. Firstly, there's nothing wrong with doing some volunteering on a tourist visa. Secondly, you're not officially working: you've not got a contract of employment and you're not earning a salary. Thirdly, volunteer visas are sometimes more difficult to obtain because they can raise suspicion and lead to all sorts of petty officialdom. As a result, volunteers tend to travel on tourist visas and can be found at the weekends popping over to their nearest border post to renew them.

Having said that, there are some organisations that prefer you to volunteer on a volunteer visa. They will either arrange one for you or ask that you obtain one. In addition, many of the charities or sending agencies that dispatch skilled volunteers overseas for long periods of time will either obtain the proper volunteer visa or a working visa on your behalf.

If you are obtaining your own tourist visa, here are a few things to bear in mind:
• The majority of tourist visas last for between three to six months and they are usually valid from the date of issue. This means you need to think carefully about when you obtain your visa, particularly if you are volunteering for a couple of months.
• Visa requirements can sometimes be affected by the transport you've used to

enter a country. For instance, if you fly into some countries you can get visas on arrival, but if you go overland you must arrange them in advance.

• In some instances, you can get a visa for a longer period of time if you apply before you travel. For instance, some countries will give you six months if you apply in your home country but only 30 days if you rock up at the border.

• If you've got an Israeli stamp in your passport from earlier travels, it can cause problems when entering countries like Iran and Lebanon (Jordan and Egypt are OK). If you are volunteering in the Middle East and have evidence of a visit to Israel in your passport, then consider getting another passport.

• If you need to extend your visa while you're volunteering, remember that many overland border crossings are open for a relatively short time during the day, so try to find out the 'opening hours' in advance. Also, they are often closed during religious holidays.

• If you want to travel after your volunteer placement and plan to obtain visas on the road, take lots of passport-sized photographs with you. Many countries require two to four photos to process a visa and it's a hassle finding photo booths abroad.

# TRAVEL INSURANCE

Obtaining travel insurance for international volunteering is not the same thing as getting it for your annual vacation. For starters, you will probably buy a different insurance policy, because it must cover the specific activities and tasks that you will be performing.

If you volunteer with a sending agency, they will advise which insurance companies to approach. However, it will also be made clear that your travel insurance is ultimately your responsibility. As such, you need to ask the right questions and be aware of the main issues.

When discussing with an insurance company which policy you need, be upfront about what you are doing and where you are going. They need to be left in no doubt that you are volunteering and that you need to be covered for anything that happens to you while you are doing this. Also be aware that if your volunteer position is regional in scope, you may be asked to travel to other nearby countries. If you intend to volunteer in a developing country, medical cover up to £2 million (US$2.5 million; A$3 million) should suffice but if you volunteer in Canada, the USA or parts of Europe then it is wiser to opt for a policy with up to at least double those figures.

On the subject of medical cover, check that the policy includes repatriation: in some cases evacuation to your home country might be safer than being taken to the nearest regional medical facility. Also, if you are volunteering in the developing world, note how large the medical excess is. This is relevant because treatment in a first-class hospital in-country will be significantly cheaper than in other parts of the world: look at policies with an excess of around £50/US$80/A$75, rather than £150/US$240/A$230 or more.

Mark Jacobs, CEO of SEED Madagascar (p168), advises:

*When taking out travel insurance, it is a good idea for volunteers to provide a couple of hypothetical scenarios to ensure they're covered for full medical costs and transport to an appropriately equipped hospital. I advise volunteers on our projects to give the following scenarios:*

*Would I be covered if…*
*1) I was crossing a 'bridge' (often a slippery log), two hours away from the nearest hospital, and inadvertently broke my leg?*
*2) I got malaria in a rural village and the standard methods of dealing with it did not get my temperature down to a safe level?*
*3) I was working with local communities making a beehive on an income-generating project and accidentally sustained some injury?*

Explaining to your insurance company exactly what you'll be doing when volunteering is key. It is particularly important to tell them if you expect to do manual labour, because you will probably need to pay an extra premium per day for this activity. And, even then, you will probably be covered only for manual labour at ground level and for the use of hand tools only (ie. not be covered for the use of heavy machinery or for anything that requires a licence to operate).

If you are volunteering on a project involving animals, make sure you grill the insurance company on what you are covered for. Monitoring, surveying and observation are usually fine but close contact with wild animals is in a class of its own.

When asking your travel insurance company volunteer-specific questions, it is also wise to bear in mind some of the following more general travel insurance points:

• **Ageism** Many policies are unashamedly ageist – often the price of travel insurance will double if you're 65 or over and on some policies restrictions apply even below that age.

• **Repatriation** Ensure this means you'll be flown home and not to the country where you bought the travel insurance (if these differ).

• **Pre-existing medical conditions** If you've got high blood pressure, diabetes, asthma etc, make sure you are covered. Usually you're OK if your condition is diagnosed and stable but all policies vary.

• **Activities** If you are working with children (or even if you're not) look at the list of sports you're allowed to play. Also, if you plan to travel at the weekends, switching from volunteer to tourist, you may want to be covered for a few adventure activities. Often you'll be allowed one or two bungee jumps within a policy but have to pay twice as much if, for instance, you want to go gliding. If you want to try snowboarding or scuba diving, ask about these activities, because often they're not included.

• **Geography** Make sure that you and your insurance company are talking the same language when it comes to geography. What do they understand by 'Europe', for instance? Are Turkey and Russia included? Cover for Europe, Australasia and most other destinations is reasonable. Premiums go way up when you are volunteering in Canada and the USA.

• **Extending cover** Most travel insurance policies cover you only for one year. However, you can purchase some policies for longer periods. If you are volunteering abroad and want to extend your placement, ensure that you can: a) extend your policy while you're away; and b) only pay for the difference between the two periods rather than needing to buy a fresh policy for your extension.

• **Baggage and personal effects** Keep receipts at home for anything you might lose or have stolen while volunteering.

• **Government travel warnings/advisories** If you go to a country that your government has advised against visiting, this will usually invalidate your travel insurance. Make sure you understand your insurance company's exact policy on this. Some insurance policies will still pay out if your claim is within seven days of your destination being named and others won't. This means you need to regularly check your government's relevant website when you're away: the **Foreign & Commonwealth Office** (www.fco.gov.uk) for UK volunteers, the **US State Department's Bureau of Consular Affairs international travel page** (www.travel. state.gov), **Canada's Consular Affairs Bureau** (www.travel.gc.ca/travelling/ advisories), or the **Australian Department of Foreign Affairs and Trade** (www. smartraveller.gov.au). This is particularly important if you are volunteering without the support of a sending agency based in your home country.

• **Acts of war and terrorism** No-one will give you cover for nuclear, chemical or biological warfare but some policies do insure you against acts of terrorism.

If your sending agency has not advised which travel insurance companies to approach, or if you are arranging your own placement directly with a local NGO, try contacting the following in the UK:
- **Blue Bear Travel Insurance** (☎44 (0)344 482 3404; www.bluebeartravelinsurance.co.uk)
- **Christians Abroad** (☎+44 (0)300 012 1201; www.cabroad.org.uk)
- **Covered2Go** (☎+44 (0)344 482 7755; www.covered2go.co.uk)
- **Insure & Go** (☎+44 (0)330 400 1383; www.insureandgo.co.uk)
- **STA Travel** (☎+44 (0)333 321 0099; www.statravel.co.uk)
- **World Nomads** (☎+44 (0)170 242 7219; www.worldnomads.com)

North American options include:
- **CSA Travel Protection** (☎+1 800 348 9505; www.csatravelprotection.com)
- **HTH Worldwide** (☎+1 610 254 8700; www.hthworldwide.com)
- **IMG** (☎+1 800 628 4664; www.imglobal.com)
- **Seven Corners** (☎+1 800 690 6295; www.sevencorners.com)
- **Travelex** (☎+1 800 228 9792; www.travelex-insurance.com)
- **TravelSafe Insurance** (☎+1 888 885 7233; www.travelsafe.com)
- **Wallach & Company** (☎+1 800 237 6615; www.wallach.com)

Australasian options include:
- **Cover-More** (☎+61 1300 72 88 22; www.covermore.com.au)
- **World Nomads** (☎+61 1300 787 375; www.worldnomads.com)

# WHAT TO PACK

There is an old travellers' adage, particularly relevant to international volunteers, that advises, 'Pack it and halve it; time it and double it.' Kerry Davies, who volunteered in Cambodia with VSO (p175), agrees wholeheartedly with the first piece of advice:

*Most people pack far too many things. It is tempting to visit a travel shop and buy lots of expensive gadgets. Most things can be obtained in the country you are working in. You will save money and support the local economy. Some things, though, are essential to take with you but this depends on your country. In Cambodia you can't get Western-sized bras and the knickers are nylon. And I still like to pack earplugs for the wedding season!*

Just like Kerry, returned volunteers mostly advise that you take items you know you can't easily buy locally. Jacqueline Hill who went to Bangladesh says:

*I took a sharp kitchen knife, vegetable peeler and Swiss Army knife. Bangladeshi cooks use floor knives which it takes quite some practice to master. Due to the abundance of fresh food, there is also little call for tins, and consequently tin-openers. I sometimes shopped in foreign food shops for treats (tins of tomatoes when the fresh ones were not in season) so the Swiss Army knife tin-opener came in handy.*

Deborah Jordan and David Spinney, who volunteered in Ethiopia, pick up on the 'kitchen knife' theme and have a few additional suggestions:

*Baggage allowance at 25 kilograms concentrates the mind. Check the climate and what is available locally to avoid taking two years' supply of tea bags or deodorant unnecessarily. And remember, family members are good at sending parcels. Invaluable was our sharp knife – all knives in the developing world bend. We also took a good supply of reading matter, a laptop (if you can use it in your placement) and some DVDs (TV serials can keep you going for weeks). We took our duvet in the second year and it was a great comfort on cold evenings.*

Clothing is another hot topic. Emma Campbell, who volunteered in Ecuador, says:

*There is no point packing clothes for volunteering. I went to the market and bought two cheap T-shirts and cheap shorts when I got there. They were ready for the bin, or the next set of volunteers, after one month.*

And Jacqueline Hill had a good solution for culturally sensitive clothing issues:

*Returned volunteers had lots of useful advice. Recognising that most of my Western clothes would be inappropriate, I bought a couple of shalwar kameez (long tunics with pants worn underneath).*

Michelle Hawkins, who volunteered on an expedition in Costa Rica and another in Ghana, found that one of the most precious things she packed was a diary:

*Even though certain memories do remain clear, the little details will fade. Journals are the best things for recalling what you felt at the time. They can also be therapeutic: writing down problems or issues you may have can help clarify your thinking and suggest solutions. Or else, sometimes writing in a diary is just like sharing a problem with a friend.*

Most importantly, don't pack things that are inappropriate for where you are going. Diane Turner, who volunteered with Coral Cay Conservation (p170) in the Philippines and in Fiji, remembers:

*Despite the list supplied by Coral Cay Conservation, one person still brought a hairdryer to a site that had no electricity!*

Diane brings up a valuable point: if you are volunteering with a sending agency you will usually be sent a detailed kit list, specific to your destination and project. However, following is a suggested packing list that assumes that you will not only be volunteering but doing some travel at the weekends or after your placement.

## SECURITY

• **Money belt** A money belt is the safest way to carry your valuables. It's wise to have one for when you're out and about in the evenings or on weekends, particularly in towns or cities. Think about its fabric: plastic sweats while leather is heavy and will smell. Cotton or polycotton are the best bet, as they're washable and the most comfortable. That said, keep your passport or other valuable papers in a thin grip seal plastic bag within the belt to keep them safe from perspiration.
• **Padlocks and a cable/chain** Good for securing your luggage and fastening the door of hotel rooms. They are also useful for attaching a backpack to the roof of a bus or the luggage rack of a train.
• **Personal security** There are loads of personal security items on the market like personal alarms, internal door guards, a Pacsafe for your backpack (a steel mesh which covers your backpack to make it unslashable and which locks onto things) and packable safes for your room (attach them to a radiator or other fixed object). Check out what's on offer at your local travel specialist.
• **Waterproof pouch** Consider one of these for your documents and money so that you can keep them on you if you choose to go swimming or snorkelling.

# SLEEPING

• **Alarm clock** To make sure you get up in time to start your volunteering day. If you usually use your mobile phone as an alarm clock, take into consideration that you may not always be able to keep it charged.

• **Mosquito net** In risky places you will be provided with one, but it's good to have your own because it is crucial that your net is treated with a mosquito killer (such as permethrine) and has no holes. Bring a 5m length of narrow guage string to tie it up if need be.

• **Pillow case** Nab one from home, just in case you stay anywhere that's a tiny bit unsavoury.

• **Sleeping bag liner/sleeping bag** A sleeping bag liner is essential. You'll use this all the time either in dubious hotels and hostels or to keep your sleeping bag clean.

• **Torch** Essential for those volunteer moments when the electricity packs it in or you're trying to read a book at night in the jungle. There are basically two types. The Maglite is the toughest but the bulbs and batteries run out quickly. Check out LED (light-emitting diode) torches, because the bulbs don't blow and the batteries last much longer. You can get an LED miner-style lamp that straps to your forehead and frees up both your hands.

• **Tealight candles** During a power cut these are safer than regular candles.

# EATING & DRINKING

• **Water bottle** Most water bottles are one litre, but two litres is what you'll probably need when you're volunteering. Buy the collapsible bladder type of water bottle, as they take up very little room in your luggage when not in use.

• **Water purification** See the Food, Water & Hygiene section (p96) for details of what to take.

• **Cup and spoon** If you're travelling at the weekends, your own cup and spoon will help you stay healthy.

# HYGIENE

• **Bath plug** A rare commodity in some parts of the world. Wide-brimmed universal rubber or plastic plugs will fit most plugholes.

• **Contraception** Condoms are sold in most countries but the quality can be variable (always check the use-by date). It's safer and easier to bring a supply with you. If you use the pill, bring enough to cover your whole time overseas, as it is difficult to get in many countries. However, you need to exercise extreme caution and restraint in sexual matters when volunteering overseas. This is especially so in any relationship with a local person in a culture that you don't completely understand.

• **Tampons, sanitary napkins or menstrual cups** Depending on your destination, these might be hard to find.

• **Toilet paper** It's best to learn how to use your hand and water, because toilet paper often blocks sewage systems in developing countries. Otherwise, take toilet paper but think about how you're going to dispose of it. Squash the roll down and put it in a plastic bag for packing.

• **Toiletries** Most items are widely available (and often cheaper than at home) but take any speciality products with you. Shower gels travel much better than soap and will often do hair and body. Decant large bottles into smaller ones if you're volunteering short-term. Plus, you can now get concentrated travel soaps which will keep both you and your clothes clean. Make sure your travel soaps are biodegradable.

• **Towel** There are two types of travel towels – ones made from chamois (which work wet and pack down to the size of a small tin of beans) and ones made from microfibre (which work dry and pack down to the size of a can of beans). Which sort you take will depend on your bathing routine. If you love wrapping up in your towel after your shower then the microfibre one is for you, but if you want pure towelling performance and don't mind something real weeny then take a chamois one.

• **Washing detergent** See Toiletries, above.

• **Washing line** A piece of string or even dental floss will do the job at a pinch, but there are relatively cheap lines on the market that don't need pegs and have suckers, hooks (or both) on the ends, making them more versatile.

• **Wet wipes & no-water washes** Handy where clean water is in short supply.

## HEALTH

• **Medical first-aid kit** See the section under Health & Hygiene (p92) for details.

## TRAVEL ESSENTIALS

• **Address book, travel journal and pens** Self explanatory.

• **Batteries** Bring spares for all your equipment and put new batteries in everything before you depart. Be mindful how you dispose of your batteries.

• **Books and DVDs** Entertainment if you're volunteering long-term overseas.

• **Camera** As you'd hate to run out of room to capture your photographic memories, it's best to bring several large memory cards. If possible, regularly download these onto your laptop as back up (avoid overwriting the cards until you're back home and have saved additional copies).

• **Earplugs** You'll never regret these if you're volunteering in a city or need a break from the blare of loud music on a 10-hour bus ride.

• **Eye wear** Take your glasses (in a hard case) and contact lenses. If you wear prescription glasses or contact lenses, take the prescription with you, along with extras such as a case and contact-lens solution. Contact-lens wearers should also take a supply of 'dailies' (disposable contact lenses) – really useful in an emergency.

• **Family photos and images of home** The people you work with will really appreciate seeing and learning more about your life back home.

• **Kitchen knife** For all volunteers who want to do their own cooking.

• **Lighter or matches** You'll need something to light your campfire, mosquito coils or candles (when the electricity blacks out yet again).

• **Short-wave radio/MP3 player/smartphone** You might be able to tune into the BBC World Service, the Voice of America or Radio Australia and it will be good to listen to something familiar if you're feeling down or homesick. Be aware that it may be difficult to keep gadgets charged in areas with no, or unreliable, electricity.

• **Pocketknife** A Swiss Army knife (or good-quality equivalent) has loads of useful tools: scissors; bottle-opener; tin-opener; straight blade and all those strange gadgets that you don't know the use of (remember not to keep the knife in your hand luggage, though, as it'll be confiscated).

• **Sewing kit** Needle, thread, a few buttons and safety pins are enough to mend clothing, mosquito nets, tents or sunglasses.

• **Gaffer tape** As Maggie Wild, who has volunteered on lots of environmental projects, says, 'It fixes everything: torn tents, torn trousers, hanging-off vehicle parts and much, much more.'

## CLOTHING

• **Keeping cool** If you're travelling in hot climates you'll need a lightweight, loose-fitting wardrobe. Cotton clothing will absorb sweat and help keep you cool. Synthetic clothing doesn't get so creased and dries out quickly but can sometimes make you feel clammy. It's your choice. Trousers that convert into shorts are good because you get two for the price of one and you can also get trousers which convert into pedal pushers. Take a hat but make sure it protects the back of your neck from sunburn.

# TEN TOP TIPS FROM TWO VOLUNTEERS

Elaine Massey and Richard Lawson have volunteered on 15 projects with Earthwatch, in country's ranging from Costa Rica to Kenya. Here are their tips:

## 1. Read the Online Briefing Repeatedly

If you don't like the heat, don't join a project in the desert, and if you like home comforts, don't join a project where the accommodation is described as 'rustic'. If you're unhappy about the prospect of sharing a dormitory, make sure you know what the sleeping arrangements are. If the project isn't right for you, you'll be miserable.

## 2. The Weather

Make sure you know what types of weather you may experience and take appropriate clothing.

## 3. Travel Arrangements

If the journey to your destination includes a long flight, try to allow some recovery time before the project starts – jet lag can impair your enjoyment of the first couple of days!

## 4. Clothing

Take clothing that you don't mind getting ruined. Most research will involve getting dirty or wet, and you won't enjoy it as much if you're worried about spoiling your clothes.

## 5. Camera

Don't forget it!

## 6. Currency

In remote villages, the shops are unlikely to be able to change US$100 notes, so try to take a supply of small denomination notes. Don't assume that credit cards will be accepted!

## 7. Your Feet (Part One)

If the project is sea based, try to take a couple of different styles of sandals, so they don't all rub in the same place!

## 8. Your Feet (Part Two)

If the project involves lots of walking, make sure your boots are properly worn in prior to travel. Also, bring a supply of good socks.

## 9. Reading List

If the project briefing includes a reading list, try to get hold of some of the books. Background knowledge will enrich your enjoyment of the project.

## 10. Packing

Try to pack light – there may not be much room to store your belongings. (But make sure you've read the 'what to take' section of the briefing!) A small bag for dirty washing is a good idea.

**Elaine Massie & Richard Lawson**

• **Keeping warm** Several layers topped by a good-quality jacket will give you the versatility you need. For starters, pack some thermal underwear. Particularly good are lightweight, cycling-style T-shirts or merino wool vests. Both will allow your body to breathe while offering good insulation. Then you need a fleece or fibrepile jacket which is lighter and less bulky than a thick jumper. Most fleeces and fibrepile jackets are not fully waterproof or windproof so you'll also need a lightweight, breathable, waterproof jacket. If you're travelling in an extremely cold environment then consider the more expensive GORE-TEX mountain jackets. Take some polypropylene or merino wool long johns and then wear your usual travel trousers over the top. Don't forget mittens or gloves, and a hat.

• **Waterproof ponchos** Whether you're going hot or cold, think about taking one of these. You can use it to cover you and your pack, as a groundsheet, a sleeping-bag cover, on your bed as a barrier between you and a mouldy mattress, or as a shade awning.

## FOOTWEAR

• **Boots or shoes** You've got the choice of three styles: a full-on high-ankle boot; a three-quarter cut boot (a cross between a shoe and a boot); and normal shoes or trainers. Unless you're going on an expedition or doing a lot of trekking, you probably don't need a high-ankle boot. If you want versatility then the mid-height boot is good because it gives you ankle support without being too heavy. Non-waterproof options are better for warm climates as your feet will breathe better. However, at the end of the day, buy what your feet feel most comfortable in. And remember to break in your footwear before you leave, so that you can deal with any blisters or rubbing in the comfort of your own home.

• **Watersport sandals** These are ideal for day-to-day wear in warm climates, even if you're doing a lot of walking. You can also wear them in dodgy showers or in the sea and leave them on your feet to dry out. There's more advice on sandals and footwear in general in Ten Top Tips from Two Volunteers (p90).

## HEALTH & HYGIENE

Needless to say, you don't want to get sick while you're volunteering overseas. If you take the right precautions both before you go and while you're abroad, you'll probably experience nothing more serious than 'Delhi belly' or 'Montezuma's revenge' (travellers' diarrhoea). Jacqueline Hill, who volunteered in Bangladesh for a year, advises:

*Be careful, not paranoid. I was only ill once – a 24-hour stomach bug in my first couple of weeks. Follow sensible precautions, especially those recommended by the volunteering agency and their in-country representatives.*

## PRE-DEPARTURE CHECK-UPS

Visit a travel clinic six to eight weeks before you depart. Your sending agency will usually advise on which vaccinations to get, but they will not be as up-to-date as a travel health specialist. They should also be able to advise whether you need an HIV test for where you're going.

Another option for those in the UK is **InterHealth** (📞+44 (0)20 7902 9000; www.interhealthworldwide.org; London), a charity that specialises in healthcare for humanitarian, development and mission workers. It provides pre-departure support for volunteers such as travel health consultations and pre-departure medicals, and also has guidance on vaccinations needed on its website.

Ensure that all your vaccinations are recorded on a vaccination certificate and take this away with you – proof of immunisation against certain diseases (yellow fever, for instance) might be needed at particular borders. Also, check that you're up-to-date with routine immunisations like tetanus and diphtheria, polio and any childhood ones like MMR (measles, mumps, rubella).

It is a good idea to check in with your doctor prior to departure and definitely with your dentist and optometrist. Tooth trouble, in particular, can be painfully inconvenient when you're in the field. At the optometrist, you may want to buy a spare pair of glasses, as you might end up wearing them more frequently than contact lenses when you're overseas.

Some charities and sending agencies will arrange all of this for you. Others might ask you to fill out a very detailed medical form and then follow up if there are any areas of concern. Mostly, however, you are responsible for your own health-related check-ups.

## FIRST-AID COURSES

Many returned volunteers advise that first-aid skills are invaluable, whether you're working on a development or conservation and wildlife project.

Some of the best courses in the UK are run by:
- **St John Ambulance** (www.sja.org.uk)
- **Lifesigns Group** (www.adventurelifesigns.co.uk)
- **Wilderness Expertise** (www.wilderness-expertise.co.uk)
- **Wilderness Medical Training** (www.wildernessmedicaltraining).

In North America, sign up for classes at:
- **American Heart Association** (www.americanheart.org)
- **American Red Cross** (www.redcross.org)
- **Canadian Red Cross** (www.redcross.ca)
- **Wilderness Medical Associates** (www.wildmed.com)

Australians should get in touch with:
- **St John Ambulance Australia** (☏+61 1300 360 455; www.stjohn.org.au).

# MEDICAL KITS

Some large sending agencies suggest you purchase specific medical kits especially designed for the needs of their volunteers. If this is the case, you will be told where you can buy them. If not, travel clinics sell a range of medical kits to suit all types of travellers (and therefore volunteers). Good ones cost in the range of £30 to £50 (US$50 to US$80; A$60 to A$100). Otherwise, what you'll pack will depend on where you're going and what you plan to do.

### Basics
- Any prescription medicines, including antibiotics and antimalarials.
- Painkillers like paracetamol (acetaminophen) and aspirin for pain and fever and an anti-inflammatory like ibuprofen.
- Insect repellent (DEET or plant-based) and permethrin (for treating mosquito nets and clothes).
- Antidiarrhoeals – loperamide is probably the most effective.
- Indigestion remedies such as antacid tablets or liquids.
- Oral rehydration sachets and a measuring spoon for making your own solution.
- Antihistamine tablets for hay fever and other allergies or itches.
- Sting-relief spray or hydrocortisone cream for insect bites.
- Sun block and lip salve with sun block.
- Water-purifying tablets or water filter or purifier.
- Over-the-counter cystitis treatment (if you're prone to this).
- Calamine lotion or aloe vera for sunburn and skin rashes.
- Antifungal cream.
- Cough and cold remedies and sore-throat lozenges.
- Eye drops.
- Laxatives (particularly if you're headed to an area like Mongolia where there's little fibre in the diet).

### First-aid Equipment

Remember to stow your first-aid kit in your luggage for flights, because anything sharp will get confiscated as hand luggage:

• Digital (not mercury) thermometer.
• Scissors.
• Tweezers to remove splinters, cactus needles or ticks.
• Sticking plasters (adhesive bandages).
• Gauze swabs and adhesive tape.
• Bandages and safety pins.
• Non-adhesive dressings.
• Antiseptic powder or solution (eg povidone-iodine) and/or antiseptic wipes.
• Wound closure strips.
• Syringes and needles – with doctor's note to avoid any difficulties.

If you're really going remote then you'll also need:

• Antibiotic eye and ear drops.
• Antibiotic pills or powder.
• Emergency splints (eg SAM splints).
• Elasticated support bandage.
• Triangular bandage for making an arm sling.
• Dental first-aid kit.

Hopefully, you'll end up not using most of what you've packed. However, you never know. Phil Sydor volunteered in Zambia and recalls:

*I sustained a head injury – a steel bar dropped on my head and I needed stitches. The local hospital sewed me up using the sutures we'd brought with us as part of our medical kit. This way the local supplies weren't depleted and we were confident that the equipment was sterile.*

## MALARIA

Sian Davies, who volunteered with Doctors of the World in Tanzania, says:

*Don't be too paranoid about getting sick. If you live in a place you have a lot more control over issues such as food, water and mosquitoes than if you're just passing through. However, having said that, I had malaria four times (despite taking prophylaxis).*

Malarial risks and antimalarial drug-resistance patterns change constantly. If you're headed to a malarial area, you need to get expert advice from your travel clinic on how to avoid catching this potentially fatal mosquito-borne disease.

There are a number of antimalarial medicines on the market and they all have their pros and cons (see www.fitfortravel.scot.nhs.uk for a full list). A travel clinic will discuss these with you and come up with the best solution for where you're going and the type of volunteering you're doing. Remember, if you need to take antimalarial pills, they generally have to be started before you arrive at the destination and continued after you depart the malarial area.

It is easy to forget that antimalarials do not stop you getting malaria, they just suppress it if you do. This means that you need to combine antimalarials with proper precautions against being bitten in the first place. These should include:
• Changing into permethrin treated long sleeved tops, trousers and socks at dusk.
• Using a DEET-based inspect repellent on any exposed skin at dawn and dusk. Reapply every hour in hot and humid conditions.
• Burning mosquito coils in your room or under restaurant tables.
• Spraying your room with a knock-down insect spray before bed at night.
• Sleeping under a permethrin-treated mosquito net.
• Volunteering in the height of the dry season – the risk of being bitten and therefore catching malaria is far less at this time.

How do you know if you've caught malaria? You'd think this was an easy question to answer. It isn't. What you need to remember is that any flu-like symptom could be malaria. If you're feeling off colour in a malarial area then go and get a blood test. In many parts of the developing world, local hospitals will test you on the spot – it takes 20 minutes and costs almost nothing. However, there are now a couple of self-testing malarial kits on the market (ask your travel clinic about these), which can be useful if you're far away from medical help.

### Long-term Use of Antimalarials
Travellers normally take antimalarial tablets for three months. However, if you're volunteering for longer in a malarial area, you will need to take your antimalarial medicine for longer. With the exception of chloroquine which has been known to cause retinal problems, there is no evidence that the extended use of antimalarial medication will increase side effects or decrease effectiveness. It is best to take all the antimalarial medicine you'll need with you from your home country (check expiry dates), although sometimes these drugs will be available where you're going.

## OTHER INSECT-BORNE DISEASES

It isn't only malaria which is transmitted by mosquitoes but also diseases like yellow fever, Japanese encephalitis, zika and dengue fever. This last disease is a problem because the carrier is a daytime mosquito, which means you have to practice bite avoidance (eg covering up and reapplication of insect repellent) during the day too, which can be hard. Dengue has been an increasing issue in South America since 2010, with numerous outbreaks in Brazil, with Colombia and Argentina also affected (the latter experiencing an outbreak in 2016). The Asia Pacfic region has also had more cases since 2014, with Philippines, Japan, Thailand, China and even Hawaii recording cases. There are no prophylactic tablets or treatment for dengue. As most of these areas are also malarial, it means you'll have to make sure you're not bitten 24 hours a day.

## FOOD, WATER & HYGIENE

On your volunteer placement you will mostly prepare your own food, accept the hospitality of people you know, or eat in local restaurants that you trust. However, what happens at the weekend when you travel or after your placement?

Hepatitis A, typhoid, diarrhoea and dysentery (bloody diarrhoea) are all transmitted by poorly prepared food and impure water. As you never know what might be buried in your food, here are a few tips to inwardly digest:

• Always wash your hands prior to eating.

• Avoid food that has been peeled, sliced or nicely arranged by other people because it means it's been handled a lot.

• Remember that food can get contaminated by dirty dishes, cutlery, utensils and cups. Blenders or pulpers used for fruit juices are often suspect.

• Raw fruit and vegetables are hard to clean. Eat them only if you know they've been washed in clean water or if you can safely peel them yourself. Bananas and papayas are safe to eat in the tropics.

• Eat only food that's freshly prepared and piping hot – avoid hotel buffets like the plague.

• Be wary of ice cream and seafood – although for different reasons.

• Think twice before you drink water from the tap or brush your teeth in it.

• Drink sealed bottled water or canned drinks where possible.

• Avoid ice cubes in drinks: they may have been made from contaminated water.

• The simplest way of purifying water is to bring it to a 'roaring boil' for three to five minutes; otherwise use chlorine, iodine or a water purifier.

Despite all these precautions, it's likely you will get a stomach upset. When you do, drink as much as you can to ensure you don't become dehydrated. In addition, use oral rehydration salts to rehydrate more quickly and drink sweet milkless tea and eat salty crackers (if possible).

## Health-related Documents

When volunteering, keep the following information in a safe place in your room (or under your hammock):
- Vaccination certificate
- Travel insurance emergency number and the serial number of your policy.
- Summary of any important medical condition you have.
- Contact details of your doctor back home.
- Copy of prescription for any medication you take regularly.
- Details of any serious allergies.
- Your blood group.
- HIV test documentation (if applicable).
- Prescription for glasses or contact lenses.
- Letter from your doctor explaining why you're carrying syringes in a medical kit to avoid any hassles.

## More Information

Although self-diagnosis is never a good idea, it might be wise to invest in a practical book on travellers' health. Try the latest edition of Travellers' Health: How to Stay Healthy Abroad by Dr Richard Dawood. If you're volunteering off the beaten track, one of the best books is called Where There Is No Doctor: A Village Health Care Handbook by David Werner.

Also, before you go, do as much research as you can online. The useful **Australian Travel Doctor** website (www.traveldoctor.com.au) has free online travel health advisory reports with recommended vaccination lists for every country based on the time of year and the duration of stay.

# MONEY

There are three main ways of taking or accessing your money while abroad: debit and credit cards; pre-paid travel cards; and cash. Travellers cheques are a fourth option, though the use of them is in great decline, with fewer and fewer places abroad accepting them. Check with your volunteer organisation if they

# TOP TIPS FOR FEMALE VOLUNTEERS

1: Pack your common sense and have your wits about you at all times. If you wouldn't normally walk down a dark alley or deserted street at night in your home town, don't do it when you're volunteering overseas. Jacqueline Hill remembers the following incident in Bangladesh:

*I was careless one evening and had my bag strap around my shoulders with the bag on full view as I travelled through Dhaka on a rickshaw. A taxi drove up alongside me and a hand came out of the window and attempted to snatch my bag, resulting in my being pulled out of the rickshaw as the taxi tried to make off. I was badly shaken and bruised but hung onto my bag.*

2: Be informed about where you are going, so that you have a rough idea of a town's layout and any areas that may be unsafe. (This is particularly relevant if you travel to a larger town to change money or if you travel at the weekends.) Poonam Sattee, who volunteered in Guatemala City recalls:

*There are a lot of areas within the city that are incredibly unsafe and without prior knowledge, it is easy to accidentally wander into these. Gang rivalry also operates within the city and you don't want to get caught up in their activities.*

3: Pay close attention to your instincts. If you're in a situation that feels wrong, even if you don't know why, move to a place where you feel more secure. Michelle Hawkins, who volunteered in Ghana and Costa Rica, remembers:

*I was suddenly surrounded by four little old ladies. They were all muttering Americana. Being British, I was a bit confused. I was confused further when they started pushing in on me from all sides, with hands grabbing my waist for my money belt. After a comic half-hearted fist fight, I fought my way out of the ambush. Had I really been overrun by little old ladies? I took my daypack off, and saw that it had been slashed with a knife – just centimetres from my ribs.*

4: If you feel like having a few too many drinks then do so in a safe environment (your room, your friend's house or the bar at your hotel).

5: If you're going out at night on your own, tell someone (another volunteer, your host family etc) where you're going and what time you expect to be back.

6: Instead of going out after dark on your own to explore, make the most of your waking hours and get up really early in the morning.

7: If you're a self-funding volunteer and fixing up your own accommodation, make sure you do so in a safe part of town. If you're on a trip at the weekend, pay a little extra to stay in a hotel in a better area. Poonam Sattee advises again:

> Guatemala City is not safe and I do not recommend that anyone lives in the city. It is better to live in Antigua, which is a 45-minute commute on a bus. Although Antigua is touristy, it has none of Guatemala City's problems, due to the high levels of tourist police operating there.

8: Pay attention to what you wear and cover up. In many regions of the world, skimpy shorts and T-shirts relay a very different message to what you may be used to at home. Poonam Sattee again:

> Don't wear jewellery of any type – even if it is only studs in your ears or religious symbols. It attracts attention – I was mugged a number of times and on one occasion, had the studs taken out of my ears (they weren't even gold or silver).

9: Take a taxi more frequently than you might at home but make sure it is bona fide. Ensure you always have enough cash on you to get home this way if you need to.

10: Think about doing a course in travel safety before you leave your home country. In the UK you can arrange one through **Objective** (www.objectivegapyear.com). Australians can prepare themselves for difficult situations by doing a course with **RedR** (www.redr.org.au) which offers intensive personal security in emergency training.

can be of use in your chosen destination. If travellers checks are an option, remember to keep receipts in case they're needed as proof either within the country you're volunteering in or when you leave.

If your volunteer placement is rural, it is possible that you'll rely mainly on cash (make sure to get some small-denomination notes). Robin Glegg, who has volunteered in Siberia, Namibia and Oman, advises:

*Take cash in US dollars. Most people will accept US dollars in developing countries. You can usually exchange hard currency for local currency when you arrive at the airport.*

And from Mike Laird, who volunteered in Bolivia:

*I would advise people on two things: take US dollars and American Express travellers cheques. I have been in situations where UK travellers cheques and pounds sterling have not been accepted. The greenback is welcome everywhere. Clean, crisp notes are sometimes worth more.*

But, on a day-to-day basis, what do you do with your cash? Where do you put it? Sharon Baxter, who volunteered in Tibet, remembers:

*In Yushu itself, there was no way to cash travellers cheques or change money. Whilst there, I just kept my cash under the mattress. My bedroom door had a lock, so I kept it locked most of the time.*

Kerry Davies, who volunteered in Cambodia, was in a similar position:

*I kept my money locked in my house, as my landlady and the dogs were always around.*

In fact, volunteers who are placed in remote locations become adept at operating in a cash society and hiding their money just becomes part of everyday life. Jacqueline Hill, who volunteered in Bangladesh, recalls:

*There were no ATMs in the town where I lived and I did not set up a bank account. My stipend was paid monthly in cash and I kept little stashes of notes all over the flat. When in Dhaka, I could use ATMs to withdraw local currency.*

Volunteers in rural areas often have to make a special trip to a city to use an ATM or change some travellers cheques. In Tibet, this was Sharon Baxter's experience:

*The nearest place to get money was Xining, which was a 16- to 22-hour bus ride away. I took some cash from England and the rest of my money in travellers cheques which I cashed in Xining. When travelling, the cash was in a secret pocket in my jeans, sewn inside the cuff of one leg. The only way anyone could have got that was to take my jeans off and, if it came to that, I didn't think money would be my main concern.*

Security is an issue that Ian Flood was concerned with in Bolivia. He says:

*I used ATMs all the time without problems. However, take a friend to stand next to you when taking money out, as sometimes the money can be snatched right out of your hands.*

And security was also very important to Poonam Sattee when she accessed her money while volunteering in Guatemala City:

*I opened up a Guatemalan bank account on arrival and had money transferred from my UK bank account (the transfer instructions were set up before leaving). I had a passbook and used this to withdraw money from the bank. There were branches everywhere. The only drawback was that I had to take my passport as ID, which I didn't like doing in Guatemala City as it is not safe. So I got a copy of my passport stamped and signed by a lawyer in Guatemala (this guaranteed it was an authentic copy) and I used this to withdraw money. But I didn't put my money in a money belt because thieves there know all about money belts. After withdrawing cash, I would stuff it in my shoes, socks, bra, wherever, and if I'd withdrawn a large sum, get a cab home (from a trusted source – not just hailing one).*

Kate Sturgeon avoided taking out large sums of money when volunteering in Zimbabwe:

*We received our stipend to live on in the field once a month in US dollars. We then gave it to the project coordinator or logistician, who would change it for us. Because inflation was so high, we would change money on a weekly basis rather than all at once. This is definitely advisable in countries where the currency is unstable.*

However, what happens if you volunteer with a charity or sending agency on an organised volunteer programme? David Grassham, who volunteered in rural India, remembers:

*As everything was included, the only thing I bought was the occasional chocolate bar or soft drink.*

If you are volunteering on a conservation or wildlife project the situation will be similar. The reason for this is summed up nicely by Vikki Cole, who volunteered on a conservation project in the Borneo jungle:

*We were quite literally miles away from civilisation so taking credit cards or substantial amounts of cash was futile. We were advised to bring only a tiny amount of local currency. We were told we would need this for the last day when we were able to access a bar in a motel. Needless to say, we drank them dry within an hour!*

The organised skilled volunteering programmes offered by the Australian Government provide volunteers with a monthly allowance which is deposited into an Australian account. Overseas withdrawal fees start at A$4, so it's worth considering how you're going to access your cash if you're on a long-term assignment, and compare rates across banks. Also, if you find yourself in Asia trying to secure long-term accommodation, you may have to pay up to three to six months rent in advance, so a cash contingency plan is essential.

## CREDIT & DEBIT CARDS

If you want to find out how near your volunteer programme is to a local ATM, log onto an online ATM locator. The one for MasterCard is www.mastercard.us/en-us/consumers/get-support/locate-an-atm.html. For Visa it's www.visa.com/atmlocator.

The rate of exchange for cash withdrawals from ATMs is often pretty good but it's offset by hefty transaction charges. What you need is a card which doesn't charge you each time you get cash out. It may be worth opening an account before you leave. For those in the UK, MoneySavingsExpert document the best accounts for international withdrawls (www.moneysavingexpert.com/travel/overseas-card-charges). In Australia, check Savings Guide's website (www.savingsguide.com.au).

## PREPAID TRAVEL CARDS

Prepaid travel cards are much like travellers cheques but without the same hassles. You load them prior to travel and then use them as you would a debit card when abroad, either by paying for goods or withdrawing cash. If the card is lost or stolen, as long as you contact the provider, you won't lose any money. An advantage over debit cards is that you can lock in a rate of exchange if you so choose. There are numerous providers, so shop around as fees and rates of exchange vary. MoneySavingsExpert in the UK provides up-to-date rankings of the various providers (www.moneysavingexpert.com/credit-cards/prepaid-travel-cards). In Australia, Finder provide a similar overview (www.finder.com.au/travel-money).

## TRAVELLERS CHEQUES

Experienced travellers know that one of the disadvantages of travellers cheques is that you're usually charged a commission when you buy them, a commission when you convert them, and on top of that they rarely attract a decent rate of exchange. Nevertheless, if you are volunteering somewhere without ATMs (and where banks still cash them) you might rely heavily on travellers cheques.

Remember to ask for a good quantity of cheques in smaller denominations, so you have the choice of changing either a large or a small amount of money. Needless to say, the equivalent of US$100 in some local currencies is a lot of money.

## KEEPING IN TOUCH

The advent of mobile internet and wifi has revolutionised the communication age. Even if these aren't available in your area, you shouldn't have difficulty tracking down somewhere to log on. There are still some internet cafes lurking out there.

The social networking revolution has made it easier than ever for travellers to keep friends and family up-to-date with their adventures. Forget the days of spamming your loved ones with epic group emails: Facebook and apps such as Instagram and Snapchat allow for easy sharing of information and images, and Twitter is perfect for bite-sized updates.

Make sure that you are aware of your volunteer program's social networking policy (if it has one) and when you're online always be mindful about how you are representing the organisation for which you are working. Also beware of uploading photos of people, especially children, without their or their guardian's permission.

Some organisations even utilise volunteers in maintaining their social media presence, so do include this in your application if it is something you are interested in doing as part of your volunteer work.

As you would imagine, email is how the majority of volunteers keep in touch with friends and family. In Bangladesh, Jacqueline Hill remembers:

*I mostly kept in touch through emails and my online diary. I would go to the internet cafe, download my emails onto a disc and reply to them on my PC at the flat. I would then copy my replies, go back to the internet cafe and attempt to send them. Erratic opening times, phone lines and electricity supplies made this a lengthy and often frustrating process.*

There are two interesting things about Jacqueline's experience. Not only did Jacqueline write a blog (for more on this, see p106) to keep people in the loop about her experiences, she also beat the problem of erratic electricity supplies in a developing country. If you don't take a laptop overseas, you can still avoid writing lovely long emails only to lose them when the internet connection drops out: write in Word, then copy and paste the text into an email when you've finished.

Ann Noon, who volunteered in Peru, used internet cafes as chat rooms – but she wasn't chatting to strangers:

*Thank goodness for live messening. It makes you feel like your family are just across the road somewhere rather than thousands of miles and three flights away. Skype was another handy invention…*

Indeed it is. Online video call platforms such as Skype and FaceTime provide an easy way of keeping in touch and staving off any pangs of homesickness. They do rely on access to a reliable internet connection, however this is less of an isssue than in years past. For more information on these services, see p108). The question of whether to pack your mobile phone is not straightforward to answer. If you have a tri-band, quad-band or penta-band GSM handset then it will work in most parts of the world. If you've got a dual-band phone, you may want to think of upgrading before you depart. For more detailed information on where your phone will and won't work, check **Mobile World Live** at (http://maps.mobileworldlive. com/). This will also let you know if the country you're volunteering in has a GSM 'roaming agreement' with your service provider. Having said this, Phil Sydor, who volunteered in Zambia, had no problems:

*We walked down to the end of the garden and the reception was quite good. Land lines were terrible, but many people had mobile phones. We bought a local SIM card and used that as it was cheaper than roaming.*

Unless you want to shell out a fortune paying an international roaming tariff, local SIM cards are a must for international volunteers. Before departing, find out whether your mobile is SIM locked. If it is, get the code to unlock it so that you can purchase a local prepaid SIM card when you're abroad – it will make your mobile calls significantly cheaper. You can buy local SIM cards almost everywhere in Asia and Africa and in most other places from telephone or service-provider shops.

Be aware that using online or location features on smart phones will chew through data frighteningly quickly. Investigate what the data charges are on a local prepaid SIM or international roaming plan before using your phone overseas to avoid any expensive headaches later on. It's also a good idea to turn off data in your phone's network settings while you are away and only turn it on when you need to access features that use it. (You will still be able to get text messages.)

However, if you're volunteering on a conservation or wildlife project, your mobile might not be so useful. Robin Glegg, who volunteered in Siberia, Namibia and Oman, points out:

*In the Altai mobile phones did not work in the mountains, as we were fairly remote from civilisation. Biosphere Expeditions operates a satellite internet and phone link, so you can send and receive urgent messages or make urgent phone calls. Remember you may be going to remote places and you don't want mobile phones ringing every five minutes (if they work at all) as it spoils the atmosphere.*

If you want to communicate quietly (and cheaply) on your mobile phone then this is what Kerry Davies did in Cambodia:

*Texting. After hating all those people with mobile phones at home I admit I am now addicted to texting. Often a text arrives so quickly you can have a conversation.*

And then there's the humble land line. Jacqueline Hill had a good arrangement with her relatives:

*My parents called me once a week at the office (I had no phone or internet connection in my flat) and, as it only had one phone, this had to be carefully timed.*

If you can't arrange for incoming calls to a land line near you, don't underestimate the international calling card. These usually work by giving you a freephone number which connects you to another service provider who can offer you a better rate on your call than the local provider can. These cards are often sold in local newsagents and shops, particularly in touristy areas. There isn't one card which works everywhere, although the Global Phonecard from ekit (www.ekit.com) works from 40 countries; this company also has a few other communication services that may interest you.

To help cut the costs of calls, Mike Laird, who volunteered in Bolivia, has some good advice:

*One of the best things is to have a cascade (or telephone tree) set up so you only have to make one phone call (ie you call your folks, they call your brother and sister, they call two of your friends etc). I know it means you don't get to speak to all your family and friends but there may be times when you don't have enough money.*

In addition to these methods, many international volunteers rediscover the ancient art of letter writing. Robert Driver, who volunteered in the jungles of Belize, remembers keeping in touch this way:

*By letter during the jungle phase and by phone and letter during the rest of the time. It was quite refreshing keeping in contact this way.*

And, of course, if you're out in the wilds, you may agree with Michelle Hawkins, who volunteered in Costa Rica. She says:

*In Costa Rica I didn't keep in touch, as there was no electricity or postal system. It was actually quite liberating not to be contactable by phone, email or post.*

## BLOGGING

If you want to share more than just the odd status update or photo with friends and family, you might want to start your own travel blog. These days there are lots of sites that allow you to publish a blog for free and most don't require more than basic computer skills to get it looking like it was put together by a professional.

- **Blogger** (www.blogger.com) Part of the Google portfolio, it's a reliable and trustworthy option. Set up is a snap with step-by-step instructions, and there are plenty of customisation options.
- **Medium** (www.medium.com) Another good option, Medium works well for story telling.
- **Penzu** (www.penzu.com) This site offers three different types of journals. Choose between a public 'Daily Diary', private 'Expressive Journal', or 'Travel Journal'.
- **Tumblr** (www.tumblr.com) This is perhaps the best site to choose if you plan on featuring visuals. Images, videos and music are easy to incorporate.
- **WordPress** (www.wordpress.com) A very popular platform, it is incredibly flexible regardless of whether you want to use it for writing, photography or both. It's also possible to upgrade if you want your own domain name.

If you are planning to use your smartphone while you are volunteering, you can download apps that will allow you to blog on the go rather than having to be in front of your computer:

- **BlogPress** (iPhone and iPad) This app supports almost all popular blogging platforms including Blogger, Tumblr, WordPress and more. Features include a simple image and video uploader and a social media site integration.
- **Blogsy** (iPad) This is one of the most popular blogging apps, which is compatible with Blogger, Tumblr, WordPress and many other platforms. It is specifically designed for the iPad and iPad mini.
- **Tumblr** (iPhone and iPad) Much like the website, a good option for those dealing with images and videos.
- **WordPress** (iPhone and iPad) This app pairs well with the WordPress site for seemless blogging on your mobile device.

If you're not at all tech-savvy, you can purchase a travel blog package for a small fee per month. Blogging companies offer differing features and functions, but most include interactive maps, space for online entries, digital photo albums and personal message boards. Be sure to find out whether you can download the content of your blog once you are back home, as you won't want all those memories of your time volunteering to just disappear into the ether. Some companies offering travel blog services include: **MyTripJournal** (www.mytripjournal.com), **Off Exploring** (www.offexploring.com) and **Travel Pod** (www.travelpod.com).

## CHATTING ONLINE

There is a range of 'Voice over Internet Protocol' (VoIP) services that use the internet to deliver phone calls. If you have a laptop or smartphone and a broadband connection, you can use your device to chat. If you're relying on internet cafes, keep at eye out for the terminals with headsets: they're for accessing chat services. You can chat face-to-face via a video call if the internet connection is fast and stable and there's a webcam; if not, keep it to just a voice call to help prevent frustrating 'freezing', lags between image and sound, and connection dropouts.

All the VoIP services are easy to sign up for and are user friendly. Services include:
• **Skype** (www.skype.com) Still very popular, can be used for video and voice calls to others on Skype, as well as calls to mobiles and landlines.
• **ooVoo** (www.oovoo.com) Works across most platforms.
• **FaceTime** (www.apple.com/ios/facetime) Only works on Apple devices and relies on access to wi-fi or broadband connection.
There are also some great apps for text, voice and video:
• **Facebook Messenger** (Android, iPhone and iPad)
• **Google Hangouts** (Android, iPhone and iPad)
• **GrooVe IP** (Android and iPhone)
• **ooVoo** (Android, iPhone and iPad)
• **Rounds** (Android and iPhone)
• **Skype** (Android and iPhone)
• **Tango** (Android, iPhone and iPad)
• **WeChat** (Android and iPhone)

## IF IT ALL GOES WRONG

It isn't often that you have to get used to a new job, a new culture, a new country, new living arrangements, new colleagues and a new support network all in one go. But this is what you do when you become an international volunteer.

At first it can be hard. During the first few days (and often weeks) you will need to give your mind and your body time to adapt. In all likelihood you will also have to reassess your personal expectations and those related to the job. Jacqueline Hill, who volunteered for a year in Bangladesh, wisely advises:

*Find out as much as you can but be prepared for all your learning and assumptions to be challenged once you are there. Recognise that you are not single-handedly going to change the world in one trip and that what you expect to do may not be what you actually do once you get there. Don't expect lots of feedback on how you are doing or what impact you're having but recognise that just by being there and sharing you are helping the people to understand one another better. Accept that you will feel that you probably got more from the experience than the people you went to work with did.*

As mentioned before, nine times out of 10, the reason why an international volunteer placement goes wrong is because the expectations of a volunteer do not match the reality of the placement. This doesn't mean there's anything wrong with the placement, or anything wrong with the volunteer. However, it might mean that the volunteer and the placement were ill-matched and that the volunteer was ill-advised and/or inadequately prepared. This is why it is so important to make sure that you volunteer with a reputable organisation that knows both you and their partner programmes well.

In addition, it is one of the reasons why patience, flexibility and adaptability are all key skills to have as an international volunteer. If your volunteer programme is significantly different to the one you signed up for, you will definitely need all three to see if you can still make things work for both you and your host organisation.

However, if you have given your situation time and you genuinely can't make the placement work, you do have a few options. If you have volunteered with a sending agency in your home country, you need to talk to their in-country representatives. Assuming there is no improvement, you will then need to contact the organisation itself in writing. If you asked for a job description prior to departure (see p32) you will be in a better position to point out the mismatch between the volunteer programme you were sold and the one you ended up with. You will then need to decide whether to go home early. This is not a decision to be taken lightly.

However, if coming home is your choice, any reputable volunteering organisation should discuss with you either a refund or free placement on another volunteer programme in the future. If this does not happen, you might like to forward your complaint to one of the professional or self-regulatory bodies that the organisation is part of. In the UK, for instance, this might be **The Year Out Group** (☎+44 (0)1380-816696; www.yearoutgroup.org). While

**Volunteering Australia** (☎+61 3 9820 4100; www.volunteeringaustralia.org) and **Volunteering New Zealand** (☎+64 4 3843636; www.volunteeringnz.org. nz) are peak bodies concerned mostly with national volunteering, they might be able to offer advice. There's no all-encompassing volunteer organisation association in the US, but the **International Volunteer Programs Association** (☎+1 201 221 4105; www.volunteerinternational.org) does count several dozen major organisations as members and might be able to offer advice on how to deal with uncooperative operators.

# USEFUL WEBSITES

• **CIA World Factbook** (www.cia.gov/library/publications/the-world-factbook/index.html) Find out all the stats from the country you're volunteering in.

• **ClimateCare** (www.climatecare.org) Offset the $CO_2$ emissions of your flights by funding sustainable energy and reforestation projects.

•**Department of Foreign Affairs and Trade** (Australia) (www.smartraveller. gov.au) Travel advisories for Australians listed by destination, travel bulletins, information on getting help overseas plus the low-down on visas and passports. The site also offers general travel and travel health tips. Register for email notification about changes to the safety status in the country you're volunteering in.

• **Embassy World** (www.embassyworld.org There's a lot more to this site than just the location of embassies around the world.

• **Lonely Planet's Thorn Tree** (www.lonelyplanet.com/thorntree) Join one of the largest online travel communities and hear first-hand what you can expect in the country you're volunteering in.

• **Lonely Planet's destination pages** (www.lonelyplanet.com/destinations) This site has information on nearly every country in the world.

• **New Zealand Ministry of Foreign Affairs and Trade – Manatū Aorere** (www.safetravel.govt.nz) Log on for travel advice and New Zealand passport and visa requirements. Travellers from the 'Land of the Long White Cloud' can register so the Ministry can contact them in an emergency.

• **Timeanddate.com** (www.timeanddate.com) Offers a world clock and also the times of sunrise and sunset, international country codes and city coordinates.

• **The Travel Doctor** (www.tmvc.com.au) Health reports, email notification service of health issues and details of clinic locations across Australia and seven locations in New Zealand.

• **xe.com** (www.xe.com/ucc) Monitor the rate of exchange for the country you're volunteering in with this universal currency converter.

# 04

## Tying up Loose Ends

Whether it's sorting your moggie or your mortgage, planning is the key to a successful volunteering venture. This may be a once-in-a-lifetime experience, so you don't want to spoil it by leaving loose ends trailing at home. This chapter outlines some of the 'life stuff' that may need finalising before you go.

# JOB

Negotiating time out from work is the most important, and potentially hardest, loose end to tie up. Bungle your approach to the boss and you could blow your volunteering dream out of the water – unless you've decided that you'll resign anyway. Planning your conversation carefully is crucial, especially if you work for a company that doesn't have a policy on volunteering or where no precedent has been set.

Before doing anything else, do your homework. If you work for a large organisation, consult your company's staff handbook, staff intranet and human resources department to get yourself up to speed on its leave provisions. Investigate if anyone else has taken time out and, if so, discreetly sound them out. Find out the company's general attitude to people taking extended periods of leave: is it openly supportive or the reverse? Armed with this information, you can plan your negotiation strategy accordingly.

Work out exactly what you're going to ask for and what you can offer in return. Do you want the same job once you return? Smaller companies may be able to accommodate this, but larger ones are unlikely to unless you're only going for a short period. Instead they will normally only promise employment at the same level and salary. If your company won't give you what you want, are you willing to quit? If so, are you going to be upfront about this, or will threatening to resign be the secret weapon that will give you leverage in your negotiations? If you opt to keep your job, are you asking for unpaid or paid leave or a mixture? How much time off do you need to volunteer? If the company doesn't agree to the period of time you are requesting, will you settle for less and, if so, how much less? Evaluate your worth to the company, as this will determine how accommodating they are likely to be. Have you worked there for long enough to prove your worth? (Many companies set two years as a minimum requirement for negotiating extended leave.) Draw up ways in which you can be replaced temporarily so that continuity is ensured and minimum expense incurred by the company. In this way you will be making life as easy as possible for your boss by doing the thinking and planning for them. Finally, put your case for how volunteering abroad is going to benefit both your company and you: in many cases a volunteering stint teaches you skills that are crucial in the workplace (such as communication skills, leadership and diplomacy skills). The aim is to present your volunteering as a win-win situation.

How long in advance should you pop the question? Antonia Stokes, a conference organiser who took a four-month break in Namibia to work for Raleigh International (p151), found her employers wanted over a year's notice. She says:

*I would advise giving as much notice as possible about your plans, even up to a year in advance, so they can arrange proper cover for you. Be as honest and accommodating as possible, especially if you want your old job back.*

The danger of giving plenty of notice is, of course, that you might be left out of any forward-planning meetings and effectively replaced long before you go. To avoid this scenario, other volunteers suggest giving only three to six months' notice.

Amanda Allen-Toland, who volunteered to work as a youth ambassor with the Thailand Business Coalition on AIDS as part of the Australian Volunteers for International Development (AVID, p155 & p164) programme, was fortunate that her workplace was well disposed to her proposed time off:

*I gave four weeks' notice. I work for a public service agency that encourages staff to enhance their skills in either volunteer or paid roles which can add value to the government's work.*

When negotiating it's wise to stick with well-worn tactics such as listening, expressing your wishes without being aggressive and showing that you can see things from your employer's point of view. Even if you've decided to quit if you don't get what you want, leaving on good terms will pay dividends in the future.

Once you've got agreement in principle from your employers, get it in writing. Make sure this includes the dates of your leave of absence, how much of your time off is paid or unpaid, what position (or level of position) and salary you'll return to and whether your pension or other company benefits are affected (see also the following 'Finances' section).

Of course, you may just decide to resign. Jacqui Pringle volunteered in Sri Lanka as a youth ambassador under AVID, and worked as a communications adviser for the Sewalanka Foundation (a rural development agency). She adopted the following tactics when leaving her job:

*I wanted to run straight to my boss and tell her that I would be leaving, as volunteering overseas was something I had always wanted to do and I wasn't enjoying my job at the time. There could be no guarantees the placement would go ahead, though, so I put off telling my employer just in case any last-minute hitches occurred. In the end I gave them two weeks' notice giving myself a week off before leaving for Colombo.*

Of course, if you get wind of the fact that your company is looking to cut costs and staff, get in first and offer to take a voluntary redundancy package and you might just leave with a nice, fat cheque to help fund your volunteering adventure.

# FINANCES

Once you've decided you're heading off to volunteer, it's crucial to sort your finances out well in advance. This may not be the most scintillating part of your preparations, but if your affairs aren't in order it could ruin your time away or leave you confronting a messy situation once you return. It's wise to get the ball rolling by discussing your affairs with an independent financial adviser. Whatever financial arrangments you make, it's important to keep some savings for when you get back, as that will make settling back in much easier. A small number of volunteering organisations offer resettlement grants when you return home but it's a good idea to make your own provision too.

Below are some particular financial issues you may want to address.

## PENSION AND SUPERANNUATION

Even if they don't excite you, you must check how your pension or superannuation scheme will be affected by your time out of the workforce. If you are taking extended leave to volunteer and you're part of a pension or superannuation scheme at work, get all the details in writing. If you've quit your job, ask your scheme trustee or financial adviser what the options are – there are numerous different schemes and they all have different rules and regulations.

In New Zealand, for instance, people with National Super and participating in recognised volunteer programmes like Volunteer Service Abroad (p165) can generally keep their entitlements for three years if volunteering overseas. In the UK, personal pension and stakeholder schemes are the most flexible for those volunteering, as you can often reduce your contributions or take a complete pension 'holiday' without penalty. And in the USA, for breaks of two years or less, most employees with some seniority can easily alter their contribution levels without incurring any penalties. If you're considering leaving the company permanently, rolling your 401(k) assets into a Roth IRA is probably your best option. In any case, it's essential to consult a financial adviser about your specific situation and needs.

## COMPANY SHARE SAVE SCHEMES

If you work for a large company you may belong to a share save scheme. In the USA these are called ESRP (Employee Stock Retirement Plans) or ESOP (Employee Stock Ownership Plans). If you are going away but intend to return, you should check how your scheme will be affected by a break in employment and ask for the advice to be put in writing. You will almost certainly have to opt out of the scheme while you are away, but your goal should be to re-enter it as soon as you return. Many companies require employees to have worked for two years before they qualify for such schemes, so you may decide to wait until you've notched these up before volunteering overseas. Some also have set dates during the year on which you can enter the scheme, so, again, take this into account.

## MORTGAGE

See the 'House' section (p120) for details on the best way to deal with your mortgage while you're away.

## INVESTMENTS

Sometimes friend, sometimes foe, it is impossible to predict whether the stock market will be up or down when you return from volunteering. If you own stocks and shares and are counting selling them when you return, it may be prudent to transfer some of your money to more secure investments. Again, it pays to consult your financial adviser when considering the options. If you are likely to be away for more than three years, most financial advisers will recommend that you invest in a mixture of bonds and cash as well as equities.

If you live in the UK and your volunteering placement is shorter than a full tax year, think about buying a cash ISA (individual savings account) up to the value of £15,240 and you'll get your interest tax-free. Otherwise any interest above £1000 per year for basic rate taxpayers (or £500 for higher rater taxpayers) will be subject to income tax.

## LOANS

If you have loans, put standing orders or direct debits in place to pay these while you are away and ensure that you have left enough funds in your account to cover the payments. You can try to freeze them but lenders are unlikely to allow this.

If you are a young volunteer with a student loan, check whether your student loan lending agency has any special arrangements for international volunteers. For instance, in New Zealand, legislation grants interest-free status to the student loans of New Zealanders volunteering on specific programmes. Australians should check their HECS-HELP status at http://studyassist.gov.au/sites/StudyAssist or contact the **Australian Taxation Office** (www.ato.gov.au). UK volunteers could contact the **Student Loans Company Ltd** (www.slc.co.uk) for further information on assessment of any income they earn while overseas. In the US, federal and many private student loans allow principal and interest deferment during periods of unemployment (and self-funding volunteer trips fall into this category) or public service (such as work with the Peace Corps and other qualifying organisations). Click over to the **Department of Education** (www.ed.gov) or check with your lender for details.

## BANK ACCOUNTS

You might want to allow a family member or friend to access one of your accounts while you're away. To do this, you need to nominate them as a signatory by filling out forms held by your local bank branch.

## TELEPHONE & ONLINE BANKING

Thanks to online banking, tracking your finances from another country has never been easier. Online banking lets you check balances, pay bills, transfer money between accounts, set up direct debits and standing orders, and increase an overdraft. Most banks also have a telephone backup service which you can ring 24 hours a day if you experience any problems with online banking. Check if your bank can text you your bank balance – this could be useful, particularly if you have limited access to the internet and you're in danger of becoming overdrawn.

Security, however, may be a concern. Internet cafes are notoriously insecure environments to do your banking in, so consider using your own device with internet access or telephone banking instead. Also, ask your bank for its international helpline numbers in case something goes wrong.

If there's no alternative to an internet cafe in the middle of Mali or Madagascar, be cautious (for starters, use a different password for each of your accounts).

## BILLS

If you are keeping your house and car set up direct debits online for items such as insurance, tax or registration and other bills. For more details relevant to house and car owners, see 'Mortgage' (p121) and 'Vehicle' (p124).

Paying your credit card bills while you are away is simple. There are three ways to do it: arrange for them to be paid by a friend who has access to one of your accounts; set up a direct debit for either the minimum payment, the full amount or a fixed amount; or pay the bills online. It's a good idea to alert your credit card company before you go abroad, because you don't want your card provider to assume the card has been stolen and cancel it.

Amanda Allen-Toland, who volunteered in Thailand for a year, found credit card fees to be a headache:

*Unfortunately I didn't plan well and got stung by overseas credit card withdrawal fees. As a volunteer, that really hurts. Before you go, look into setting up an account with a bank that doesn't charge steep fees.*

## DIRECT DEBITS & STANDING ORDERS

Go through any reccurring payments you have and reassess them; cancel ones you don't need and set up new ones. Have you remembered to sort your car repayments, for example?

## INSURANCE POLICIES & INCOME PROTECTION

Check your life or private health insurance policy for any exclusions before you go, as certain insurance companies deny cover if you are going to 'undesirable' areas. Be aware that getting insured after you've returned home from these areas can be difficult. It is unlikely that you'll be able to suspend payments while you are away, as most policies become void if you fail to make regular payments, but some companies are more flexible. In Australia, check with your tax adviser regarding suspending private health insurance, as pausing payments may have implications at tax time.

## MAINTENANCE PAYMENTS

Before you go abroad notify your child support agency, if relevant, otherwise you risk building up arrears or even jail time. Your payments will be reassessed on the basis of your volunteer status. Be sure to contact the agency upon your return.

## SUBSCRIPTIONS

If you're going away for a long time remember to cancel subscriptions to newspapers and magazines. If you're going to be volunteering in a developing country your media diet may be limited, so consider taking out subscriptions to international publications like *The Economist* or *TIME Magazine*.

Trekking in the Himalayas on an expedition with British Exploring Society

Photo: © British Exploring Society

# TAXATION & NATIONAL INSURANCE

## TAX

Completing a tax return is the last thing you want to be doing while you are volunteering overseas. If you can, deal with it before you go. If you do need to file a tax return while you are away, work out exactly how you're going to do this. If possible, pick up a form from your local tax office, fill it in and post it off before you go or complete one online. In the UK, you can file your return online via the **HM Revenue & Customs** (www.gov.uk/government/organisations/hm-revenue-customs). US and Canadian citizens can 'e-file' their federal income tax payments online using privately produced software (some of which you can obtain for free). For Americans, the website of the **Internal Revenue Service** (www.irs.gov) website has comprehensive information. Canadians should check out the **Canada Revenue Agency** (www.cra-arc.gc.ca). Australians can file their tax returns online with the **Australian Taxation Office** (www.ato.gov.au). New Zealanders should check out **Inland Revenue** (www.ird.govt.nz).

Your tax status is unlikely to be changed by volunteering internationally if the break is for less than a complete financial year, but check this with a tax adviser or your local tax office. You should also seek advice if you intend to earn money abroad to support your volunteering, or if you intend to dispose of any assets (eg your home or shares) before leaving or while abroad.

## NATIONAL INSURANCE

For UK residents, sorting out your National Insurance (NI) situation before volunteering internationally for an extended period is vital. If you are going abroad for more than a year you may have to make voluntary contributions while you are away to avoid losing entitlement to full maternity or unemployment benefits, or to a full state pension upon retirement. Some organised volunteering programmes will pay your contributions for you.

## HOUSE

You may own a house or flat that you'll be leaving behind. In this case you may choose to let it, leave it empty (rather dodgy, particularly as regards your insurance), or even sell it. If you're renting, you'll probably simply give notice and put your stuff into storage.

# MORTGAGE

If your mortgage won't be covered by rent from tenants while you are away, think about switching to a flexible mortgage with online facilities. This is the perfect mortgage for international volunteers as you can pay bigger monthly payments before you leave or after you come back, and in return make smaller payments or even take a complete mortgage 'holiday' while you are abroad. Ideally, you should start making additional repayments a year in advance so that the pressure is off, both while you volunteer and once you return.

# SELLING

The beauty of selling your home (and maybe some possessions too) is that you're free of worries; you have no truculent tenants to potentially make your time volunteering any more challenging than it may already be. If you invest the money in an interest earning account, you may be able to keep your savings safe so that you are in a position to buy another home on your return. The risk is that if property prices rise faster than your savings, you may be forced to downsize when you buy back into the market. Don't underestimate the cost of buying again either – taxes, agent and legal fees all add up. For these reasons, selling your home is probably only a sensible option for long-term volunteers.

# LETTING (LEASING) YOUR HOME

Most international volunteers who own property decide on this option. With luck your tenants' rent will cover your mortgage, your bills and even give you a modest income while you are away. Bear in mind, though, that rental income is taxable.

Here are some things to consider when letting your house or apartment.

### Tell Your Mortgage Lender

Look carefully at the small print in the terms and conditions section of your mortgage document and it will invariably stipulate that you need to notify the lender if you let your home.

### Finding Tenants & an Agent

You may decide to let privately and to find your tenants by advertising in local papers, shops or websites (universities often have websites that are referred to by visiting teaching staff, for example). Remember to obtain character references and bank statements (or payslips from an employer) and a watertight tenancy agreement. Although renting to friends can seem the easiest option, it can be disastrous: if something goes wrong with the rental arrangement, your friendship may be knocked on the head forever.

The other option is to let your property through a reputable agent. Although this will cost you more, it can be a safer option. Check the agent is well-established and affiliated to a respected industry body which imposes minimum standards. Whether you use an agent or go it alone, you should start looking for tenants around four to eight weeks before leaving.

## Safety Issues

When you let your home in the UK you need to comply with certain legal obligations regarding safety. These usually entail having your gas, electrical appliances and fixed electrical installations tested for safety. If you are letting through an agent they will normally arrange for these checks to be carried out, for a fee.

## Tax

If you let your home while you are abroad, remember that you'll be taxed on any profit, minus expenses like wear and tear, decorating and repairs. If you are going away for more than six months, you will probably have tax deducted from your rental income. Whether you own another house, whether you let it, and whether you live in your home again on your return will also have an impact, so check out your status with a tax adviser.

## Storage of Personal Effects

Should you decide to put your personal effects into storage, shop around, get quotes and ask lots of questions. For instance, find out how much notice is needed to collect your stuff; what insurance cover is offered; if insurance is included in the price; if the price includes tax; what the storage conditions are like; and if you can see the place where it will be stored (look out for damp areas that could damage your valuables). It could also be relevant to find out whether you can get access to your belongings while they are in storage and, if so, how much it costs. It's normally cheaper if you book storage for a long period of time (rather than constantly renewing) and don't need access. Never put precious items like jewellery, money or documents into storage – use a safe-deposit box instead.

## Inventory

An inventory is essential for avoiding potential conflict when you reclaim your home. You can draw one yourself or pay an agent to do it as part of their service. If you are doing it yourself be meticulous: for example, write down the exact make and model of stoves and fridges and make a note of every blemish so there's no dispute later. It's a good idea to take electronically dated photographs of your contents as a backup, but don't rely on them: they are no defence in court as dates can be tampered with.

## Building & Contents Insurance

If you tell your insurer that you're letting your house, they will almost certainly not offer to cover contents. However, do not despair: there are specialist insurers who will cover both buildings and contents. Premiums will probably be around 10 to 20 per cent more; ask an insurance broker to get quotes. It is hard, however, to get insurance cover for a period of less than three months.

## Tenancy Agreement

This agreement between you and the tenant (also known as a rental or lease agreement) is the key safeguard of your precious asset, so make sure it's done properly. If you are letting through an agent, they will issue their own version. If you are letting privately in the UK, you can buy off-the-shelf agreements from high street stationers or newsagents. In the US, major chain stores like **Office Depot** (www.officedepot.com) do sell standard rental agreements, but smaller outfits won't carry them. Far better, however, is to get a solicitor to draw up a watertight agreement. Make sure you have agreed who is paying contentious costs like water rates and council rates. There is usually no legal minimum period to let a property, but there may be a minimum notice period if you wish to end a tenancy agreement.

## Rent

When the tenancy agreement is signed, you or the agent will probably ask for a month's rent in advance, plus one or possibly two months' rent as a deposit against damages or unpaid bills. In the UK you can insist that the tenant sets up a standing order for rent payment, which will give you far greater peace of mind. If you are paying an agent to manage your property, they will collect rent monthly and forward it to your bank.

**Utilities**

If you are using an agent, in the UK they will transfer accounts for utilities like gas, electricity and water into the tenant's name. Otherwise, the tenants will need to do it themselves once you have arranged for utilities to be disconnected. If you are volunteering only for a short time, you may prefer to leave accounts in your own name and get bills forwarded to the tenant to pay. The risk, though, is that the tenant won't cough up, in which case the responsibility is yours. The telephone is the biggest gamble; you may decide to stipulate that the tenant use their mobile and stop your line or switch it to incoming calls only.

**Inspections & Repairs**

If you are letting privately, you would be wise to appoint a friend to be on stand-by should anything go wrong, such as the hot water breaking down. Ask them to inspect the property – every three to six months is the norm for estate agents. If you are employing a managing agent, they will normally do this, but it is still advisable to ask a friend to be your agent's main point of contact.

## LEAVING YOUR HOUSE EMPTY

If you are volunteering for a short period, it may not be feasible to let your house and you may decide to leave it empty. If so, be sure to appoint a friend to keep a regular eye on it. One of the biggest problems with leaving a house empty is insurance. Most normal policies state that a house must not be left empty for more than 30 days (some say 60).

## HOUSE-SITTERS

Another option is to get a friend or relative to look after your house, pets and garden in return for rent-free accommodation. There are also a number of companies that provide professional house-sitting services, but this is an expensive option and probably not feasible for more than a couple of weeks.

## VEHICLE

What you do with your car, van or motorbike depends on how long you intend to be away. If it's just a few months, your best option is to leave the car in the garage or at a friend's or relative's place and ask them to drive it around the block once or twice. Note that they need to be nominated drivers on your insurance policy.

Many volunteers going away for a year or two decide to sell their cars, adding welcome cash to their volunteering funds. Another option is to lend the car to a friend while you are away, but there can be insurance snags involved.

## OTHER TRANSPORT

If you have a seasonal transport pass and are leaving before it expires, you can try applying for a refund by returning to the ticket office where it was bought.

## PARTNER & CHILDREN

If you have a partner and children, you may need to time your volunteering to fit in around them. In the case of your partner, there may be an optimum time for you to volunteer abroad simultaneously, or you may decide to spend the time apart. Antonia Stokes, who spent four months in Namibia, had just started a relationship when she left the UK:

> I'd been planning the trip for over a year so decided to go ahead with it and leave my boyfriend behind. A break of three or four months can improve a relationship, or at least expose the issues in it. It definitely pushes you to make decisions about your future.

Volunteers with Restless Development working as part of the International Citizen Service

Photo © Restless Development

Alternatively, of course, you may be wanting to volunteer abroad because you have just split up with a partner. Travel can be a great healer and spending time away an ideal way to cement the break.

Volunteering with children is slightly more complicated, depending on their ages and whether they are at school or not. Some parents decide to volunteer during the school holidays, which is easier than longer-term volunteering where you'll need to make decisions about schooling your child abroad. Teaching your children yourself is not an easy option if you are volunteering full-time. For information about international schools or local schools, contact your embassy in the country you plan to be in. And, as always, health and safety issues will be paramount with children. Lonely Planet's *Travel with Children* contains more information on being abroad with a family.

## MAKING A WILL

It may not be the cheeriest subject, but if you don't have a will you should make one before you depart (the country that is, not this world). If you don't make one and you die intestate (ie will-less), your family and loved ones could end up with little. Your partner is particularly vulnerable if you are cohabiting but not married.

Volunteers heading out to sea
on an Earthwatch expedition

Photo: © David Gaspard / Earthwatch

You can buy a DIY will kit from stationers or newsagents. However, solicitors claim they make more money out of unravelling DIY wills than they do drawing them up. So, for a fee, why not do it properly and get yourself a solicitor? Whatever method you choose, give your friends and relatives copies of your will, or tell them where copies are kept – your will is of little use if it's never found.

In the UK you can choose from hundreds solicitors to draw up your will for a suggested donation (£95 for a basic single will; £150 for a pair of basic mirror wills) during the month of November as part of the **Will Aid** (www.willaid.org.uk).

## POWER OF ATTORNEY

If you are volunteering long-term, you might want to think about giving a trusted friend or relative power of attorney over your affairs while you are away, in case you are incapacitated or out of contact. It's not a step to take lightly, as it gives the person power to do anything from selling your house or taking out a mortgage in your name. If you are thinking of taking such a step the rule is, as ever, seek professional advice first.

## VOTING

If you're leaving for a while but still want a say in how your country is run, decide how you're going to vote. In the UK, consult the **Electoral Commission** (www.electoralcommission.org.uk). The **Federal Voting Assistance Program** website (www.fvap.gov) has information on absentee voting for Americans (also see www.fec.gov), and Canadians should consult **Elections Canada** (www.elections.ca). In Australia, **Australian Electoral Commission** (www.aec.gov.au) covers frequently asked voting questions for anyone heading overseas. If you're from New Zealand, get the low-down from **Elections New Zealand** (www.elections.org.nz).

## POST

While you are away, your local mail authority may be able to forward your mail either to your address abroad (if you have a fixed one) or to a reliable friend or relative in your home country who is willing to sift through it for you. And don't forget to send out change-of-address cards or emails before you go.

# USEFUL WEBSITES

The following list of websites may help you get organised and on your way sooner:

## UK Websites

- **The Career Break Site** (www.thecareerbreaksite.com) Everything you ever wanted to know about putting your life on hold while you are abroad.
- **Carers UK** (www.carersuk.org) Information for those caring for elderly relatives.
- **Driver & Vehicle Licensing Agency** (www.gov.uk/government/organisations/driver-and-vehicle-licensing-agency) Check with the DVLA when deciding what to do about your vehicle while you're away.
- **Education Otherwise** (www.educationotherwise.net) A useful site about home schooling if you decide to do this with your kids.
- **Home Education Advisory Service** (www.heas.org.uk) This organisation produces an informative leaflet on your options for home schooling abroad. Online subscribers (£16 per year) can also read the latest in UK home education network news, download resources and access up-to-date articles.
- **Post Office** (www.postoffice.co.uk) Contact to have your mail re-directed.

## North American Websites

- **Canada Post** (www.canadapost.ca)
- **Care Pathways** (www.carepathways.com) For those who look after elderly relatives, this site hosts a searchable database of recommended providers of assisted living, continuing care, independent living and nursing-home care.
- **Kelley Blue Book** (www.kbb.com) Kelley's online Blue Book is full of practical advice about how to price, sell or trade in your car.
- **Nolo Press** (www.nolo.com) Nolo Press publishes superb plain-English self-help legal books and provides a wealth of free online information on everyday legal topics such as wills, tenancy agreements, limited power of attorney.
- **United States Postal Service** (www.usps.com) Re-directing your mail.

## Australasian Websites

- **Association of Superannuation Funds of Australia** (www.superannuation.asn.au) Information on different types of funds.
- **Australian Furniture Removers Association** (www.afra.com.au) AFRA-registered businesses to take care of your beloved belongings in transit.
- **Australia Post** (http://auspost.com.au) Will hold or forward your mail.

- **Carers NSW** (www.carersnsw.asn.au) For those who look after elderly relatives, Carer Resource and Carer Respite Centres exist in each Australian state; they are all linked through this website.
- **Drive** (www.drive.com.au) Check this site out before you put up a 'for sale' sign on your car.
- **Australian Department of Human Services (**www.humanservices.gov.au/customer/themes/families) You may lose your Family Tax Benefit if you leave Australia without notifying the FAO. Check the website for details.
- **Law Council of Australia** (www.lawcouncil.asn.au) The Law Council of Australia represents 40,000 legal practitioners across the country (who can provide power of attorney and other legal advice).
- **National Insurance Brokers Association** (www.niba.com.au) Find around 500 brokers in Australia who specialise in everything from car or house and contents insurance to travel, life and terrorism insurance.
- **Self Storage Association of Australasia** (www.selfstorage.com. au) The SSAA represents over 1100 storage centres across Australia and New Zealand.
- **Your Mortgage** (www.yourmortgage.com.au) The online version of Australia's Your Mortgage magazine, with broker listings and all sorts of mortgage advice.

A Greenpeace volunteer talking about the organisation at Glastonbury Festival, UK

# 05

## Organised Volunteer Programmes

If you've picked this book up, chances are that a little voice may have asked, 'Can I really do it?' The prospect of volunteering abroad can seem daunting, but it can be made much less so when it's arranged through a structured, organised programme. Choosing this route to a volunteer placement means that, in most cases, you'll pay a single fee and – voilà – everything from the pre-departure orientation to the little bag of peanuts on the flight home is arranged for you. Whether your calling is to protect turtles in Ecuador or teach grammar in Bangkok, there's a wide assortment of organised placements to choose from, offering opportunities to those who take comfort from a 'packaged' approach.

Most of these organisations have a few key characteristics in common, offering as part of the package pre-departure and in-country support and accommodation and food. Some also include travel insurance and visas, and others will organise your international airfare. But beyond these basic characteristics, the permutations are many and varied.

In many cases, the costs of organised programmes are high. However, it is difficult to generalise, because a number of voluntary organisations sending skilled volunteers abroad do not charge for placements and even offer a small monthly stipend. There are differences in the scale of organisations too. Some organisations, like International Federation of the Red Cross and Red Crescent Societies (p179), have offices and programmes around the world, and send millions of people abroad on projects of every stripe. Others, like PEPY Empowering Youth (p162) accept less than 10 volunteers a year. Some organisations specialise in particular fields, such as Operation Smile (p177) only offering placements in medicine, for example, while others like VSO (p137) allow participants to pick and choose from a smorgasbord of offerings. It's these variations in size, scope and types of project that can make or break your volunteering experience. One volunteer's dream placement doing hands-on entomology research is another's nightmare assignment swatting at bugs.

Some of the organisations listed in this chapter have programmes for everyone. Others are suitable only for people wanting to volunteer long term or for those trained in a particular profession. However, these can easily be sorted into two broad categories: expeditions and placements. We'll start by defining these terms.

# HOW DO THEY WORK?

## EXPEDITIONS VS PLACEMENTS

Anyone who has dipped a curious toe into the volunteering world knows that jargon and acronyms abound. In this book, the word 'expedition' is not to be confused with the kind of solo caper that involves slashing your way through the jungle with a machete. In volunteering parlance, expeditions are usually team-oriented exercises, where participants live, travel and work together in groups of 10 or more volunteers, accompanied at all times by qualified staff. Expeditions of this type often combine a service-based experience with an adventure element – activities such as trekking, climbing or rafting. Organisations offering these kinds of combined packages include Outlook Expeditions (p159), Quest Overseas (p150) and Raleigh International (p151). Personal development is usually a key component of expedition-style volunteering. Laurence Gale travelled to Ghana with Raleigh International and says:

*I did a 10-week expedition. As soon as we arrived in Accra we went to base camp and were immediately put into groups. The first week was spent doing icebreakers and learning basic first-aid and camping skills. Then we had three projects to work on: community, adventure and environmental projects. My community phase was spent on the border with Burkina Faso building pit latrines in a village. The adventure phase involved doing 260km over land and lake Volta in two and a half weeks. It was an awesome challenge and great fun for someone like me who loves running around outdoors. We also spent a lot of time in village schools teaching HIV/AIDS awareness. In my final (environmental) phase I spent the nights combing a sandy beach for olive ridley and giant leatherback turtles. We slept in big army tents along with various bugs, snakes and grass rats. Woohoo!*

However, most organisations in this chapter offer placements, not expeditions. Simply put, for a placement the organisation acts like a temping agency, matching your requirements, skills, abilities and interests with projects in need. You may work independently, but more often than not you'll work alongside a handful of fellow volunteers. Placements are more self-determined than expeditions; you can have more freedom to shape your placement and make what you will of it, though you can still expect a high standard of in-country support. For example, most organisations have a local staff member who looks after a number of volunteers in a particular area and, in addition, there is a representative in the country of origin who is little more than a satellite phone call away should you need help. Two such placement organisations are The Leap (p146) and Projects Abroad (p142). Louise Ellerton, who travelled to Ghana with Projects Abroad, describes her experience of being part of an organised placement:

*I did voluntary work in a veterinary practice, as this is the field that I will be going into. You have to be prepared for things to be different and accept that it's not always what you expected. I found the people very laid-back and a lot of the day was spent sleeping. At first this frustrated me, as I was there to gain experience, but you learn to make the most of the times when you do get to see a case or an operation. I went alone but in the knowledge that I was going with a gap-year company who would be there for me when I arrived and had sorted out my placement and accommodation for the year. It was very easy to meet other volunteers doing the same thing through the company and you had ready-made friends who knew the country better than you did.*

Claire Fulton, who volunteered in Africa with The Leap, appreciated the in-country support during her placement:

*The in-country staff were invaluable and they made it that much more enjoyable. They prevented many near-catastrophes from happening! They would have done anything for us. As a group, we were all so glad that they were there.*

## COSTS

While some of the more selective programmes like the Peace Corps (p178) don't charge for their placements, many of the programmes mentioned in this chapter are expensive. In many cases, the price covers a truckload of inclusions, sometimes incorporating flights, in-country support and pre-departure training.

A proportion of the (often hefty) price tags attached to expeditions allows for first-class equipment, whether this comes in the form of a tent that won't leak or a guide who can read a map. Want to feel a warm inner glow from shelling out your life savings? Just keep in mind that all development and conservation and wildlife projects rely on volunteers' money to keep their projects afloat.

## SELECTION & ELIGIBILITY

Some of the programmes in this chapter – particularly the ones in the 'Skilled Volunteering' and 'Emergency & Relief' sections – are selective, requiring such highly specialised training that they're simply not an option for many people. Others such as World Expeditions (p156) require little more than an interest in the project and a financial commitment.

## LENGTH OF PROGRAMMES

There are organised programmes of every length: from a volunteering stint during a week-long vacation to an assignment that will last several years. Be sure you have a general idea of the time commitment you'd like to make before you begin your research because, while some programmes offer flexible time frames, others require very structured time commitments.

## WHAT TO LOOK FOR

Make sure you check whether costs such as airfares and travel insurance are included in the programme fee. Also, if you think you might like to do some independent exploring, find out how much time you'll be allowed off from the volunteer programme. It's a good idea to request the contact details of former participants, who can provide objective answers to any of your specific questions.

## PROS & CONS

Regardless of whether you choose an expedition or a placement, there are some significant pros and cons attached to organised volunteer placements that you should weigh up before committing yourself.

## PROS

**You're guaranteed a structured and packaged volunteering experience**
By definition, organised volunteer placements offer inclusive packages that take care of almost everything. In exchange for a sizable financial commitment,

usually in the form of a flat fee, you're relieved of spending months trawling through guidebooks and foreign-language websites for information about your destination. You're also relieved of much of the burden of pre-departure planning, because your accommodation, food, local support and the project itself are all usually prearranged for you.

### Higher standards of in-country support make you feel more secure

Safety is often a chief consideration for anyone about to jet off to an unfamiliar part of the world. Obviously, no-one can guarantee that things won't go wrong, but placement organisations have systems in place to prevent a crisis from turning into a tragedy. Expeditions are accompanied by experienced team leaders and sometimes a doctor or a nurse. If you're on a placement there will be in-country representatives who can provide support in an unfamiliar setting and who will follow established procedures in the event of an emergency.

### You'll likely get thorough pre-departure training & briefings about your project

Many organisations take great pride in thoroughly preparing volunteers for their expeditions or placements. Many have training weekends, workshops on cultural awareness, language training, risk-assessment sessions and lengthy discussions on health and safety issues. Attendees are better prepared when they arrive at their destination and most hit the ground running from day one.

Also, when you live and work in the developing world where living conditions are, well, developing, it's important that you understand what to expect. Living without electricity or running water shouldn't come as a shock to you, as it did to Claire Loseby, who volunteered in China. She says:

*Everything seemed a bit daunting at first because I never expected to live in such horrible conditions (no toilets, for example) but you soon adapt to it.*

### You'll work with like-minded volunteers & local communities

Programmes that attract school-leavers or recent graduates can be great places to make new friends. Volunteers who live and work together, alongside their local partners, can become like tight-knit family groups. Tabitha Cook, who taught English and worked at an orphanage in Sri Lanka with Travellers Worldwide (p159), really appreciated being around like-minded people her own age and says:

*If you're thinking of volunteering, look at who you'll be living with, whether you're placed in a homestay or living with other volunteers. I chose to live with other volunteers because I wanted to be around people that I could moan to if it all got on top of me, and so if I made a cultural faux pas I wouldn't offend those I was living with. It was the best decision I have ever made. I made so many friends and learnt a lot, plus we had some great house parties.*

### You can find programmes geared toward personal development

Providing personal development opportunities for volunteers is a goal of many volunteering ventures aimed at young people. Encouraging volunteers to develop their skills, whether as part of a team or in a leadership capacity, is a key component of organisations such as Raleigh International (p151).

### Your nearest and dearest are likely to worry less about you

Organisations aimed at the under-30 set are used to dealing with hand-wringing parents while you are halfway around the globe. Some go to great lengths to ensure that both you and your parents are kept happy while you're away, for example providing secure blogs on their websites so that friends and family can track your itinerary.

## CONS

### The costs

As we have mentioned, some of these programmes are expensive, though many organisations offer help in raising the programme fees. But if you get a thrill from not knowing where the next meal is coming from or where the next bus is going to, there are plenty of programmes that offer a less structured approach, along with a more affordable price tag.

### You're locked into a pre-paid commitment for a rigid period of time, and you may be too coddled

Programmes vary in length, but some, like Project Trust (p150), require very specific and restrictive time commitments. If you're fresh out of school or college, these structured commitments might feel too institutional. Consider this carefully, because with many organisations, if you decide to pack up your bags and leave early, it's very unlikely your money will be refunded.

**You're worried about not interacting enough with local people**

Sometimes a group-based volunteer experience might not provide you with enough exposure to the local people and culture. Are you sure you want to be surrounded by compatriots when you go abroad? A good way to ensure interaction with local people is to live with a host family, so check if this is an option with the programme you're interested in. Otherwise, an immersive placement, where you work on your own or in pairs, might be more your cup of tea.

**You came halfway around the world to do volunteer work, not for this personal development nonsense**

If you're serious about rolling up your sleeves and committing your time to a charitable organisation in the developing world, you might be better off volunteering with an outfit that's focused on intensive volunteer work, rather than on a combination of volunteering and personal development.

# MAJOR INTERNATIONAL PLACEMENT PROGRAMMES

When you think of volunteering abroad, a handful of well-established, long-standing organisations probably spring to mind. Agencies like VSO and the Peace Corps are heavy hitters with well-organised programmes, elaborate support systems, and decades-old relationships with their host countries. It's worth bearing in mind, however, that smaller, grassroots organisations usually offer more flexibility than these large organisations.

## VSO

VSO is a leading independent, international development charity working to alleviate poverty in 24 countries across Africa, Asia, South America and the Pacific. It mobilises international, regional, corporate, youth, short-term and long-term volunteers to make a difference in some of the world's poorest communities. In 2015, along with its 400 local partners, VSO helped better the lives of more than 2.2 million people.

This work is done by volunteers sharing their skills with local people and empowering them to change lives in the areas of health, education and employment. It accepts applicants between 18 and 75 from a variety of professional backgrounds, such as healthcare, teaching, business, IT, project management, engineering and agriculture. VSO provides accommodation and a basic allowance. They cover the cost of flights, insurance, medical costs and visas.

For people without professional expertise, VSO has a volunteering programme aimed at people aged between 18 and 25: the International Citizen Service (p145). To apply or for more information visit www.vsointernational.org.

## VSO KNOWLEDGE EXCHANGE

Recently started, this programme allows employees from companies who have signed up to the scheme to volunteer abroad for approximately two months and share their professional skills with communities in the world's poorest countries. The companies release their staff on the understanding that they still have a job to come back to. Examples include Syngenta workers helping to transform farming communities, IBM staff improving local IT systems and Citibank employees teaching better business practice.

For more information visit www.vsoknowledgeexchange.org.

## PEACE CORPS

Founded in 1961, Peace Corps (www.peacecorps.gov) is an independent federal agency of the US Government, and has sent more than 220,000 Americans on 27-month volunteer assignments around the world. It's unique among service organisations because their volunteers live and work at the community level with a focus on integration and sustainable change. Any USA citizen over 18 can apply. There is no upper age limit, but the average age of volunteers is 28.

Placements vary widely and volunteers currently serve in 63 countries worldwide. You may work with small-scale farmers and families to increase food security in a remote African village or work with non-governmental organisations and municipalities to encourage economic opportunities in communities in Eastern Europe – it all depends on the needs of your community and your skills. Peace Corps volunteers come from all kinds of backgrounds. They range from recent college grads to mid-career professionals to retirees with many years of experience.

Ryan Andersen joined the Peace Corps as a break from a career in finance:

*I served as a Peace Corps volunteer for two years in the Dominican Republic and transferred and extended for a third year to help launch a new project in Zambia. The overarching goal of my project in the DR was to teach business skills to farmers, women's groups and youth groups. In Zambia I lectured at a college on farm management and worked with the Zambian Ministry of Education to develop a new distance-learning programme for orphans and vulnerable children.*

*The experience surpassed my expectations – almost every week I get emails and handwritten letters that have traversed half the world carrying a stamp that cost a quarter of a day's wages. These letters reaffirm the bonds that I went to Zambia and DR to build. The Peace Corps gave me a great new perspective. In some ways it made me more motivated to take advantage of all the opportunities that I have here and it also made me reassess what is truly important in life and where I should focus my priorities.*

Peace Corps' service time is 2 years plus 3 months of training. It also offers specialised, high-impact, short-term assignments to experienced professionals through Peace Corps Response and the Global Health Service Partnership. The Peace Corps provides each volunteer with housing and a living stipend that enables them to live in a manner similar to people in their community of service. Unlike other international volunteer programs, there is no charge to participate in the Peace Corps. There is no application fee, although costs may only be partially covered for required medical examinations during the application process.

Serving as a Peace Corps volunteer is a professional opportunity with many benefits so the application process is competitive. But the application process is now simpler, faster, and more personalised. Applicants can now choose their country of service and apply to specific programs through an online application that can be completed in about one hour. Assuming you receive an invitation to serve, you'll be assigned a placement matching your skills. Your assignment could be in any of the over 60 countries where Peace Corps volunteers serve and could focus on agriculture, community economic development, environment, health, youth in development, or education. The whole process – from completing your application to departing for service – should take about 6 months.

## EUROPEAN VOLUNTARY SERVICE (EVS)

European Voluntary Service is funded by the European Union's Erasmus+ programme and will pay you to volunteer full-time in another country. The funding covers everything from travel and accommodation to food and insurance, as well as giving you a small monthly allowance, up to €145.

EVS placements are between two weeks and 12 months, and are coordinated by the sending organisation (usually from the volunteer's home country) and the host organisation (usually the one where you are volunteering). The wide variety of opportunities includes work in the social, environmental or cultural sectors. EVS gives you the chance to experience other cultures and languages and the opportunity to try out different types of work and develop new skills. Plus, international experience will enhance your CV.

To take part, you need to be between 17 and 30 and live in an eligible country – which is the 28 EU member states plus Iceland, Norway, Turkey, Liechtenstein and the former Yugoslav Republic of Macedonia. In addition, some EVS projects take place in 'partner regions' neighbouring the EU.

If you are interested in taking part in EVS, either on your own or in a group, you first need to find an EVS-accredited sending organisation or a project you are interested in. There are two lists: one of organisations (https://europa.eu/youth/volunteering/evs-organisation_en) and one of projects (http://europa.eu/youth/volunteering/project_en) on the European Youth Portal website.

In the UK, EVS is administered by the Erasmus+ UK National Agency (☎+44 (0)121 212 8947; erasmusplus@ecorys.com; www.erasmusplus.org.uk/volunteer-abroad).

Hanging out in the tree canopy of the Amazon with the British Exploring Society

Photo: © British Exploring Society

# OPTIONS FOR THE UNDER 30S

Even though it's less common in the USA than in most of Europe and the UK, many youngsters take a year out to see a bit of the world, either before starting higher education or after completing it. The following organisations (often referred to as 'gap-year organisations') cater mostly to the under-30 set, and send as many as 200,000 young people abroad every year. While some of the following opportunities are tailored to 17- to 25-year-olds looking for a taste of the world beyond academia's walls, many also accommodate older volunteers.

## INTERNATIONAL ORGANISATIONS

### BUNAC

London, UK

☎ +44 (0)33 3999 7516

enquiries@bunac.org.uk

www.bunac.org

Better known for working holiday and summer camp programmes, BUNAC also offers 11 volunteer programmes. Among these are wildlife conservation in South Africa, construction in Nepal and marine conservation in Mexico.

**Status:** Limited company.

**Timing & Length of Placements:** Placements last from five weeks to six months (there are monthly group departures). Apply at least 10 weeks prior to departure.

**Destinations:** Cambodia, India, China, South Africa, Nepal, Thailand, Vietnam, Mexico, Australia, New Zealand and Ecuador.

**Costs:** Five weeks from about £799, usually

including: programme literature, an arrival orientation course, UK and in-country support, accommodation and food (check with BUNAC for full details). Flights, travel insurance and pocket money are not covered.

**Eligibility:** Minimum age is 18 and some programmes require you to be a student or recent graduate. South Africa and Cambodia are only open to British or Irish nationals; all programmes require that you be a UK resident. For the Peru and Costa Rica placements, you need to speak conversational Spanish. If working with children, you'll also need a criminal background check.

**Groups or Individuals:** Individuals.

**Annual no. of Volunteers:** 300 to 500.

**Partner Programmes:** In all six regions, BUNAC partners with local NGOs.

**Selection & Interview Process:** Volunteer programme participants pay a deposit and are enrolled onto the programme.

**In-country Support:** Different projects have varying levels of in-country supervision. All volunteers will receive an arrival orientation and BUNAC's local partners provide guidance and supervision throughout the trip. Emergency phone lines are operated 24/7 both in-country and also in the UK.

### Cross-Cultural Solutions

Tower Point 44, North Rd, Brighton, UK

☎ +44 (0)845 458 2781/2

New Rochelle, NY, USA

☎ +(0)1 800 380 4777

info@crossculturalsolutions.org

www.crossculturalsolutions.org

Cross-Cultural Solutions offers volunteer programmes in eight countries around the world. Placements are based on an individual's skills and interests and the needs of the local community. All work is with locally designed projects, usually in the fields of education, healthcare and social service. Strong emphasis is placed on cultural exchange, and participants are given the chance to be immersed in the culture of their host region through travel, activities and seminars.

**Status:** In the UK, Cross-Cultural Solutions is a registered charity and limited company. In the USA it's a social enterprise.

**Timing & Length of Placements:** Placements are from one to 12 weeks and can be extended. There are start dates throughout the year. Apply 60 days in advance.

**Destinations:** Costa Rica, Ghana, Guatemala, India, Morocco, Peru, Tanzania and Thailand.

**Costs:** The cost of a two-week programme is approximately £1930, and each additional week comes in at around £350. This includes lodging, meals, in-country transportation, airport transfers, full staff support, medical insurance, language training and cultural excursions (but not international flights).

**Eligibility:** The minimum age of independent volunteers is 18, and there are exclusive summer programmes for high school students. Children between the ages of eight and 16 must be accompanied by a parent, legal guardian or a person appointed by a parent or guardian. All volunteers are run through a sex offender database.

**Groups or Individuals:** Depends on placement.

**Annual no. of Volunteers:** 2000-2500.

**Partner Programmes:** More than 200 partner programmes worldwide.

**Selection & Interview Process:** Anyone with a desire to volunteer internationally is encouraged to apply and placements are designed to accommodate all kinds of skills and levels of experience. Volunteers wishing to apply their specific skills to local community projects may do so through a customised placement developed by the country director.

**In-country Support:** Professional, local staff to provide orientation, safety, supervision and guidance throughout each volunteer's stay. A staff member is always present and available and the country director is available in case of emergency at all times. For the convenience of friends and families of volunteers, there is a toll-free 24-hour emergency hotline in the US.

## Projects Abroad

Goring, Sussex, UK

☑ +44 (0)1903 708 300

info@projects-abroad.co.uk

www.projects-abroad.co.uk

Projects Abroad is a large global organiser of overseas voluntary work placements. It has a huge variety of projects available: animal care, archaeology, business, care, conservation, culture and community, journalism, language courses, law and human rights, medicine and healthcare, sports, teaching, veterinary medicine.

**Status:** Limited company.

**Timing & Length of Placements:**
Placements can range from two weeks to 12 months and volunteers can move from one placement to another, if they wish. There are programmes year-round and departure dates are flexible. Try to give at least three months' notice.

**Destinations:** The many destinations include Argentina, Bolivia, Cambodia, China, Ethiopia, Ghana, Jamaica, Mexico, Mongolia, Nepal, Peru, South Africa and Thailand.

**Costs:** Two-week projects start from £995, which includes food, accommodation, airport transfers, transport to and from work where required, insurance and in-country backup. International flights are extra.

**Eligibility:** Those aged from 16 to 70 are eligible. A criminal background check is required for positions dealing with children or vulnerable adults.

**Annual no. of Volunteers:** 10,000.

**Annual Projects:** More than 200.

**Partner Programmes:** 50.

**Selection & Interview Process:** After being selected on the basis of their application forms, participants reserve placements with a £195 deposit that goes towards their fundraising target.

**In-country Support:** There are full-time, paid and trained staff in every destination.

## Restless Development

London, UK

☎ +44 (0)20 7976 8070

info@restlessdevelopment.org

www.restlessdevelopment.org

Restless Development is an international development charity that runs the International Citizen Service (p145) in partnership with VSO (p175). It has worked for 25 years with both international volunteers and young people across the world to deliver programmes tackling some of the most pressing issues facing young people today, such as HIV and unemployment.

# UK ORGANISATIONS

## British Exploring Society

London, UK

☎ +44 (0)20 7591 3141

info@britishexploring.org

www.britishexploring.org

Founded in 1932 by a surviving member of Scott's Antarctic expedition, BES aims to provide opportunities for young explorers to access remote areas of the world on immersive expeditions with a development focus. Explorers work within groups of 12 on a variety of environmental and research projects led by volunteer leaders who may be scientists, teachers, media professionals or outdoor leaders. Expedition destinations vary each year but typically include the Amazon, Arctic, Himalayas and desert environments.

**Status:** Charity.

**Timing & Length of Expedition:** It runs three- and five-week summer expeditions which depart in late July.

**Destinations:** It varies each year but typically include the Amazon, Arctic, Himalayas or desert environments.

**Costs:** The costs for expeditions vary from

£2400 to £3900 plus flights. Fundraising support is given and reduction in cost is possible through volunteering.

**Eligibility:** Applicants must be aged 16 to 25 at the time of the expedition but are encouraged to apply up to 24 months in advance. Some experience of camping, hill walking and outdoor activities is desirable but not a prerequisite.

**Groups or Individuals:** Individuals.

**Annual no. of Volunteers:** 250.

**Annual Projects:** Vary, but always combine adventurous activities with environmental conservation projects.

**Selection & Interview Process:** Applications are online and followed up with a phone interview.

**In-country Support:** Each expedition has an experienced chief leader, multiple medics (depending on destination), chief scientist, media leaders, base-camp manager and two adventure leaders for every group of 12. Also, there is a 24-hour UK response team, International SOS repatriation and emergency cover.

## Changing Worlds

Bristol, UK

☎ +44 (0)20 8123 8702

info@changing-worlds.com

www.changing-worlds.com

Changing Worlds offers travel experiences for individuals looking to take part in placements overseas during a gap year, student holiday or career break. Placements range from internships and work experience, courses and qualifications, paid work options and community volunteering, to cultural and adventure tours.

**Status:** Limited company.

**Timing & Length of Placements:** Start dates happen most weeks of the year. The minimum stay is 14 days, with the average length of placement being four weeks.

**Destinations:** Argentina, Australia, Cambodia, Canada, China, Costa Rica, Fiji, Germany, Ghana, India, Indonesia, Laos, Kenya, Malaysia, New Zealand, Philippines, South Africa, Sri Lanka, St Lucia, Thailand and Vietnam.

**Costs:** Start from £495 for two weeks, with an extra charge for each additional week you stay. This generally includes all accommodation, food, airport pick-up, training and induction, support and a donation to the project you work on. Fees do not include flights, travel insurance, vaccinations, visas and personal spending money but Changing Worlds provides guidance with this.

**Eligibility:** The minimum age is 17; most volunteers are school and university leavers but some are on a break from careers. Criminal background checks are made for some applicants who will be working with children. References are also required.

**Groups or Individuals:** Individuals, but you can go out as part of a group.

**Annual no. of Volunteers:** 500 plus.

**Annual Projects:** 200.

**Selection & Interview Process:** Applications can be made online or over the phone.

**In-country Support:** 24-hour UK and in-country support is available through project managers and in-country coordinators. Full travel advice and inductions are provided pre-departure and during the project.

## International Citizen Service

London, UK

www.volunteerics.org

www.restlessdevelopment.org

Managed by VSO (p175) and Restless Development (p143), ICS is funded by the UK Government and offers teams of youngsters the opportunity to volunteer for three months on projects in developing nations. Volunteers work side-by-side with local volunteers and stay with host families in the local community to make sure they become part of the community.

ICS projects include improving access to good education, raising awareness about health issues, creating more employment opportunities, strengthening environmental resilience and promoting the rights of marginalised communities. Projects are designed in partnership with the local community and delivered through local partners.

Status: Charity

Timing & Length of Placements: Placements start throughout the year, and last 10 to 12 weeks or six months if a team leader.

Destinations: Africa, Asia and Central America.

Costs: Volunteers are asked to fundraise at least £800, which goes towards the programme. ICS covers volunteers' medical costs, training, flights, accommodation, food, visas, insurance and a basic allowance.

Eligibility: Applicants need to be between 18 and 25 and able to communicate in English. They must also be a resident of the UK; although residents of the EU, Norway, Liechtenstein or Iceland qualify if they've lived in the UK for a year or more, or are a resident of a country in which ICS programmes are delivered. Criminal record checks are also required if working with children or vulnerable persons. For team leaders, applicants need to be 23 to 35 years of age.

Groups or Individuals: Individuals.

Annual no. of Volunteers: 8585.

Selection & Interview Process: ICS chooses its volunteers based on their personal qualities and potential. You don't need cash, skills or qualifications to apply for ICS – just the ambition to make a difference.

In-country Support: Volunteers are supported before they go and while they are overseas. Quality training from ICS means they can support projects effectively and understand how they contribute to a wider programme of development work.

## Inter-Cultural Youth Exchange UK

London, UK

✆ +44 (0)20 7681 0983

info@icye.org.uk

www.icye.org.uk

ICYE-UK is a user-led charity working in the field of personal, social and community development. ICYE is part of the ICYE International Federation, which has been recognised as an 'International Peace Messenger' by the UN General Assembly and has earned consultative status with Unesco. Volunteer placements include working in HIV clinics and orphanages, with disabled people and in primary schools. If you're interested in volunteering in Europe, ICYE-UK is an EVS-affiliated sending organisation (see p139).

**Status:** Charity.

**Timing & Length of Placements:** Placements last from three weeks to 12 months. The shorter placements run year-round but the longer ones (six or 12 months) depart in January and August. Apply with three months' notice.

**Destinations:** Many around the world, including Bolivia, Brazil, Colombia, Costa Rica, Europe, Ghana, Kenya, Mozambique, Nepal and New Zealand. Also Mexico, Honduras, Uganda, Morocco, Nigeria, India, Taiwan, Japan, Indonesia, Vietnam and South Korea.

**Costs:** A six-month placement costs from £3795 and a 12-month one from £4495, including international flights, living costs, health insurance, pocket money, a language course and pre-departure, on-arrival and evaluation training seminars. If you're 18 to 30 and going to Europe then your trip could be funded through the EVS.

**Eligibility:** Long-term international placements are open to those aged 18 to 30; EVS is open to 18- to 25-year-olds; and shorter term placements to those 18 and above. All applicants must pass a criminal background check.

**Groups or Individuals:** Individuals.

**Partner Programmes:** Unesco, European Commission's 'Youth In Action' Programme, the Council of Europe (European Youth Directive) and Mobility International.

**Selection & Interview Process:** Many applicants start with informational recruitment days. Contact the organisation for details.

**In-country Support:** After an orientation with in-country staff, volunteers have the full support of paid local staff.

## The Leap

Marlborough, Wiltshire, UK

☎ +44 (0)1670 519922

info@theleap.co.uk

www.theleap.co.uk

The Leap specialises in team volunteer placements that combine conservation, community and ecotourism projects. Each placement offers a variety of environments (eg beach, rainforest, mountain) and volunteer work, including teaching English and sport, caring for orphans, building clinics and wells, assisting rangers on safari and taking part in reforestation projects. In addition, some placements also include language lessons and an adventure expedition element.

**Status:** Limited company.

**Timing & Length of Placements:** Placements are for six and 10 weeks. Some departures are flexible, while others take place in January, April, July and September. You need to apply at least a month before you leave.

**Destinations:** Madagascar, Namibia, Tanzania, South Africa, Borneo, The Philippines, Cambodia, Peru, Costa Rica, Ecuador and Cuba.

**Costs:** Starting from £2067 depending on whether you stay for six or 10 weeks. Everything except flights and insurance is included. Approximately 60 per cent of this fee goes straight to the place where you are volunteering.

**Eligibility:** You must be at least 17 at the time of departure; solo volunteers are usually between 22 and 24 years old.

**Groups or Individuals:** Individuals and team placements are available.

**Annual no. of Volunteers:** 360.

**Annual Projects:** 11.

**Partner Programmes:** 11.

**Selection & Interview Process:** Each potential Leaper is called by the country manager on application who will talk them through the programme to ensure they're joining the most suitable placement. If the volunteer and country manager are happy they will be accepted on to the programme.

**In-country Support:** Each placement is co-ordinated by an in-country manager who will ensure that projects are completed, time is spent efficiently and, most importantly, that volunteers are kept safe.

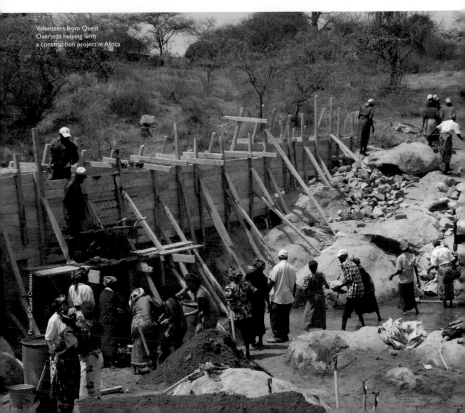

Volunteers from Quest Overseas helping with a construction project in Africa

Photo: © Quest Overseas

## Madventurer

Newcastle upon Tyne, UK

☎ +44 (0)191 232 0625

team@madventuer.com

www.madventurer.com

Madventurer combines volunteering activities in urban and rural areas of the developing world with a travel adventure. You choose how long you want to travel to create a customised experience. Projects range from building schools and teaching in rural communities to coaching sports and working on conservation initiatives. Some adventure travel opportunities include hiking up Kilimanjaro or joining a Machu Picchu trek in Peru, all of which raise funds that go towards local development projects.

**Status:** Private limited company.

**Timing & Length of Placements:** You're recommended to apply between three and nine months in advance of travel, but often late applications can be accommodated. Projects and challenges last anything from one week to one month and run year-round. Adventure travel components last from three to 10 days.

**Destinations:** Fiji, Ghana, India, Kenya, Peru, Sri Lanka, South Africa, Tanzania, Thailand, Togo and Uganda.

**Costs:** A two-week volunteering project costs from £1250 and includes the following: all food and accommodation overseas; a donation to the communities that you'll be supporting; full-time overseas project support crew; and in-country travel. International flights, visas, travel insurance and personal kit are not included.

**Eligibility:** Open to those aged 17 and over. Volunteers who are working directly with children unsupervised in schools must undergo a criminal record check.

**Groups or Individuals:** Individuals and

A Quest Overseas' volunteer working with a puma in the Amazon.

Photos: © Quest Overseas

groups may apply; project work takes place in groups of five to 12 people.

**Annual no. of Volunteers:** 100.

**Annual Projects:** 10-15.

**Partner Programmes:** 'Yoga Volunteers', 'MAD Challenges' and 'Development Expeditions'.

**Selection & Interview Process:** You can book over the phone or online.

**In-country Support:** Volunteers will have full-time crew members looking after their needs 24 hours a day. Pre-departure, volunteers will receive support from a full-time crew member at a regional HQ.

## Outreach International

Compton Dundon, Somerset, UK

☎+44 (0)1903 746 900

info@outreachinternational.co.uk

www.outreachinternational.co.uk

Outreach International is a social enterprise that has been connecting volunteers with ethical, community-led projects overseas for almost two decades. Its volunteers range from gap year students to professionals and retirees. Outreach supports grass roots projects working in education, social welfare, health and conservation. Its approach is to offer each volunteer personal support, with unlimited consultation before they book (for students and parents), to help them identify the project that will suit their experience and ambition. It is a member of the Year Out Group, an industry association created to deliver best practice in the volunteering and gap year market, as well as a member of Social Enterprise UK.

**Status:** Social enterprise.

**Timing & Length of Placements:** Placements are from one month to six months plus. Dates can be tailored to each volunteer's requirements, with an option to choose multiple projects. Apply at least three months before departure.

**Destinations:** Mexico, the Galápagos Islands, Sri Lanka, Costa Rica, India, Nepal, Kenya, Tanzania and Cambodia.

**Costs:** Refer to the costs page on the Outreach International website.

**Eligibility:** The minimum age is 17 and there is no maximum. All volunteers are assessed for their suitability based on their experience, skills, preferences and ambition. Volunteers must be fit, healthy and pass a criminal records check as appropriate.

**Groups or Individuals:** Placements are suitable for individual volunteers or those travelling together (friends and partners). You may also work alongside other volunteers in some projects if you choose.

**Annual no. of Volunteers:** 100.

**Annual Projects:** 50.

**Selection & Interview Process:** All volunteers are offered an online consultation, using Skype or FaceTime, to help them understand the choices available and to ensure they are matched with the right project.

**In-country Support:** There is a full-time coordinator in every country, providing comprehensive support. All volunteers have unlimited health insurance, a 24-hour emergency line and full air evacuation in emergencies.

## Project Trust

Isle of Coll, Argyll, Scotland, UK
☎ +44 (0)1879 230444
info@projecttrust.org.uk
www.projecttrust.org.uk

Project Trust aims to empower young people to be confident, effective, creative, independent and resilient through a challenging volunteering experience overseas. Acting as responsible global citizens, volunteers make a positive difference to their overseas host communities and to their own community upon return by sharing their learning and understanding.

**Status:** Educational charity.

**Timing & Length of Placements:** Project Trust runs a 12-month programme that departs during August and an eight-month programme that departs in January.

**Destinations:** Twenty destinations, including Honduras, Dominican Republic, Guyana, Chile, Senegal, South Africa, Swaziland, Ghana, Nepal, India, Sri Lanka, China, Cambodia, Malaysia, Thailand and Japan.

**Costs:** The fee of £6200 for the 12-month programme and £5500 for the eight-month programme covers flights, insurance, training, accommodation, living expenses and overseas support.

**Eligibility:** Project Trust works with young people who are between the ages of 17 and 19 during their placement overseas. You just need to have the desire, motivation and aptitudes required to succeed (and have a clean criminal background check).

**Groups or Individuals:** Individuals.

**Annual no. of Volunteers:** 280.

**Annual Projects:** 120.

**Selection & Interview Process:** After submitting an application, volunteers attend a four-day selection course on the Hebridean Island of Coll. Those who are successful attend a five-day briefing and training course specifically for their country group.

**In-country Support:** There are in-country representatives on hand for emergencies.

## Quest Overseas

Brighton, UK
☎ +44 (0)1273 777206
info@questoverseas.com
www.questoverseas.com

Specialising in gap-year projects and expeditions, Quest Overseas has been sending teams to South America and Africa since 1996. Two- to three-month combined expeditions depart between September and April, and include time spent working on long-term project partnerships, followed by an expedition such as trekking, scuba diving, jungle exploration or ice climbing. In South America, this can also include a language-training phase. Its shorter trips in July and August (four to six weeks) are either just a project or an expedition. Projects include working with children in a shanty town in Lima, Peru; caring for wild animals in the Bolivian Amazon; or working with orphans in Malawi, among others. Each project partnership has been established to ensure the work teams do is genuinely beneficial, and funds are provided to make sure they are sustained.

**Status:** Limited company linked with registered charity (Quest4Change).

**Timing & Length of Placements:** Three-month combined expeditions depart between September and April every year. Four- to eight-week projects or expeditions run in July and August.

**Destinations:** Peru, Bolivia, Ecuador, Kenya, Rwanda, Malawi and Tanzania.

**Costs:** From £1910 for a four-week project to £5500 for a three-week combined project and expedition. All expenses are included on the ground, but not flights and insurance.

**Eligibility:** No restrictions. However, typical age is between 18 and 24. Team leaders are background checked.

**Groups or Individuals:** Led group expeditions.

**Annual no. of Volunteers:** 120-150.

**Partner Programmes:** Six projects, all long-term partnerships.

**Selection & Interview Process:** Choose an expedition programme, then apply via online applications to start the booking process.

**In-country Support:** Teams have project and expedition leaders with them, as well as an extensive local project and expedition support network.

## Raleigh International

London, UK

☎ +44 (0)20 7183 1270

info@raleighinternational.org

www.raleighinternational.org

Raleigh International is a sustainable development charity committed to creating lasting change in Asia, Central America and Africa. Raleigh works with young volunteers, local governments and project partners to deliver projects focusing on providing access to safe water and sanitation, raising awareness of effective hygiene practices, promoting the effective use of natural resources and building the resilience of vulnerable communities. There are three phases in each placement: community volunteering, environmental volunteering, and an adventure trek.

**Status:** Registered charity.

**Timing & Length of Placements:** Expeditions depart three times throughout the year (spring, summer and autumn). Volunteers can choose between five-, seven- or 10-week expeditions and volunteer managers can choose between eight- or 13-week placements. It's recommended that volunteers apply six to 12 months in advance to allow plenty of time for fundraising and preparation. However, spaces are sometimes still available at shorter notice. Volunteer managers should apply as early as possible to increase their chances of securing their chosen role.

**Destinations:** Costa Rica, Nicaragua, Malaysian Borneo, Nepal and Tanzania.

**Costs:** As a registered charity, the programme is completely dependent on fundraising activities to cover costs. The fundraising targets for the five-, seven- and 10-week placements are £1850, £2550 and £3150 respectively. For volunteer managers, the fundraising targets are £2350 for 13 weeks (or £1950 for expeditions starting in June) and £1750 for eight weeks. This includes all training, food, accommodation, insurance and in-country support.

Eligibility: Open to ages 17 to 24. Those aged 25 or over can join as volunteer managers who lead and support young people in a variety of roles. DBS checks for criminal records are required for volunteer managers.

Groups or Individuals: Individuals.

Annual no. of Volunteers: 700.

Selection & Interview Process: After completing an application and being selected, volunteers reserve their place with a £200 deposit that goes towards the fundraising target. Volunteer manager applicants must attend an assessment weekend.

In-country Support: Raleigh has an extensive in-country support system, including medical professionals, 24-hour radio communications, in-country volunteer staff and a comprehensive emergency and evacuation plan.

# NORTH AMERICA ORGANISATIONS
## Amigos de las Américas

Houston, TX, USA

☎ +1 800 231 7796, +1 713 782 5290

info@amigosinternational.org

www.amigosinternational.org

For over 40 years, Amigos de las Américas has run community service projects involving more than 20,000 youth volunteers and thousands of communities in Latin America. Through its programmes, high-school and college-aged volunteers jump in to lend a hand on collaborative projects working with a vigorous network of Pan-American partner agencies and local host communities. These same volunteers often return to lead programmes in Latin America as project staff. Amigos aims to be a youth-led organisation in which creativity, initiative and multicultural understanding are highly valued.

A volunteer social worker in Mongolia with Scope Global as part of the AVID programme.

Photo: Scope Global

Status: NGO.

Timing & Length of Placements: Volunteers spend five to eight weeks living and working in one of nine Latin American countries. Project dates vary from year to year between the months of June and August (five-, six- and eight-week projects all have set dates, although these vary from summer to summer).

Destinations: Nine different countries in Latin America: Brazil, Costa Rica, Dominican Republic, Honduras, Mexico, Nicaragua, Panama, Paraguay and Uruguay.

Costs: Volunteers pay US$5150 as a participation fee, which goes directly towards training, equipment, transportation and support costs. The fee includes international airfares from Miami or Houston, all project-related expenses, materials, in-country lodging, transportation and meals. It also includes international medical insurance, staff training and a 24-hour on-call emergency system.

Eligibility: Participants must be 16 or older by 1 September of the year of service, and at least a sophomore in high school. They must also have at least two years of Spanish or Portuguese or an equivalent fluency level.

Groups or Individuals: Volunteers travel to and from their countries as a group.

Annual no. of Volunteers: About 750.

Annual Projects: 14.

Partner Programmes: Amigos partners with 21 other agencies.

Selection & Interview Process: Depending on whether the volunteer works with a local chapter, they will either have phone interviews or interviews in person.

In-country Support: Each project is equipped with a project staff member on call 24 hours a day. In many countries there are partnerships in place with the Ministry of Health, which assists volunteers when they are sick or in case of emergencies.

## Amizade

Pittsburgh, PA, USA

☎ +1 412 586 4986

volunteer@amizade.org

www.amizade.org

Amizade is a non-profit organisation dedicated to promoting volunteering, community service, collaboration and cultural awareness throughout the world. Amizade offers a broad range of international volunteer opportunities for individuals and families, and regularly customises programmes for groups.

Status: Non-profit organisation.

Timing & Length of Placements: One or more weeks with regular departures throughout the year. Some placements can be extended for up to six months.

Destinations: Bolivia, Brazil, Jamaica, Poland, Northern Ireland, Tanzania, Trinidad and Tobago, Puerto Rico, the Navajo Nation, Northern Ireland, Ghana and the USA.

Eligibility: The minimum age is 18, or 12 if you are accompanied by a parent or guardian; there is no nationality requirement. Some sites are more suitable than others for disabled volunteers. Background checks are required.

Groups or Individuals: Groups of six to 30

volunteers work alongside host-community members.

Annual no. of Volunteers: 1000.

Annual Projects: 50.

Partner Programmes: 16 community partnerships in 16 different sites.

Selection & Interview Process: Volunteers are assigned to projects and communities that best match both their interests, skills and local needs.

In-country Support: Upon arrival in the country, on-site personnel provide a formal orientation to familiarise volunteers with the programme, location and logistics. A staff member remains with the group for the duration of the project to coordinate and provide assistance as needed.

## Global Volunteers

St Paul, MN, USA

☎ +1 800 487 1074

email@globalvolunteers.org

globalvolunteers.org

Global Volunteers is a large organisation that has placed more than 30,000 volunteers since it was founded in 1984. It offers short-term service programmes in 17 countries on five continents – at the invitation of local host organisations, under the direction of local leaders and hand-in-hand with local people. Volunteers help deliver essential services to enable children to reach their full potential. Projects include teaching conversational English; counselling pregnant women and new mothers; teaching nutrition and disease prevention – as well as nurturing at-risk babies and toddlers – and repairing and painting community buildings.

Status: Global Volunteers is a private, non-profit, non-sectarian international organisation.

Timing & Length of Placements: Programmes are one to three weeks long and are offered year-round. There are specific departure dates throughout the year.

Destinations: China, the Cook Islands, Costa Rica, Cuba, Ecuador, Greece, India, Italy, Mexico, Peru, Poland, Portugal, Romania, St Lucia, Tanzania, USA (Appalachia, Blackfeet Reservation) and Vietnam.

Costs: Fees are tax-deductible and cover all meals, lodging, ground transportation in the community, project expenses, an emergency medical evacuation service and the services of a trained team leader. Airfares are extra, but all project-related costs, including airfares, are tax-deductible for USA taxpayers. There are discounts for students, returning volunteers, families and groups.

Eligibility: Families with children as young as five can serve in some countries, and there are no upper age limits or language and expertise requirements. You can serve as long as you are in good health, sufficiently mobile and have a curiosity about other cultures, a flexible attitude and a willingness to serve. Education, health care, business and building trade professionals can directly apply their skills on most programmes. Criminal background checks are required for some volunteer positions.

Groups or Individuals: Volunteers can work in teams of up to 35 in some communities or join a team solo to work one-on-one with local people in the host country. Family and group applications are accepted.

Annual no. of Volunteers: Around 2000.

Annual Projects: Each year nearly 200 teams of short-term volunteers are sent to work on long-term development projects worldwide.

Partner Programmes: Global Volunteers works with more than 40 community organisations in the USA and overseas.

Selection & Interview Process: Volunteers must fill out an online registration, attest they are in good health and sufficiently mobile, and provide three character references.

In-country Support: The international staff is made up of indigenous, in-country team leaders and consultants. All team leaders and country managers are available 24 hours a day for medical emergencies, are trained in CPR and first aid, and are acquainted with medical facilities in their communities.

# AUSTRALASIAN ORGANISATIONS

## Scope Global

Kent Town, SA, Australia

☎ +61 (0)8 8364 8500

info.volunteers@scopeglobal.com

www.volunteering.scopeglobal.com

Scope Global manages volunteer programmes to enable positive change by building the capacity of people and organisations in developing countries. Scope Global is a delivery partner of the Australian Volunteers for International Development (AVID) programme, an Australian government initiative funded by the Department of Foreign Affairs and Trade. The AVID programme provides opportunities for skilled Australians to contribute to the Australian government's aid programme.

Status: Private company, owned by the Government of South Australia.

Timing & Length of Assignments: Typically, assignments are designed for the volunteer to spend 12 months in-country, although there are also shorter term assignments and assignment extensions depending on host organisation requirements. Volunteers are mobilised throughout the year.

Destinations: Bhutan, Cambodia, Fiji, Indonesia, Kiribati, Laos, Mongolia, Nepal, Philippines, Samoa, Sri Lanka, Tonga, Vanuatu and Vietnam.

Costs: The AVID programme is fully funded. It provides comprehensive pre-departure financial support, including medicals, visas and insurance, as well as travel costs to the host country. Once in-country, you'll receive living allowances to help establish yourself and to live a moderately comfortable lifestyle.

Eligibility: Applicants must be aged over 18 years and be an Australian citizen, New Zealand citizen with a special conditions visa or Australian permanent resident. Participants must have relevant experience to support capacity development. All volunteers are required to submit a National Police Check form that is confirmed by the Australian Federal Police.

Groups or Individuals: Volunteers generally

assist host organisations individually, though may occasionally assist as a part of a team.

**Annual no. of Volunteers:** In 2015/16, Scope Global mobilised 779 volunteers.

**Annual Projects:** 552.

**Partner Programmes:** In addition to AVID, Scope Global works with a range of other organisations (including universities and private sector organisations) to design and deliver international volunteering programmes.

**Selection & Interview Process:** Openings are posted on the website. The online application form is followed by phone interview if your qualifications and experience are suitable for the advertised assignment. Host organisations are involved in the selection process.

**In-country Support:** Scope Global's In-Country Management teams provide volunteers with 24-hour welfare support. Scope Global also supports volunteers and host organisations with assignment development and progress as required. It also supports volunteers to transition back to Australia through a debrief process and ongoing alumni engagement opportunities.

## World Expeditions

Sydney, NSW, Australia

☎ +61 (0)2 8270 8400

info@worldexpeditions.com.au

Auckland, New Zealand

☎ +64 (0)9 368 4161

enquiries@worldexpeditions.co.nz

www.worldexpeditions.com

www.communityprojecttravel.com

World Expeditions is an Australian adventure-travel outfit which offers community project travel trips, exposing travellers to new cultural experiences. It asks that all travellers make a donation, which funds the acquisition of the materials required for the project and the wages of a local expert to oversee the project work. Volunteers from the host community work alongside the travellers to complete a project. Projects include installing piping for water and rebuilding schools in Nepal. World Expeditions promises an 'interactive, philanthropic, educational and uplifting' experience. Certainly, working alongside villagers on the 'roof of the world' could lend a new meaning to the term 'workplace high'.

**Status:** Limited company.

**Timing & Length of Assignments:** Departure dates are advertised on www.worldexpeditions.com and www.communityprojecttravel.com. Trips range from four to 21 days; there are departures year-round for selected projects.

**Destinations:** Nepal, Peru and Vietnam.

**Costs:** A$1500 to A$3290.

**Eligibility:** Participants must be fit and healthy, as some trips entail a two-day trek to remote communities. Teenagers can participate if they travel with a guardian. Adults working at a school community for longer than 24 hours are expected to sign the World Expeditions Code of Conduct and provide a criminal record check.

**Groups or Individuals:** Individuals are placed on group trips; private group arrangements are possible.

**Annual no. of Volunteers:** 40.

**Annual Projects:** Varies.

**Partner Programmes:** World Expeditions works alongside on-the-ground operators and remote communities.

**Selection & Interview Process:** A normal trip-booking process applies, with no selection prerequisites or interview necessary. A medical clearance is required for pre-existing illnesses and travellers over a certain age.

**In-country Support:** Experienced on-the-ground operational staff and crew.

## OVERSEAS ORGANISATIONS
### Volunteer in Africa

Accra, Ghana

☎ +233 20 198 3724

voluinghana@gmail.com

www.volunteeringinafrica.org

Formerly known as the Save The Earth Network, this organisation aids programmes that promote environmental preservation, sustainable development and international cultural exchange through voluntary work placements and host family home-stays in Ghana. Working four days a week, volunteers help teach children English or maths, care for orphans or abandoned children, educate people about AIDS, help with reforestation or work in healthcare clinics and hospitals.

**Status:** Not-for-profit organisation.

**Timing & Length of Projects:** Placements are from one to 12 weeks. Join year-round.

**Destinations:** Ghana.

**Costs:** A one-week stay costs US$195 and a four-week stay costs US$500. After that the costs rise by US$100 each successive week.

**Eligibility:** Criminal record checks are required for all positions involving work with children.

**Groups or Individuals:** Applicants may apply in pairs, and will usually work in a group of between four and 30 people.

**Annual no. of Volunteers:** 30.

**Annual Projects:** 7.

**Partner Programmes:** 7.

**Selection & Interview Process:** Applications can be made via the website and are followed by a telephone interview.

**In-country Support:** 24-hour support.

## VOLUNTEERING PLUS

Volunteering Plus listings are mostly aimed at people under 30. They combine service opportunities with structured classes in a wide variety of subject areas, including language and culture. For instance, Travellers Worldwide (see p159) may teach you to tango while at the same time allowing you to work on a conservation project. Asociación Pop Wuj (p160) will help you hone your Spanish skills while giving you the opportunity to do something for the common good, working on a community-development project.

## UK ORGANISATIONS
### Gapforce

London, UK

☎ +44 (0)207 736 2769

info@gapforce.org

www.gapforce.org

Fast friends: an orangutan and volunteer with Travellers Worldwide in Malaysia

Gapforce is a for-profit expedition organisation that evolved out of the UK-based charities Trekforce Expeditions and Greenforce. Keen to continue the charities' legacies, Gapforce puts over 25 years' worth of experience towards its structured gap year programmes, volunteer projects and extreme expeditions. Its overseas volunteer projects aim to enable young people to become global citizens and make a real impact on the world.

**Status:** UK-based organisation.

**Timing & Length of Placements:** Programmes run from four to 16 weeks, with regular start dates through the year.

**Destinations:** Africa, Asia, Europe, South America, Central America, Caribbean, Australia and the South Pacific.

**Costs:** From £1500 for four weeks up to £8000 for leadership training courses.

**Eligibility:** There is no upper age limit, but most volunteers are between 18 and 24. It requires criminal background checks for its courses and if minors are taking part.

**Groups or Individuals:** Individuals and groups.

**Annual no. of Volunteers:** 500-700.

**Annual projects:** 25.

**Partner Programmes:** In every country Gapforce partners with local project partners and NGOs.

**Selection & Interview Process:** As long as you are medically fit, joining an expedition is by self-selection.

**In-country Support:** Gapforce expedition leaders run its programmes with support from local partners. These leaders have completed the company's extensive four-month expedition leader training course.

## Outlook Expeditions

Bangor, Gwynedd, UK

☎ +44 (0)845 900 2989/+44; (0)1248 672 760

info@outlookexpeditions.com

www.outlookexpeditions.com

Outlook Expeditions is the youth arm of Jagged Globe Ltd, the first British company to run guided expeditions to climb Mt Everest. It offers a wide programme of overseas educational expeditions. A typical itinerary includes a challenging adventure element (trekking to a mountain summit, sea kayaking etc) and a rewarding project, which could be helping to conserve precious environments and wildlife or working with local communities. Expeditioners have the opportunity to develop new skills as they work in a team towards identifiable goals. The programme fulfils the expedition requirements of the Duke of Edinburgh's Gold Award and the Queen's Scout and Guide Awards.

**Status:** Limited company.

**Timing & Length of Projects:** Ten- to 30-day adventures offer the option of joining a community project. Applications should be sent six to 12 months in advance of departure, though destination options are available year-round.

**Destinations:** Morocco, Tanzania, Kenya, Nepal, India, Kyrgyzstan, Borneo, Ecuador, Argentina, Peru, Bolivia, Canada, Corsica, Spain, Greenland, Slovakia and the Alps.

**Costs:** The adventure phase costs between £1500 and £2000, flights and in-country costs included. The volunteering phase costs roughly an additional £200 per month.

**Eligibility:** Applicants must be 16 or older; but most are school leavers.

**Groups or Individuals:** Groups of between 12 and 15 are most common. Larger groups can be accommodated, but may be split.

**Annual no. of Volunteers:** Varies.

**Annual Projects:** 18 expeditions.

**Partner Programmes:** Thornbridge Outdoors, Undercover Rock, Young Explorers Trust.

**Selection & Interview Process:** Individual or group applications, beginning with an online query.

**In-country Support:** Groups are led by a team leader and an in-country English-speaking guide.

## Travellers Worldwide

Worthing, West Sussex, UK

☎ +44 (0)1903 502595

info@travellersworldwide.com

www.travellersworldwide.com

Although Travellers Worldwide offers the standard fare – teaching English or sports, aiding in wildlife conservation efforts, community development, veterinary medicine, journalism or law in the developing world – it also has a range of 'off-the-wall' projects such as learning to tango, doing a photography course, renovating community buildings and temples, or cage diving with great white sharks.

**Status:** Limited company.

**Timing & Length of Placements:** Placements can be as short as two weeks or as long as a year. Some can be arranged with only four weeks' notice but the most popular need to be booked between six and 12 months in advance. Programmes run throughout the year with flexible start dates.

**Destinations:** Argentina, Australia, Brazil, Cambodia, China, Costa Rica, Ghana, India, Indonesia (Bali), Malaysia, Morocco, New Zealand, Peru, South Africa, Sri Lanka, Thailand, USA, Zambia and Zimbabwe.

**Costs:** Projects start from £750 for two weeks and longer. Pricing varies depending on the length of project and which country it's in. Prices include accommodation, food, transport, airport pick up, induction and in-country support. International flights and travel insurance are not included.

**Eligibility:** Open to anyone over 17. CRM/DBS criminal checks required for anyone working with children.

**Groups or Individuals:** Both.

**Annual no. of volunteers:** 1000.

**Annual Projects:** 300.

**Selection & Interview Process:** Online application, CV and motivation letter required.

**In-country Support:** There are support staff 24/7 in all destinations worldwide and a 24-hour emergency international telephone line direct to the head office. Each site has regular risk assessments and evaluations.

## OVERSEAS ORGANISATIONS
### Asociación Pop Wuj
Quetzaltenango, Guatemala

☎+502 7761 8286

info@pop-wuj.org

www.pop-wuj.org

Owned and operated by a cooperative of Guatemalan directors, Asociación Pop Wuj is a non-profit Spanish school that offers immersive classes and runs community development projects in and around the city of Quetzaltenango. All profits go to the projects. Visitors volunteer either as students, who have daily one-on-one classes for around four hours, or as interns for a minimum of three months. Regular Immersion Program students can build safe stoves and spend supervised time with children at the Family Support Center. Students in specialised courses receive a week of cultural competency and then volunteer alongside Guatemalan staff. The medical and social work Spanish programmes work in Pop Wuj's own medical and social/educational projects, and Spanish for Teachers students teach in a local public school. Interns receive cultural competency and volunteer at least 40 hours each week in all projects or with a speciality, overseen by staff at Pop Wuj and partner non-profit EntreMundos (www.entremundos.org).

**Status:** Non-profit organisation.

**Timing & Length of Placements:** No minimum for Regular Immersion; four weeks for specialised programmes; three months for internship.

**Destinations:** Guatemala.

**Costs:** Regular immersion is US$140 per week; Medical Spanish Program is from US$205 per week; Social Work Program is US$170 per week; Spanish for Teachers Program is US$155 per week. Prices include daily activities. Room and board with host family available for US$45 per week. Lifetime registration fee is US$65 for Regular Immersion and US$150 for specialised programmes. Internships are US$300, split between EntreMundos and Pop Wuj.

**Eligibility:** Students of all backgrounds, Spanish levels and ages welcome. Guardians must accompany minors or submit release form. Most internships require intermediate Spanish (see EntreMundos for detailed requirements).

**Groups or Individuals:** Both individuals and groups are encouraged to apply.

**Annual Projects:** 7.

**Selection & Interview Process:** Applications begin online. Pop Wuj encourages early applications due to limited space, especially for popular summer months. Interns submit a written application via EntreMundos and have a follow-up interview with them and Pop Wuj staff.

**In-country Support:** Provided by school staff and host family. EntreMundos facilitates all internships.

## Institute for Central American Development Studies

San Pedro de Montes de Oca, Costa Rica
☎ +506 225 0508
info@icads.org
www.icads.org

ICADS is a Central American research and learning centre, dedicated to social and environmental issues. Its main areas of focus are women's issues, economic development, environmental studies, public health, education, human rights and wildlife conservation. With the four programme areas in ICADS you may study Costa Rica's rich flora and fauna, Spanish conversation with an ecological bent, or work to protect threatened rainforests, all while earning academic credit. Spanish classes have a four-person size limit; field courses have a 15-person limit. People enrolled in the Spanish immersion programme are only allowed to volunteer if they have sufficient language skills and spend a month or more with the programme.

**Timing & Length of Placements:** Placements start at two weeks, though most are a month long. There are programmes year-round. Apply at least two months in advance for the popular summer months.

**Destinations:** Costa Rica and Nicaragua.

**Costs:** Tuition for the four-week programme includes room and board and is approximately US$1800. There are additional fees for transferring college credits to your academic institution.

**Eligibility:** Minors need to be accompanied by a guardian. Most students are college age. Criminal background checks are required for interns.

**Groups or Individuals:** Projects are typically group-oriented work.

**Annual Projects:** Four ongoing projects.

**Selection & Interview Process:** There is a selection process for field courses; no selection process for other programmes. Interested applicants can submit an enrolment form with a deposit to secure placement.

**In-country Support:** Teachers, staff and project leaders are on hand at all times.

## PEPY Empowering Youth

Siem Reap, Cambodia

☎ +855 63 690 5465

contact@pepyempoweringyouth.org

pepyempoweringyouth.org

PEPY's mission is to empower young Cambodians to pursue careers that will improve the quality of their lives. To enable this it connects them to the skills, opportunities and inspirations needed to reach their potential. It has three progammes: the Learning Center, where the students learn ICT, English and Youth Empowerment; the Dream Class, where they attend classes that provide career resources, mentorship and group workshops; and the Scholarship Program that provides university and vocational training scholarships for selected students. Volunteers will mostly be administrative helpers in PEPY's communications department and Dream Class project.

**Status:** NGO.

**Timing & Length of Projects:** Volunteers must commit to at least six months. Openings are on a per need basis, and announced on www.idealist.org.

**Destinations:** Cambodia.

**Costs:** There are no costs associated with volunteering. While PEPY does not cover living, food or flight expenses, it does provide a monthly allowance (cost depending on hours and responsibility involved) and visa and work permit assistance to the volunteers.

**Eligibility:** Criteria depends on placement, with details given on each posting.

**Groups or Individuals:** Individuals.

**Annual no. of Volunteers:** Fewer than 10.

**Annual Projects:** 3.

**Partner Programmes:** PEPY partners with educational, environmental and health organisations in Cambodia.

**Selection & Interview Process:** Applicants must submit a CV, meet the eligibility check and pass a final interview.

**In-country Support:** PEPY connects volunteers with the local community for accommodation, and offers the use of its motorcycles and bicycles for your transport. The management team and staff are ready to assist with any emergencies.

# DEVELOPMENT PLACEMENTS

As you'll see, development can mean almost anything – this multidisciplinary field can encompass picking fruit one day and working in social development the next. But the common goal of all these organisations is to alleviate difficult living conditions through sustainable social programmes and increasing the effectiveness of healthcare and educational institutions and infrastructure (that's where the latrines come in).

## UK ORGANISATIONS

### Cuba Solidarity Campaign

London, UK

☎ +44 (0)20 7490 5715

office@cuba-solidarity.org.uk

www.cuba-solidarity.org.uk

CSC organises volunteers for

International Solidarity Brigade camps near Havana. British volunteers (or brigadistas, as they are called) work alongside Cubans and groups from other countries. Volunteers carry out five to six sessions of light agricultural work on local cooperative farms, such as picking oranges, preparing seedlings, planting and preparing ground. There is a full programme of activities, including visits to factories, hospitals, trade unions, schools and educational or political events.

**Status:** Non-profit organisation.

**Timing & Length of Placements:** The brigade camps last for 18 to 21 days and are run three times a year, in April, July and December.

**Destinations:** Cuba.

**Costs:** The trip costs around £600 to 650, which does not include international flights.

**Eligibility:** Applicants must be 18 or over.

**Groups or Individuals:** Both.

**Annual no. of Volunteers:** 60.

**Annual Projects:** 3.

**Selection & Interview Process:** Those interested must complete an application form, send £100 deposit and join the Cuba Solidarity Campaign (£20 waged/£8 unwaged). A preparatory weekend takes place four to six weeks before departure.

**In-country Support:** The trip is organised in conjunction with ICAP (Instituto Cubano de Amistad con los Pueblos), which runs the programme in Cuba and provides full support.

## International Voluntary Service

Edinburgh, Scotland, UK

☎ +44 (0)131 243 2745

info@ivsgb.org

www.ivsgb.org

IVS promotes peace and social justice through volunteering. The projects focus on conservation, inner-city children, orphanages, community arts projects and people with disabilities. Some of its projects have a strong study element on peace, human rights and climate change. Volunteers join a team of six to 20 volunteers who live and work together on the project. IVS works on the principle that the more understanding there is between people, the less conflict there will be.

**Status:** Registered charity and limited company.

**Timing & Length of Placements:** Short-term projects are two to four weeks long. Long-term projects are two to 12 months. Most of the short-term projects run between April and October.

**Destinations:** Projects are located in more than 70 countries in Europe, Asia, Africa, the Americas and Australia.

**Costs:** Projects abroad cost £150 to £245 and projects in Britain cost £55 to £155. Food and accommodation are provided by the host. Volunteers pay their travel costs.

**Eligibility:** Volunteers need to be at least 18 to go abroad. There are some places on British projects for those aged under 18 who are residents of Britain. DBS checks required for all UK projects and those involving children or vulnerable adults in other nations.

**Groups or Individuals:** Volunteers travel alone to their placements, but work in groups. In some cases it's possible for volunteers to work with requested partners.

**Annual no. of Volunteers:** 200.

**Annual Projects:** 1000.

**Partner Programmes:** Approximately 90.

**Selection & Interview Process:** Selection is by application form. Volunteers must attend a preparation day and an evaluation day. Extra information is needed when the project is in the North/South Programme.

**In-country Support:** All projects are sourced locally by the local branch. The local branch and local host work closely together to provide in-country support.

## AUSTRALASIAN ORGANISATIONS
### AVI

Fitzroy, VIC, Australia

☎ +61 (0)3 9279 1788; 1800 331 292

info@avi.org.au

www.avi.org.au

The best known of Australia's volunteer programmes, AVI is a not-for-profit organisation committed to achieving economic and social development outcomes across Asia, the Pacific and Africa. Operating since 1951, it has recruited more than 10,000 Australian volunteers to participate in Australian government, university and corporate volunteering programmes. AVI supports and co-designs locally driven initiatives that help stimulate sustained outcomes so that rewarding relationships between Australians and international peers are made.

**Status:** A not-for-profit organisation, limited by guarantee and registered as a charity.

**Timing & Length of Assignments:** Volunteers work on long-term placements that are six to 18 months, departing year round. There are some shorter term assignments.

**Destinations:** Asia-Pacific region and Africa.

**Costs:** Volunteers apply for travel, living and accommodation allowances, visas and medical insurance.

A VSA volunteer sharing a laugh on Pele Island in North Efate, Vanuatu.

Photo: © Murray Lloyd / VSA

Eligibility: Volunteers must be aged over 18 and are required to have at least two years' work experience in their field or profession. Participants need to be Australian citizens or permanent residents, or New Zealand citizens currently and permanently residing in Australia. People with disabilities are encouraged to apply. All deployees are required to provide an Australian Federal Police check that includes a working with children check.

Annual no. of Volunteers: In 2015/16, AVI managed 670 volunteers.

Annual Projects: 6.

Groups or Individuals: Most AVI assignments are for individuals. In some instances, volunteers can be accompanied by partners and families.

Partner Programmes: AVI manages a number of volunteer programmes providing new experiences for Australians that have an ongoing positive impact. AVI delivers a range of programmes including the Australian Government-funded Australian Volunteers for International Development (AVID) programme, the AVI/VSO partnership, university programmes run in partnership with The University of Melbourne and Macquarie University, and Indigenous programmes.

Selection & Interview Process: New opportunities are advertised on www.avi.org.au on the first day of each month and are open for application for three weeks. AVI's recruitment process involves making sure applicants meet the selection criteria, a skills assessment and expertise evaluation, and checking personal and professional references. If selected, candidates must attend a two-day pre-departure briefing in Melbourne.

In-country Support: AVI has support staff for each country it works in, and offices in Timor-Leste, Fiji and the North Pacific, South Africa, the Solomon Islands, Papua New Guinea, Myanmar and Indonesia.

## Volunteer Service Abroad (VSA)

Wellington, Aotearoa, New Zealand

☎ +64 (0)4 472 5759

vsa@vsa.org.nz

www.vsa.org.nz

Volunteer Service Abroad (VSA) is New Zealand's oldest and most experienced volunteer agency working in the field of international development and is always on the lookout for people with the diverse skills needed by its partner organisations overseas, from beekeeping to nursing.

Status: Registered Charity.

Timing & Length of Assignments: Varies – from a few weeks up to two years. Volunteers depart throughout the year.

Destinations: Timor-Leste, Autonomous Region of Bougainville, Cook Islands, Fiji, Kiribati, Papua New Guinea, Samoa, Solomon Islands, Tokelau, Tonga and Vanuatu.

Costs: VSA volunteers are paid a monthly living allowance during their assignment. An establishment grant is offered and at completion a resettlement grant is provided for each month the volunteer was away on assignment. Accommodation, flights, insurance cover, medicals, visas and permits are also paid for.

**Eligibility:** VSA volunteer applicants have to be New Zealand citizens, permanent residents, or have right of re-entry to New Zealand. They need experience in a specialist field, or a recognised professional, trade or commercial qualification. VSA volunteers range from 20 to 75 years of age. Criminal records checks and identity verifications are done on all VSA candidates.

**Groups or Individuals:** Volunteers are individually assigned to partner organisations. Where there's a skills-fit, a volunteer's partner may be placed on longer-term assignments.

**Annual no. of Volunteers:** 150.

**Annual Projects:** 150 plus.

**Partner Programmes:** 150-200.

**Selection & Interview Process:** Shortlisted applicants to positions advertised on www.vsa.org.nz are invited to a series of interviews over two days. Once selected, they must undertake a three-day-long briefing before departing.

**In-country Support:** VSA has field offices in six countries. The remaining nations are visited regularly by VSA programme staff.

# CONSERVATION & WILDLIFE PLACEMENTS

To be honest, it's rare to find large organisations that don't have conservation or wildlife management programmes in their portfolio of opportunities. But the following organisations all have a conservation-centric bent. Burgeoning Dr Doolittles will delight in the plethora of hands-on wildlife management opportunities available, such as protecting endangered marine environments with Coral Cay Conservation (p170). For animal-lovers who want to stay on dry land, organisations like Operation Wallacea (p171) offer placements in Africa's Rift Valley. If your taste is for trees rather than cheetahs, look to the many ecological programmes, including Rainforest Concern's work in the Ecuadorian Amazon (p172).

# UK ORGANISATIONS

## African Conservation Experience

Wotton-Under-Edge, Gloucestershire, UK

📞 +44 (0)1454 269182

info@conservationafrica.net

www.conservationafrica.net

This programme offers conservation placements in game and nature reserves in southern Africa. These are ideally suited to anyone interested in zoology, animal care, environmental sciences and veterinary medicine – especially those on leave from school and students considering a career in conservation and environmentalism. Placements are not limited to students only, though, as anyone with an interest in wildlife conservation is welcome.

**Status:** Limited company.

**Timing & Length of Placements:** Placements are available year-round and usually last from two weeks to three months.

Volunteers with Coral
Cay Conservation doing
an underwater survey in
the Philippines

**Destinations:** South Africa, Botswana, Namibia and Zimbabwe.

**Costs:** Placement costs vary depending on duration and project choice. Shorter placements start at £2535 to £3100, including flights from London to Johannesburg, transfers, all meals and accommodation. Additional weeks typically cost £400 to £700.

**Eligibility:** Applicants must be over 17 and enthusiastic about conservation. There's no upper age limit.

**Groups or Individuals:** Couples can be placed together at some projects and families with children aged 12 and over can be accommodated on a case-by-case basis.

**Annual no. of Volunteers:** Approx 500.

**Annual Projects:** 14.

**Partner Programmes:** None.

**Selection & Interview Process:** There's no formal interview, but a comprehensive application form must be filled out. Following this, an ACE team member will schedule a phone chat to help choose the project best suited to your wishes and qualifications.

**In-country Support:** An African Conservation Experience staff member is available 24 hours a day, and coordinators are based on each project continually. Full support is given in emergencies in terms of first aid and transport to a doctor or hospital. A staff member accompanies volunteers at all times. There is a Major Incident Protocol and chain-of-communication in place to deal with emergencies.

## SEED Madagascar

London, UK

☎ +44 (0)20 8960 6629

info@seedmadagascar.org

www.madagascar.co.uk

Formerly called Azafady, which is a Malagasy word meaning 'please', this registered charity changed its name to SEED Madagascar in early 2016 (an acronym of Sustainable Environment, Education and Development). Founded in 1994, it has placements available in grassroots conservation, development and sustainable livelihoods projects in southeastern Madagascar. Projects focus on local needs, human or otherwise, and the work is extremely diverse, ranging from digging wells and latrine pits, to teaching English, conducting field studies and community centred conservation initiatives on endangered species. All volunteers have the opportunity to learn basic Malagasy enabling them to integrate with the community. Programmes can also be taken as internships.

**Status:** Registered charity.

**Timing & Length of Placements:** Assignments last from two to 10 weeks and start in January, April, July and October. Apply giving at least one month's notice.

**Destination:** Southeast corner of Madagascar.

**Costs:** Volunteers are required to contribute a minimum donation between £695 and £2,495 depending on the programme. As this is a direct charitable donation, volunteers are encouraged to actively fundraise this with the hands-on help of the UK team, while raising awareness about Madagascar. The fee

Surveying leatherback turtle nesting sites in Ecuador with Rainforest Concern

Photo: © Rainforest Concern

excludes flights, vaccinations and visa

**Eligibility:** Must be 'able bodied' and over 18. Criminal background checks are required for those working with children.

**Groups or Individuals:** Volunteers work within a team of approximately four to 10 volunteers, but many more Malagasy staff.

**Annual no. of Volunteers:** Approximately 100.

**Selection & Interview Process:** All volunteers must fill in an application form and send it in to the SEED Madagascar London office, which may request answers to further questions or an interview before the assessment process is completed.

**In-country Support:** Each team is accompanied by a field coordinator and supported by an administration coordinator. SEED has a team of Malagasy guides and works closely with specialists for support on specific projects. SEED Madagascar's staff are trained in all types of potential emergency response; risk assessments are updated quarterly and teams always have supervision.

## Centre for Alternative Technology

Powys, Wales, UK

☎ +44 (0)1654 705950

www.cat.org.uk

CAT is Europe's leading ecocentre, which inspires, informs and enables people to live more sustainably. Key areas of work are renewable energy, environmental building, energy efficiency, organic growing and alternative sewerage systems. There are two volunteer schemes. One is for long-term volunteers who come for six months and work in a specific area or department, which may include woodlands, building, engineering, gardening, media or visitor engagement. The second is for short-term volunteers who come for a week or two and help with general outdoor, practical work (mostly gardening).

**Status:** Limited company.

**Timing & Length of Placements:** Short-term programmes are normally one to two weeks (with a maximum of four weeks). The long-term six-month placements begin either in spring or autumn. Due to the popularity of the programme, it's a good idea to apply six months in advance.

**Destination:** Powys (Wales).

**Costs:** Short-term volunteers pay £10 per day for full board. Some long-term volunteers can be accommodated on-site and there's no fee payable to CAT (they may also take on CAT's courses that are concurrent with their stay).

**Eligibility:** For those aged 18 and over.

**Groups or Individuals:** Individuals; groups by negotiation for specific projects.

**Annual no. of Volunteers:** Approximately 50 short-term volunteers and 20 long-term volunteers.

**Annual Projects:** Ongoing site maintenance, biodiversity surveys, energy monitoring, research projects and development of visitor engagement tools.

**Partner Programmes:** GWIRVOL and European Voluntary Service (p139).

**Selection & Interview Process:** Long-term volunteers spend a trial week with the department they wish to assist, following submission of their CV. Short-term volunteers are interviewed either in person or via a telephone.

**In-country Support:** Support is provided by the personnel department and a friendly, supportive atmosphere. Many long-term staff are former volunteers.

## Coral Cay Conservation

Tongham, Surrey, UK

☎ +44 (0) 207 620 1411

info@coralcay.org

www.coralcay.org

Coral Cay Conservation (CCC) runs expeditions to collect scientific information in some of the most beautiful coastal areas of the Caribbean and the Philippines. Participants help to protect some of the most endangered marine and tropical habitats in the world on cutting-edge programmes that work hand in-hand with NGOs from the host countries. CCC runs projects at the invitation of local governments and in collaboration with in-country NGOs, so it is purely coincidental that the locations happen to look like a slice of paradise.

**Status:** NGO.

**Timing & Length of Placements:** Most CCC projects run throughout the year. The minimum commitment for volunteers is one week for terrestrial expeditions and two weeks for marine expeditions. Ongoing projects have 12 start dates a year.

**Destinations:** Philippines and Montserrat.

**Costs:** Costs start from £315 for terrestrial based projects and £825 for marine projects, though CCC pricing is defined by project costs and location. Marine expeditions include UK briefing sessions, field accommodation, food, buoyancy control devices, regulators, dive training, tanks, air, weight belts, expedition and research training and field staff supervision. Fees do not include international flights, manuals and dive certification, insurance, visa (if needed), airport departure taxes or your personal diving or trekking equipment.

**Eligibility:** There is no upper age limit, but volunteers must be 18 or over (or 16 if part of a school group). The ability to speak and read English is important. No previous experience is required since professional CCC expedition staff will provide all necessary training on-site, including scuba training.

**Groups or Individuals:** Volunteers are never on their own. Typically, you'll work in expeditions of between three and 20. If there is space available on the desired expedition, volunteers can be placed together. Groups of 10 or more will also secure a 10 per cent fee reduction or a free place for the organiser.

**Annual no. of Volunteers:** 150.

**Annual Projects:** 2.

**Selection & Interview Process:** No selection process, just a compulsory medical. For staff that are office-based, interviews are conducted at the CCC head office in Surrey.

**In-country Support:** All expedition sites have a full-time staff team comprising a field base manager, project scientist, science officer, and scuba instructor, plus local staff. All sites have a comprehensive medical inventory, an up-to date evacuation plan and a CCC crisis management plan for major emergencies.

## Operation Wallacea

Spilsby, Lincolnshire, UK

☎ +44 (0)1790 763194

info@opwall.com

www.opwall.com

Operation Wallacea is a series of biological and social science expedition projects that operate in remote locations across the world. These expeditions are designed with specific wildlife conservation aims in mind – from identifying areas needing protection, through to implementing and assessing conservation management programmes.

**Status:** Limited company and charitable trust.

**Timing & Length of Placements:** Expeditions run from late June until mid August. Volunteers can stay from two to eight weeks.

**Destinations:** African Rift Valley, Croatia, Cuba, Dominica, Ecuador (including Galápagos), Fiji, Guyana, Honduras, Indonesia, Mexico, Madagascar, Peru, South Africa and Transylvania.

**Costs:** Ranging from £1225 (US$1900) for two weeks to £3950 (US$5925) for eight weeks. All food, accommodation, transfers, training courses and medical and evacuation insurance are included in the price. Airfares are not included.

**Eligibility:** General surveyors must be 18 years and over if joining the expedition on their own, and have an interest in conservation and biodiversity as well as a good fitness level. People with disabilities can apply.

**Groups or Individuals:** Volunteers work in teams according to the area of interest. Minimum and maximum numbers also depend on the scientific component.

Individuals who wish to volunteer with friends or partners are welcome.

**Annual no. of Volunteers:** More than 2000.

**Annual Projects:** There are hundreds of different projects in 14 countries.

**Partner Programmes:** More than 10.

**Selection & Interview Process:** Most applicants come via universities and are undertaking a biology or geography degree or as high-school groups studying similar subjects. However, any volunteer showing an interest in conservation is welcome.

**In-country Support:** All volunteers are accompanied by staff members at all the sites and while out in the field. All sites are staffed by qualified scientists and have a medical officer. There are well-rehearsed evacuation procedures.

## Rainforest Concern

Bath, UK

☎ +44 (0)1225 481151

info@rainforestconcern.org

www.rainforestconcern.org

Rainforest Concern's objective is to conserve threatened rainforests and the biodiversity they contain. Most volunteers are placed in Costa Rica at a coastal reserve for the protection of the leatherback turtles. In Ecuador, volunteers might assist with scientific research, species auditing, reforestation, socio-economic work with local communities and teaching conservation issues to schools. Volunteers in Chile assist with the maintenance of a reserve, including maintaining trails.

**Status:** Registered charity.

VSO volunteers working with locals on their International Citizen Service project in Tanzania.

© Andrew Aitchison / VSO

**Timing & Length of Placements:** In Costa Rica the minimum stay is two weeks and volunteers are accepted from mid-March until late August. Length of stay for volunteers sent to the Ecuador and Chile projects depends on availability of places and time of year.

**Destinations:** Costa Rica, Ecuador and Chile.

**Costs:** Contact for cost and details.

**Eligibility:** An interest in conservation is a must. As some programmes require hiking to work sites, a degree of physical fitness may also be required.

**Groups or individuals:** Volunteers work in teams, so individuals are welcome to apply with friends or partners.

**Annual no. of Volunteers:** 75-100.

**Annual Projects:** 18.

**Selection & Interview Process:** Placements can be made through Rainforest Concern and directly with the project staff.

**In-country Support:** Volunteers work with trained staff who often live and work with volunteers.

## Scientific Exploration Society

Shaftesbury, Dorset, UK

☏ +44 (0)1747 853353

jbs@ses-explore.org

www.ses-explore.org

Founded in 1969 by Colonel John Blashford-Snell OBE and his colleagues, SES supports the scientific expeditions of its members, which take place around the world. Some of these are run by the founder himself, involving conservation, community aid and scientific studies,

and occur worldwide. Helping out community aid projects – and often assisting charities such as safe water campaigners Just A Drop – usually form part of his expeditions.

**Status:** Registered charity and limited company.

**Timing & Length of Placements:** Colonel John Blashford-Snell OBE usually does two expeditions per year, each lasting up to three weeks.

**Destinations:** Worldwide (except polar regions).

**Costs:** A three-week expedition costs approximately £3000, depending on the location, and includes everything, bar international flights.

**Eligibility:** Applications welcome from anyone aged 18 and over, though those with professional skills (archaeologists, doctors, dentists, engineers, nurses, biologists, agriculturists) are preferred.

**Groups or Individuals:** Volunteers work in teams of about eight to 24 people.

**Annual no. of Volunteers:** Fewer than 50.

**Annual Projects:** 2.

**Partner Programmes:** In-country scientific organisations and British charity Just a Drop.

**Selection & Interview Process:** Apply for an application form via email. This will be followed with an interview by phone or in person. A briefing weekend is held in Dorset several months before each expedition.

**In-country Support:** All teams have an expert related to the project, and an expedition team doctor and dentist (to assist the local community).

# AUSTRALASIAN ORGANISATIONS

## Cape Tribulation Tropical Research Station

Cape Tribulation, QLD, Australia

📞 +61 (0)7 4098 0063

www.austrop.org.au

If doing ecological and animal research in paradise appeals to you, look into this station on the Coral Coast of Queensland, which is considered to be the jewel of the Australian Wet Tropics World Heritage Area. The station is focused on issues of adaptation to climate change, both as it affects the environment and the human community. You might be radio-tracking bats, counting figs, stomping grass for forest regeneration, constructing station buildings, digging holes, manning the visitor centre or even working on the coral reef. This is a very special area of rainforest sandwiched between the fringing reef and the coastal mountain range, and is home to a wide variety of animal habitats.

**Status:** Non-affiliated, funded by the not-for-profit, tax-exempt Austrop Foundation.

**Timing & Length of Placements:** Typically two to three weeks up to 6 months, but extensions are rarely denied.

**Destinations:** Australia.

**Costs:** Volunteers pay about A$35 per day, which covers accommodation and food. Airfares are not covered. There are also interns and student positions for those wishing to carry out a research project.

**Eligibility:** The station prefers volunteers aged over 20; people with trade skills are especially welcome. Minor physical disabilities are OK. Volunteers must be proficient in English.

**Groups or Individuals:** Typically individuals, but student groups of 18 people are also catered to.

**Annual no. of Volunteers:** About 45.

**Selection & Interview Process:** Email CV and application form. Applicants are rarely refused.

**In-country Support:** Station staff support volunteers 24 hours a day.

# OVERSEAS ORGANISATIONS

## ARCHELON, The Sea Turtle Protection Society of Greece

Athens, Greece

📞 +30 210 523 1342

volunteers@archelon.gr

www.archelon.gr

If rescuing turtles and spending time on the shores of Greece sounds palatable, this could be the opportunity for you. The primary aim of ARCHELON is to protect sea turtles in Greece through monitoring and research, management plans, raising public awareness and rehabilitating sick and injured turtles. Volunteers must bring their own tents to stay on designated campsites. The organisation was instrumental in the establishment of the National Marine Park of Zakynthos, and is a world leader in its specialised area of marine wildlife research. When asked about his most memorable experience on the programme, Mian Vich, who was with the programme for a month, says it was 'the sensation you have the first time you see a turtle getting out the water and see her laying that huge amount of eggs, just 40cm from you'.

**Status:** Not-for-profit organisation.

**Timing & Length of Placements:** The advised participation length is six weeks (minimum of four weeks). Departure times vary according to the type of volunteer work, and are listed on the website.

**Destinations:** Greece, particularly at Zakynthos island, Kyparissia Bay in Peloponnese, Amvrakikos Bay and Crete.

**Costs:** Once accepted, applicants pay a non-refundable participation fee of €250, with a further €150 to €590 depending on the project. A communal food system is used to keep living expenses to around €4 per day. Airfares to Greece are not included.

**Eligibility:** No special qualifications are required, although a driving licence, boating licence or English-language skills will be appreciated. Volunteers need to be over 18 years old.

**Groups or Individuals:** Participants work in teams but applicants are not accepted in groups larger than two.

**Annual no. of Volunteers:** 760.

**Annual Projects:** 10.

**Partner Programmes:** ARCHELON is a member of the European Union for Coastal Conservation (EUCC), the European Environmental Bureau (EEB) and a partner to UNEP/Mediterranean Action Plan. Also, members of Archelon participate in the IUCN Marine Turtle Specialist Group.

**In-country Support:** Volunteers are trained and supervised by field leaders and experienced project members.

# SKILLED VOLUNTEERING

Fancy escaping the rat race and the daily grind of a nine-to-five lifestyle? Salvation could lie in a volunteer placement that will dovetail with your individual skill-set and culminate in a rewarding escape. This is a particularly attractive option for professional career-breakers or students who have just completed a degree programme. From programmes offered by Challenges Worldwide (CWW, listed right) to the fairly self-explanatory Lawyers Without Borders, the following listings are only a smattering of career-specific opportunities. If you don't see a good fit with your professional skills, don't worry – with a few well-aimed internet searches you're likely to find that there are niche opportunities out there for almost anyone.

## INTERNATIONAL ORGANISATIONS
### VSO

London, UK

☏ +44 (0)20 8780 7500

enquiry@vsoint.org

www.vsointernational.org

VSO is an international development charity that works to alleviate poverty in the developing world by recruiting professional volunteers from countries around the world. Participants in the international volunteer programmes are typically skilled professionals who spend one or two years living abroad and applying their skills training and advising colleagues in an area of expertise. For more information about VSO, see p137.

# UK ORGANISATIONS

## Challenges Worldwide

Edinburgh, UK

☎ +44 (0)131 2259 549

info@challengesworldwide.com

www.challengesworldwide.com

Challenges Worldwide is a pioneering social enterprise placing volunteers in the International Citizen Service (p145) to work as business support associates for 10 or 12 weeks. Those taking part play a key role in delivering sustainable development projects through delivery of the Challenges Worldwide Enterprise Support Framework (ESF). Volunteers do not need previous business experience as they'll receive face-to-face training accredited by the Chartered Management Institute (CMI). After the programme, volunteers will be invited to complete an assessment and gain their Level 5 qualification in Professional Consulting.

**Status:** Registered charity.

**Timing & Length of Placements:** Departures for 12-week placements take place in January and September, while 10-week placements leave in June to allow more flexibility for students. Research placements are usually organised in conjunction with applicants' universities.

**Destinations:** Ghana, Uganda and Zambia.

**Costs:** ICS placements are fully funded by the UK Government, volunteers must raise a minimum of £800. These funds are used to maintain the ICS programme. This programme includes accredited training. Those wishing to gain a Chartered Management Institute qualification post programme can do so at a discounted rate.

**Eligibility:** The programme is open to 18 to 25-year-olds who have been resident in the UK for the past 12 months. There are a small number of Team Leader positions which are open for 23 to 35-year-olds.

**Groups or Individuals:** Individuals.

**Annual no. of Volunteers:** 100 plus.

**Annual Projects:** 675.

**Partner Programmes:** 675.

**Selection & Interview Process:** Applicants submit an online application via the ICS website (www.volunteerics.org). Applicants need to select that they heard about the opportunity through Challenges Worldwide and that they have an interest in 'Business and Livelihoods'. Applicants will be invited to an assessment day in either London or Edinburgh and if successful they will be invited to attend the three-day pre-departure preparation and training session in Edinburgh.

**In-country Support:** Support is provided through in-country teams of UK and local employees. Full mentor support is provided by a network of senior business professionals, and an overseas officer with 24-hour contact is available in emergencies.

# NORTH AMERICA ORGANISATIONS

## Lawyers Without Borders

Hartford, CT, USA

☎ +1 203 823 9397

info@lwob.org

www.lwob.org

This organisation is dedicated to rule-of-law

projects and initiatives, including legally oriented issues in the human rights arena. Its principal work involves justice sector capacity-building and community oriented access to justice. Core activities include trial advocacy training, trial observation and technical support. LWOB harnesses and leverages large-scale lawyer pro bono (volunteer) resources to support all of its programmes.

**Status:** Registered charity in USA, UK and Kenya.

**Timing & Length of Placements:** One week to six months.

**Destinations:** Latin America, the Caribbean, Africa and Asia.

**Costs:** Generally all travel and associated costs self-funded by volunteer.

**Eligibility:** Most volunteers have a law degree or are currently enrolled in law school. All must be over the age of 21.

**Groups or Individuals:** Typically, travel is solo or in small teams of two up to 10.

**Annual no. of Volunteers:** 50-100.

**Annual Projects:** 10.

**Selection & Interview Process:** This depends upon the nature of the assignment and volunteer qualifications. Initiate application with a covering letter and detailed CV.

## Operation Smile, Inc.

Virginia Beach, VA, USA

☎ +1 757 321 7645

www.operationsmile.org

Throughout the world, Operation Smile volunteers repair childhood facial deformities while building public and private partnerships that advocate for sustainable healthcare systems. Its goal is to create smiles and change lives. Each Operation Smile international mission includes medical professionals, as well as a student team consisting of one student sponsor and two student educators. Medical professionals provide surgical care for patients of cleft lip and cleft palate. Student educators teach oral rehydration, burn care and prevention, proper nutrition and dental care to patients and families.

**Status:** Not-for-profit organisation.

**Timing & Length of placements:** International medical missions are conducted year-round and are typically two weeks in length.

**Destinations:** Bolivia, Brazil, China, Colombia, Democratic Republic of Congo, Ecuador, Egypt, Ethiopia, Ghana, Honduras, India, Jordan, Madagascar, Malawi, Mexico, Morocco, Nicaragua, Panama, Paraguay, Peru, the Philippines, Russia, Rwanda, South Africa, Thailand, Venezuela and Vietnam.

**Costs:** Each team member (both medical and non-medical) pays a team fee of US$500 per mission trip. Operation Smile arranges for air transportation, accommodation and most meals.

**Eligibility:** All volunteers must complete a screening and credentialing process; requirements depend on the medical discipline. Student volunteers who travel on international missions must be 16, attend an Operation Smile International Leadership Conference and Mission Training Workshop.

**Groups or Individuals:** Individuals.
**Annual no. of Volunteers:** Around 4000.
**Annual Projects:** In 2015, medical volunteers provided free surgery for 12,000 children through international and local medical missions in more than 25 countries.
**Selection & Interview Process:** Medical volunteers complete an application based on medical discipline and submit it to be reviewed by Operation Smile's medical advisors. All students and student sponsors must apply to attend the International Leadership Conference. Applying to volunteer is extensive and it can take eight to 12 weeks to be approved. To promote sustainability in the programme countries and longevity in the organisation, selection to attend a mission is determined by the needs of the Operation Smile International Foundations, which are responsible for all in-country mission logistics.
**In-country Support:** Mission teams are hosted by Operation Smile International Foundations, which are responsible for all in-country mission logistics.

## Peace Corps

Washington, DC, USA
☎ +1 855 855 1961
www.peacecorps.gov

In the US, the Peace Corps is one of the most readily recognised names in international volunteering. The organisation's roots go back to then-US Senator John F Kennedy's challenge to students at the University of Michigan to serve their country in the cause of peace by living and working in developing countries. Eventually, his vision gave rise to an agency of the Federal Government devoted to world peace and international friendship. Today, a placement with the Peace Corps could find you doing almost anything – from working in emerging and essential services in cutting-edge fields like information technology and communications, to the most basic community programmes in the developing world. For more information on the Peace Corps, see p138.
**Status:** Government agency.
**Timing & Length of placements:** Traditionally, two years plus three months of training, but specialised, high-impact, short-term assignments to experienced professionals are now possible through Peace Corps Response and the Global Health Service Partnership.
**Destinations:** Sixty-three developing countries in Central America, South America, the Caribbean, Eastern Europe, Africa, Asia and the Pacific islands.
**Costs:** All Peace Corps programmes provide volunteers with housing and a living stipend that enables them to live in a manner similar to people in their community of service; cost of transportation to and from their country of service; and medical and dental care that covers all related expenses. The two-year programme also offers more than $8000 (pre-tax) to help volunteers readjust to life back home at the end of their service. Student loan benefits may also be available to volunteers including

deferment, partial cancellation, income-driven repayment, or forgiveness.

**Eligibility:** Any US citizen over 18 can apply. There is no upper age limit. All applicants must complete a background check.

**Groups or Individuals:** Individual applications, but Peace Corps volunteers depart with a group to their country of service and complete their three-month training together. Depending on site placement after the training, a volunteer may serve alone in their community.

**Annual no. of Volunteers:** Around 3500.

**Selection & Interview Process:** Detailed online application.

**In-country Support:** Peace Corps medical officers are in every post to ensure volunteers' health care, and security personnel conduct regular detailed assessments of hazards, vulnerabilities, and potential impacts on volunteers' well-being.

# EMERGENCY & RELIEF

The organisations listed below are definitely not for the casual volunteer looking for a good way to while away the summer. These opportunities are strictly for skilled volunteers dedicated to a life on the frontlines of humanitarian relief. For such individuals, working on the international stage with organisations such as those listed here is a worthy long-term goal.

This list includes many of the most selective volunteering opportunities in the world. Given the fact that they mostly operate in extremely unpredictable and difficult locations – often shattered by natural disaster or military conflict – the rigorous selection criteria that apply are a necessity for the safety of everyone involved. Since factors such as destination, length of placement and in-country support vary on a case-by-case basis, this information can't always be listed.

# INTERNATIONAL AGENCIES

## International Federation of Red Cross and Red Crescent Societies (IFRC)

Geneva, Switzerland

☎ +41 22 730 42 22

www.ifrc.org

Depending on where you live, the Red Cross might bring to mind any number of community services. IFRC and its member National Red Cross and Red Crescent Societies work in disaster management – preparedness, risk reduction, response, recovery and resilience – in health, water and sanitation, livelihoods, support to migrants and refugees, shelter, social inclusion and many other humanitarian services. Many run ambulance and blood services in their own countries, and others are active in international disaster and crisis response operations.

The Red Cross and Red Crescent is non-religious, apolitical and abides by seven fundamental principles – humanity, neutrality, impartiality, independence, voluntary service, unity and universality. Those interested in participating in domestic disaster relief should contact a local chapter or branch in their country. People interested in joining international relief operations should be aware that it can take years (sometimes decades) of training and experience to be deployed on an international IFRC operation.

**Status:** The world's largest humanitarian organisation, comprised of more than 190 National Red Cross and Red Crescent Societies in almost every country in the world.

**Timing & Length of placement:** Dependent on operation.

**Destinations:** Global.

**Costs:** The Red Cross usually funds all transportation and accommodation.

**Eligibility:** Organisations under the IFRC umbrella have varying eligibility criteria.

**Annual no. of Volunteers:** More than 17 million.

**Selection & Interview Process:** Begin by contacting your local chapter. The interview, training and eligibility requirements are extremely rigorous.

**In-country support:** Varies depending on which National Society is organising the deployment.

## International Medical Corps

Los Angeles, CA, USA

☎ +1 310 826 7800

inquiry@internationalmedicalcorps.org

www.internationalmedicalcorps.org

London, UK

☎ +44 (0) 207 253 0001

info@internationalmedicalcorps.org.uk

www.internationalmedicalcorps.org.uk

IMC is a private non-political, non-sectarian organisation that assists with healthcare training and relief services in the developing world. Though it might not have the recognition that Doctors Without Borders does, IMC is a major player in the field of international voluntary medical work, currently saving lives in Afghanistan, Chad, DRC, Iraq, Somalia, Sudan and Uganda (among others).

**Status:** Non-profit organisation.

**Timing & Length of Placements:** Assignments to various locations are for a minimum of six to eight weeks, though with highly technical positions, a two- to four-week placement is possible.

**Costs:** In general, volunteers cover the cost of travel to their assignment. Per diem allowances, shared housing and emergency medical evacuation insurance are usually provided. In some instances, depending on funding, duration of contract and the person's speciality, the volunteer may be eligible for a monthly stipend.

**Eligibility:** Emergency roster volunteers are required to be ready for deployment within 24 to 72 hours and be professional doctors, nurses, lab technicians, nutritionists, EMTs, engineers or various medical administrators. There are other domestic opportunities in the USA and UK that don't require medical training. Background checks are completed for those working with children.

Selection & Interview Process: Submit a CV and cover letter via email or post. Promising applicants are then interviewed.

## Médecins Sans Frontières (Doctors Without Borders)

Geneva, Switzerland

☎ +41 22 849 8484

www.msf.org

With offices around the world, MSF is one of the best-recognised international voluntary medical relief organisations. It delivers emergency aid to people affected by armed conflict, epidemics and natural or man-made disasters and has been doing so for over 40 years. MSF is one of the first organisations to arrive on the scene of a disaster, dispatching teams with specialised medical equipment specifically suited to the assignment. Each year, MSF-affiliated doctors, nurses, water-and-sanitation experts, logisticians and other medical and non-medical professionals tackle more than 3800 field assignments, working with over 30,000 local staff and 3000 international staff.

Status: International medical humanitarian organisation.

Timing & Length of Placements: Physicians are required to be available for typically nine to 12 months, though surgeons and anaesthesiologists may be accepted for shorter assignments.

Destinations: More than 65 countries.

Costs: The organisation covers all transportation and accommodation costs and pays a monthly stipend of approximately €1200 and a per diem allowance in local currency.

Eligibility: The general criteria for working abroad are: at least two years of professional experience in a relevant, usually medically related field; availability for at least nine months; current professional credentials; and relevant work or travel experience outside of your home country, preferably in a low-income or low-resource country. Medical students are not accepted. Criminal record checks are required of all volunteers.

Groups or Individuals: An average field project team has four to 12 international volunteers working in collaboration with up to 200 local staff members.

Selection & Interview Process: After eligible applicants complete an application form, a motivation letter and a current CV, they will be contacted for an interview. Applicants who advance past that stage are moved into a pool of active volunteers and considered for deployment based on their qualifications.

In-country Support: Volunteers are briefed on the region's security situation before going to the field and are given specific security protocols on-site.

# 06

## Structured & Self-Funding Volunteer Programmes

Instead of following a leader down a plotted trail, would you rather just be handed a map and allowed to find your own way? Rather than having a portion ladled into your bowl, would you prefer to dig into the dish yourself, making sure you've snagged a little extra of your favourite bit? If you've answered 'yes' to these questions, then structured volunteering programmes may be the best option for you.

Structured programmes are the middle ground between organised and DIY programmes. They mark X on the map for you, but reaching X and deciding what to do once you arrive there are often left up to you. The majority of structured programmes are run by small, grassroots organisations who don't have the capacity (or desire) to develop and run all - inclusive, package - style programmes. Many of these organisations are based overseas in the country in which they operate, and are therefore run by locals. Volunteers usually work in very small groups or individually in conjunction with these organisations.

Structured programmes are great for people who want flexibility in their placement and don't feel the need to have their hand held. Consequently, they're popular with older volunteers, people who are taking a career break, and those who have previously travelled or volunteered overseas. These programmes can provide some of the most rewarding volunteering experiences. However, to enjoy this kind of programme you need to have particular character traits: you need to be independent and self-motivated, have initiative and relish a challenge.

Nayna Wood volunteered as a teacher with Development in Action (p203) in India. Her motivation for choosing a structured programme echoes that of many other volunteers who've chosen the same option:

*I had travelled overseas independently before and wasn't looking to have my hand held or to be restricted by a strict programme of activities. However, I wasn't sure how easy it would be to be introduced to an organisation I could volunteer with myself, or even where to start in a country as vast as India. Plus, it was good to know that there was some extra support in terms of logistics or if I needed help in an emergency situation.*

A desire for independence, cultural immersion and insights into grassroots development work are also common reasons for choosing a structured programme. Tom Wilmot, who worked as an engineer in India, explains why he chose to volunteer with Development in Action (p203):

*There were many reasons for not volunteering with a packaged expedition. I wanted the experience of working in development but without the group mentality of a working party. I felt this option would give me much more scope for engaging with the local culture. I looked at the packaged expeditions and felt that while they would have been very enjoyable, they would have offered me much less independence. Also, I wouldn't have got a well-rounded experience of development work. I like the fact that DiA is a non-profit organisation which is no frills and down to earth.*

Ben Donaldson volunteered as a teacher and also helped install a water system with a charity in Thailand. He had similar reasons for volunteering with a grassroots, structured programme:

*I wanted to be part of a smaller, more tightly knit group so I could grasp the full impact of the charity's work, and not get lost in bureaucracy and other behind-the-scenes action. I wasn't looking for a highly organised operation with no surprises or flexibility, and I didn't get one. The experience far exceeded my expectations – it was far more hands-on and offered plenty of scope for improvisation and creativity, and you could get as involved as you wanted to.*

The fluid, self-determined nature of structured programmes can be daunting to people who haven't travelled or volunteered before. If you're considering taking this route, you need to be sure you're comfortable with the level of self-reliance expected of you by the organisation you're considering volunteering with. To help ease the burden, most organisations will be happy to give you tips and advice on making your travel arrangements and can put you in touch with past volunteers who can also give you pointers.

## HOW DO THEY WORK?

## COSTS

A major feature of structured programmes is that they're self-funding. This means that volunteers not only make their own travel arrangements but also cover all their travel-related costs, including insurance. Structured programmes do charge fees but these are often much less than those of organised programmes. The amount you'll pay covers things such as organising your placement, a short orientation upon your arrival and your room and board during the placement. That's usually about all they do cover, though.

The cost of a placement depends largely on the country in which it's based, how long you go for and what work you'll be doing there. Fees charged by organisations based overseas tend to be lower than those charged by conservation projects, which need to cover equipment, training and running costs, while fees for community development projects can be next to nothing.

Some volunteers raise funds to cover the costs of their placement and travel, but as fees are often low, many volunteers can afford to pay out of their own pockets. If you do decide to fundraise, be prepared to put in a lot of time and energy. For fundraising advice see Raising the Money (p66), and the Fun, Fun, Funds box on the next page for more ideas.

## SELECTION & ELIGIBILITY

The selection process for structured placements largely depends on the type of work you will be doing and where the organisation is based. Organisations based in the volunteer's home country will often hold telephone or face-to-face interviews, while those based overseas are usually restricted to online applications. In the latter case, it is very important that you make a special effort to find out whether the organisation you're applying for a placement with is one you'd be happy working with and that seeks to match your interests and abilities with its needs. Wherever possible, talk to people who have volunteered with the organisation in the past; most organisations are happy to give out these contacts.

## FUN, FUN, FUNDS

Thinking of fundraising to cover the costs of your placement? Consider these tried-and-tested methods:

• Bring the noise and organise a night of live music.
• Add some humour to the raffle idea (see p72).
• Hold a car-boot or garage sale.
• Toast your endeavour with a pub night.
• Sing or play your way overseas by busking.
• Display your creative side and sell home-made goods.
• Get energised with a sponsored swim, bike ride, run or dance-a-thon.

For skilled positions, the selection process is fairly strict – proof of qualifications is often required and references checked – but for many structured programmes, the only requirement is that you are at least 18 years old. Some organisations state a preference for experience in a particular field, but most welcome volunteers from a wide range of backgrounds and ages. Instead of specific skills, many structured programmes list attributes like commitment, enthusiasm, a spirit of adventure and flexibility as necessary qualities. However, the two most important qualities you'll require are motivation and initiative, as the nature of these placements generally means that it is up to you to determine both what kind of involvement you want to have and your level of involvement.

Tom Wilmot's experience of volunteering in India with Development in Action (p203) illustrates just how important these qualities are:

*I found that I needed to be proactive in choosing and finding jobs to do. DiA doesn't specify what work volunteers will do, since it's entirely up to the partner organisations. At Barli it was really a case of communicating what sort of thing I wanted to do, appearing keen and motivated, and then getting on with it. This was the secret of my success as a volunteer. There were plenty of opportunities to do a wide variety of work and, depending on their skills, volunteers could exploit these opportunities and contribute in many different ways.*

Michele Moody took up a manual labour placement in Africa. She speaks of the necessity of self-motivation in a placement:

*Once on site and participating in the project, we had complete freedom over what we did and this motivated us to push ourselves harder than we may have done if we had specific tasks each day. We knew what the goal of the project was and were keen to make our mark.*

Matthew Sykes, who taught in Brazil with the Association Iko Poran (p196), also found that being pushed to take initiative was very motivating:

*Iko Poran places a lot of emphasis on individual volunteers making a unique contribution by using their particular skills and experiences. This was very challenging, but far more rewarding than simply being told what to do.*

## LENGTH OF PROGRAMMES

While some structured programmes offer two-week placements, most ask for a minimum commitment of at least a month and others require volunteers to stay for a minimum of three to six months. Almost all programmes prefer longer-term commitments. Many organisations will allow you to extend your stay.

Heather Graham did exactly this when she volunteered at Casa Guatemala (p199) on the Rio Dulce in Guatemala:

*Originally, I was only planning to stay for six months, but I ended up staying almost three years, and I still go back every year. Because of this I have participated in almost all aspects of the project, from being farm supervisor to store manager to working in the administration of the orphanage.*

## WHAT TO LOOK FOR

This depends entirely on what you're after. One of the first things you need to determine is whether to volunteer through an organisation based in your home country or one based overseas. Both options have their advantages. Sending agencies and organisations in your home country can offer face-to-face assistance prior to the placement and pre-departure support. It's often easier to discuss expectations and potential hurdles with someone from your own culture and to check out the reputation of an organisation located in your own country. On the other hand, overseas organisations often charge cheaper rates and you can be pretty sure that all of your fee is going directly to the local community. The programme is likely to be very grassroots, with all aspects of the project run and managed by locals.

It's important to have clear expectations of your experience: do you want to undertake a certain type of work; use a particular skill; be immersed in a new culture or have the opportunity to accomplish something on your own initiative? If so, will the organisation enable you to achieve your aim(s)?

Gemma Niebieszczanski volunteered in Thailand and gives this advice:

*Think about what you want to get out of your volunteer experience, where you'd like to go and what you'd like to do. For me, the aim of the trip was to get some work experience in a developing country in order to pursue a career in overseas development. Therefore, I wanted a long-term project and ideally something that would give me the opportunity to do more than just teach.*

In pinpointing a programme that suits you, try and determine what the primary aims of a given programme are. For example, is the programme focused mainly on cultural exchange and learning about development work, or on practical work? As structured programmes are generally more loosely organised and grassroots in nature, volunteers are often in a great position to gain an insight into development work, which is the focus of many placements. For volunteers who were hoping for a placement focused more on practical work, this can be frustrating: many complain of feeling 'useless' and of being unable to use their skills or get their teeth into any 'real work'. Others are happy to simply go with the flow, experience the culture and exchange knowledge, and see working as a bonus.

Peggy Melmoth took this perspective when volunteering in India:

*What I liked was the emphasis on observing and learning. I was a 'project visitor', not a 'volunteer'. This allowed me to try out lots of different types of work: I painted murals, helped with English conversation classes, taught hypnotherapy and joined yoga and Hindi classes. The overall experience was very fulfilling.*

Most volunteers look for a balance between giving through work and receiving something in return. Katie Hill, who taught in India through Development in Action (p203), feels that she found the right balance:

*DiA is a small organisation that depends on volunteers, but it focuses on development education. It's not just about going out, doing the placement and then coming back. The work done with partner organisations in India is realistic, and is as much about learning and bringing experiences back to the UK as helping out in India. I learnt far more than I could have ever given in such a short space of time. I gained an insight into development work that I wouldn't have had with a big, packaged expedition. I think this will be valuable to me, those around me, and my future career.*

Look at how many partners or projects the organisation works with. If it's only one or a few, then it's easier to determine whether the organisation can offer you what you're after. With structured programmes, particularly with overseas, grassroots organisations, having lots of partners is not necessarily a negative factor – it can be an asset. So long as the organisation has an ongoing, proven relationship with these partners, you may find exactly what you're after. As Matthew Sykes discovered in Brazil:

*The number of contacts that Iko Poran has means they can find a good fit with the skills and interests of volunteers.*

## EXPECTATIONS

According to an ancient Chinese proverb, 'The one who goes with an empty cup may have it filled. The one who goes with a full cup leaves no room for new experience.' In other words, be open to the unexpected and don't head off with such a full agenda that you miss out on opportunities to learn things or to make a difference. Volunteering with structured programmes generally means that there won't be a clearly defined task awaiting you. How the placement evolves is, to a large extent, left up to you and it's unlikely you will be guided every step of the way. Therefore, you need to expect as many stumbles as successes.

After volunteering in India, Katie Hill advises:

*Be realistic. This is difficult to begin with because of all the excitement, but soon enough reality will hit and it's best to be prepared. Things aren't going to be easy, and there are going to be days of self-doubt and frustration. Achieving anything in such a short space of time is difficult. People spend their whole lives doing work such as you may be doing – a few months is nothing really. Be realistic about why you're volunteering. You will not change the world, but you will learn a whole lot. It probably won't 'change your life', but it will be an experience that will stay with you, influence future decisions and hopefully those around you for the rest of your life.*

Structured programmes are more about the overall experience, especially as they often involve a high level of cultural immersion. It's likely that what you accomplish and take away with you – what you will look back on as your most rewarding experience – will not be what you expected.

It's worth questioning how reasonable your expectations are at the outset. Michael Best, who volunteered in Nepal, was in need of a reality check:

*I went away thinking that I would come back in a Zen state and everything would be right with the world. Well, that didn't happen. I got involved in the trivialities of life in Nepal as if I were still at home. So in a way the trip taught me one big thing: no matter where in the world you go, whether to Africa, Asia or America, you're always you. There is no big change, maybe just a little growth.*

## PROS & CONS

As with other types of volunteering experience, there are pros and cons to structured placements. While these vary between organisations, there are some common ones that can affect your volunteering experience. Consider the following information when deciding if a structured placement is for you and, in particular, if a specific organisation meets your needs.

### COST

The low cost of structured placements is a drawcard for many volunteers. Far less expensive than most organised placements, structured programmes open up international volunteering to those without a fat wallet. Even when airfares, insurance and any necessary in-country travel, accommodation and food costs are tacked on to the placement fee, structured programmes are still considerably cheaper. This is largely due to the DIY factor; you're not paying anyone to book transport for you or to act as a guide etc.

Matthew Sykes' experience of volunteering through a structured placement in Brazil reassured him that he chose the best deal:

*We thought that the fully packaged expeditions seemed overpriced for what they offered and this was confirmed after a while in Rio. Iko Poran also acts as the local coordinator for packaged firms so, essentially, we were cutting out the middle man and saving quite a lot of money. We are very independent people and didn't want any of the hand-holding that might come with a packaged scheme.*

If you are comfortable taking on the role of middle man and prefer to hunt down the best deals for flights and insurance yourself, then you may find that structured programmes suit your personality as much as your finances.

Of at least equal appeal is the fact that most organisations offering structured placements are small and do not have large overheads. Because of this, volunteers often feel that more of their money is going directly to where it is needed most. They also feel that their role as a volunteer isn't simply to feed money into the organisation, but to make a genuine contribution through both a modest placement fee and actual on-the-ground activity.

Gerrard Graf, who taught at an orphanage in Tanzania, chose a structured placement for this reason:

> I wanted to be part of a volunteer project where I could see that I was making a real and tangible difference to the people I was working with and for. With some of the fully packaged expeditions, it is questionable whether you are actually providing any real benefits aside from money. And this money in itself can sometimes be misspent or used inappropriately. The programme was extremely transparent.

## FREEDOM & FLEXIBILITY

Structured programmes offer volunteers the opportunity to create and tailor their placement to suit their own interests and skills. This appealed to Nayna Wood when she taught in India with Development in Action (p203):

> A DiA placement is very flexible, and the fact that I could have an input into where I was placed and a relatively large degree of independence during my placement was also a great bonus. I really enjoyed the freedom I had and it allowed me to make much better use of my very short time than I might have done in a more tailored environment. Some of the most interesting and enjoyable experiences I had came out of using my initiative and from being the only volunteer at the time.

However, the freedom to determine the course of your placement can also pose problems. Volunteers left to their own devices in communities where they don't speak the language, and may be suffering culture shock, can find themselves feeling bored or frustrated. The onus is often on the volunteer to plan a course of action, and if this is something they've never done before, it can be daunting. It's well worth putting some time and energy into researching and preparing for your placement to head off these potential problems.

The way in which structured placements are set up also means that volunteers have more flexibility with their itineraries. As volunteers book their own transport and travel, most tack some independent travel on to the beginning or end of their placement. This gives them the chance to round out their experience of a country, seeing it through the eyes of a short-term resident as well as those of a tourist. And as most volunteers manage to pick up a little of the language while on their placement, as well as an understanding of the culture and day-to-day practicalities, it's easy to gain the confidence to travel independently after their placement is over.

## CULTURAL IMMERSION

Most volunteers on structured programmes are placed individually or in very small groups within a local community, so cultural immersion often plays a large role in their experience. Almost all volunteers find this a rewarding part, if not the highlight of, their placement.

Michael Best speaks highly of his cultural experience in Nepal:

*I was completely embraced by the local population. As far as I'm concerned this was the 'experience'. There would have been no point in me travelling to Nepal (a country vastly different from my own) and surrounding myself with anybody except the local people. The most rewarding aspect of the experience was the sense of being integrated into the community. Over the course of the placement I got to know the parents of the children I was teaching: I bought my papers from them in the morning, sat on the bus with them in the afternoon and shared a Coke with them while watching the sunset in the evening.*

Past volunteers recommend that those after in-depth cultural immersion choose a programme that offers homestays, as it is gives you the chance to join in the everyday life of locals.

Gemma Niebieszczanski describes her experience of living with a hilltribe family while teaching in Thailand:

*All volunteers were living with local families. I shared a room with another volunteer, but we ate meals and spent our free time with the rest of the family. We really became involved in village life and gained a sense that the teaching*

Photo: © Anabelle Brooks

Two Earthwatch volunteers working
on a marine conservation project

*was only one part of our experience. A lot of it was about cultural exchange and really getting to know how these people live. People were always keen to talk to me and I made many friends, both from my village and other villages nearby; this definitely enhanced my experience: I felt I was part of the village and could really get to know the hilltribe lifestyle. I don't think there was any way I could have had more interaction with the local population, and I certainly wouldn't have changed that.*

Even if the programme you're interested in doesn't offer homestays, the flexibility of structured programmes generally means that you will have free time to immerse yourself in the culture. As with most aspects of a structured placement, the level of cultural interaction you have is largely dependent on the initiative you take, as well as on your cross-cultural communication skills.

Oliver Middlemiss, who lived and volunteered with a rural community in India, describes how he got to know the locals:

*You had to pitch the interaction at the right level. Kids were easy to get on with, as all you needed was a football or Frisbee and off you went! The adult villagers were naturally a lot more stand-offish, and you had to earn their respect. It is important not to dive straight into a community and start acting as if you've known everyone for years.*

It should, of course, be noted that if the idea of being dropped on your own into a foreign culture with people who speak a different language makes you break out in a cold sweat, then you need to think carefully about which programme you choose. There are structured programmes that always place volunteers in pairs, and others (particularly those in conservation) where volunteers work in groups. Bridging a cultural gap alone is certainly not going to appeal to everyone. If this is the case for you, it's best to recognise this before you sign up. Also, if privacy is important to you, look for a programme that offers alternatives to homestays.

## IN-COUNTRY SUPPORT

Organisations offering structured programmes are generally small and have little infrastructure. While this can be appealing in regard to transparency and cost, when it comes to support in emergencies, these programmes can suddenly appear rather less attractive. Most organisations are upfront about the support they offer and the fact that the onus is often on the volunteer to be as self-reliant as possible. It pays to be aware from the outset about what help you can expect to receive in an emergency. If you're going to be placed in the middle of nowhere, at a considerable distance from a telephone or hospital, be sure to take all precautions necessary to ensure your safety in the event of something going wrong.

While a degree of isolation may sound adventurous and exciting, Ben Donaldson, who volunteered in Thailand, paints a rather different picture:

> *An emergency arose involving my mother back in England having a terrible stroke. Due to the remoteness of my village and my not teaching for a few days, there was no easy way of contacting me, so it was five days before I heard. It hit me very badly – she had been in intensive care almost a week before I spoke to my father.*

Even if there is access to telecommunication networks, volunteers are often left largely to their own devices in an emergency. When volunteering in Africa, Michele Moody did not find a telephone a very comforting replacement for personal, in-country support:

> *We had a satellite phone that we could use in case of emergency, but I feel that as we were in such an isolated area, it would have been difficult to get help to us quickly. I would have been much happier if we had an experienced member of the organisation working with us at the project.*

But don't let such stories put you off. Most organisations do take all possible precautions, ensuring there is first aid available on site, and that volunteers are placed within a reasonable distance from a hospital and given a 24-hour contact number for emergencies. Horror stories are extremely rare, but you should still make sure the programme offers a level of support you feel comfortable with. Once you're in the field, take note of any limitations in the in-country support available and be sure to have a plan of action in case any emergencies arise.

# DEVELOPMENT PLACEMENTS

The kinds of projects working in development are as diverse as they are numerous. Work in earthquake-affected regions of Nepal; erect community buildings in Cameroon; or teach in aboriginal communities in Canada's arctic north. The possibilities for development volunteering are almost inexhaustible and the destinations span the globe. This section lists some of the most worthwhile, stimulating and exciting projects in this field. It's divided into sections according to the type of work involved.

# OVERSEAS ORGANISATIONS
# COMMUNITY DEVELOPMENT

## Association Iko Poran

Rio de Janeiro, RJ, Brazil

☎ +55 3852 2916

www.ikoporan.org

Established in 2002 Iko Poran works with its own projects to tackle specific challenges identified by local councils. Placements are incredibly diverse and developed according to volunteers' abilities and interests, but one of the main objectives is the exchange of experiences. Past volunteers have taught dance, music and circus skills; worked in health, translation, fundraising, business development and website development; and trained locals in film-making and photography. It has moved beyond Brazil and now works in 10 other countries.

**Status:** Not-for-profit organisation.

**Timing & Length of Projects:** From one to 24 weeks. Start dates vary, but generally occur on the first and third Sunday of every month.

**Destinations:** Argentina, Brazil, Ecuador, Costa Rica, South Africa, Kenya, Uganda, Tanzania, India, Nepal and Thailand. Colombia and Mexico are in the pipeline.

**Costs:** The Registration fee is US$189. Programme fees start at US$150.

**Eligibility:** The minimum age is 18 in most countries, but in South Africa and Tanzania some projects accept volunteers from 16 (with parental consent). Most projects do not require any specific skills, but a few very technical projects require CV and experience, such as the medical programme in Nepal or the marine programme in Kenya. Those with physical disabilities are welcome to apply, but some accommodations might have stairs. Criminal background checks are required.

**Groups or Individuals:** You can apply in a group of six to 30 or individually. Volunteers share accommodation in designated houses.

**Annual no. of Volunteers:** 1000.

**Annual Projects:** 200 plus.

**Partner Programmes:** 12.

**Selection & Interview Process:** Online application and email discussion to agree upon an individualised placement.

**In-country Support:** Volunteers have the competent support and advice from the local teams and project leaders, who are always available in the case of any emergency.

## Himalayan Light Foundation

Kathmandu, Nepal

☎ +977 144 25393

info@hlf.org.np

www.hlf.org.np

US Office: Poughquag, NY, USA

☎ +1 845 226 666

Working in the Himalaya and South Asia, this small, grassroots organisation works to improve the quality of life in remote villages by introducing environmentally friendly,

Photo: © Association Iko Poran

A team from Association Iko Poran working on a renovation in Rio de Janeiro

renewable-energy technologies. Through its Solar Sisters Programme (SSP), volunteers subsidise and work with local technicians to install solar electricity systems in community buildings like medical clinics, schools, health posts and monasteries. During the installation, volunteers stay with a local family. This NGO is currently focusing on earthquake effected areas.

**Status:** NGO.

**Timing & Length of Projects:** Solar Sisters Programmes are typically 10 days long, but volunteers can choose to stay up to five months to support the community or other HLF projects. Projects are open year-round.

**Destinations:** Nepal and South Asia.

**Costs:** The cost varies in each country; in Nepal the SSP costs US$2000. This includes accommodation, food, guide, an administration fee and much of the cost of the Solar Home System that the volunteer installs.

**Eligibility:** The minimum age is 18, unless accompanied by an adult. There are no required skills or experience for SSP, but volunteers must have sound health and be willing and able to trek and travel to remote areas. Volunteers must also have full insurance coverage for health and emergency evacuation.

**Groups or Individuals:** Volunteers can work individually or in a family or group of up to 15.

**Annual no. of Volunteers:** Approximately 25.

**Annual Projects:** Varies greatly.

**Partner Programmes:** HLF works with local, grassroots partners as well as South Asia Regional NGO partners.

**Selection & Interview Process:** Apply via

email, telephone or online (www.hlf.org.
np/become-a-volunteer).

**In-country Support:** Volunteers are
accompanied by HLF guide and technical
assistant who are able to provide first
aid, and have access to a 24-hour contact
person in Kathmandu.

## Mango Tree Goa

Bardez, Goa, India
☏ +91 9881 261 886
info@rokpa.org
www.rokpa.org

This charity aims to help children living
on the streets and in slums in Goa. The
Mango House project supports around
180 children every day and provides a pre-
primary school, afternoon tuition classes,
meals, recreational activities, and assists
children to gain access to the registered
school system.  Volunteers support the
teachers with all aspects of the project.

**Status:** Registered UK charity; registered
trust in India.

**Timing & Length of Projects:** A minimum
of three months; projects start year-round.

**Destinations:** India.

**Costs:** A £100 donation is required in
respect of all placements. Volunteers are
expected to be completely self-funding,
including travel and accommodation.

**Eligibility:** The minimum age is 18 and
volunteers need to be fit and healthy.
A clear, recent police check from the
applicant's country of origin is required.

**Groups or Individuals:** Volunteers can
apply either individually or as a group. All

volunteers work as a team on site.

**Annual no. of Volunteers:** 10 to 20.

**Annual Projects:** 1

**Partner Programmes:** None.

**Selection & Interview Process:** All
applicants must supply the police check,
two references, a CV, covering letter and
photo. Selection is via post or email.

**In-country Support:** All volunteers will be
met at the airport and taken to their chosen
accommodation and escorted to Mango
House on their first day.

## Rokpa International

Zurich, Switzerland
☏ +41 44 262 68 88
www.mangotreegoa.org

Working mainly in Tibetan and Nepalese
communities, Rokpa is run to a high degree
by volunteers. Its soup kitchen in Kathmandu
serves 800 meals per day during the winter
and is the main project for volunteering.

**Status:** Registered charity.

**Timing & Length of Projects:** Placements
are open from December to March,
however, volunteers can specify their
availability between these dates.

**Destinations:** Nepal

**Costs:** All volunteers must be entirely
self-funding.

**Eligibility:** The minimum age is 22.
Volunteers must be physically fit and able
to cope well with stress. Placements are not
suitable for those with disabilities.

**Groups or Individuals:** Volunteers work in
a group of up to six.

**Annual no. of Volunteers:** Varies according

to local needs; approximately 15 annually.

**Annual Projects:** 100

**Partner Programmes:** Rokpa works with local communities and local government for most of its projects.

**Selection & Interview Process:** Volunteers are selected via a questionnaire.

**In-country Support:** Volunteers in Nepal have a project leader responsible for training, who also provides support.

# EDUCATION & TRAINING

## Casa Guatemala

Guatemala City, Guatemala

☎+502 4212 8223

administracion@casa-guatemala.org

www.casa-guatemala.org

Casa Guatemala runs a children's village on the banks of the Río Dulce, where it cares for 250 orphaned, abandoned or poverty-stricken children from the surrounding villages. Volunteer placements are generally involve caring for children outside school hours, teaching English, working in the medical clinic, administration, and helping on the farm or in the kitchen. Doctors and nurses are always required.

**Status:** Not-for-profit organisation.

**Timing & Length of Projects:** Placements start year-round. Week-long placements are possible; longer term volunteers (three months plus) are welcome.

**Destinations:** Guatemala.

**Costs:** Long term: one-time tax-deductible donation of US$300; short term: US$300 per week. This covers food, lodging at Hotel Backpackers and transport by boat to and from the children's village.

**Eligibility:** The minimum age is 22. Skills or experience in teaching, medicine, computers, childcare, cooking, agronomy, animal husbandry or administration are preferred. Volunteers with minor disabilities may be accepted if possible. Basic conversational Spanish is a must, as is clear criminal background check.

Short Term: Minimum age is 18 (or younger with parental supervision) Basic Spanish is preferred but not a prerequisite. All backgrounds are welcome.

**Groups or Individuals:** Individuals, couples, friends or groups. Volunteers work together in a group of up to 50.

**Annual no. of Volunteers:** Over 150.

**Annual Projects:** 1.

**Partner Programmes:** 1 (project-run hostel).

**Selection & Interview Process:** Apply online.

**In-country Support:** Support is available at all times, and there is a volunteer co-ordinator and clinic on site.

# UK ORGANISATIONS

## Volunteer Action for Peace

London, UK

☎+44 (0)844 20 90 927

action@vap.org.uk

www.vap.org.uk

Working across all continents, VAP's short-term international workcamps bring together a group of international volunteers from different backgrounds to undertake unskilled tasks that would otherwise be impossible without

# THINKING OF TAKING THE KIDS?

Clare Wearden spent a year volunteering in Bolivia with her husband and three young children. Here, she gives some tips on how to prepare for the experience.

## 1. Make sure the organisation is positive about children

We had definite negative vibes from two other organisations before we found our ideal organisation. It put us in contact with people they knew with kids around the same age as ours, so that we could ask about schooling, the main concern for us. Also, it was willing to help with visa requirements for children as we were staying beyond the period that a tourist visa is valid for. You can't find out about these requirements easily from the UK and it was invaluable to us to have this information.

## 2. Decide how the voluntary work will fit in around your family time

We decided to put our kids into the Bolivian education system, where schooling is only on offer for one four-hour session (either morning or afternoon) and then we worked it out between us who would be with them in the afternoons. We also decided to live in a residential area with a garden, outside the town centre, so that the kids had neighbours to play with. We were very careful about food – especially with the baby – and did not eat any street food for a long time. We did all have occasional bouts of illness, but nothing serious.

## 3. Tell (and teach) the kids as much as possible before departing

Make sure the kids know where and why they are going and what the place is like, what the people look like, how it will be different etc. We got maps, videos and books about Bolivia for them. We even managed to get some children's films in Spanish – Buzz Lightyear and Toy Story – and we learnt a little bit of basic Spanish before we left. Taking them out of the UK system for five terms has had absolutely no ill effects. We did no home tutoring at all and they went to a Spanish-speaking school within two weeks of arrival. They settled in incredibly quickly.

## The Result

In the end the challenges were no greater than if we had moved within the UK – in fact it was probably less daunting as we had so much more time together as a family. It is the best thing we ever did and a totally different experience of a country than going as a single person. The kids are doing really well back at their local school now and are eager to repeat the experience – with or without us.

paid labour. These can range from construction work on public buildings, to environmental conservation and social projects involving children, the elderly or refugees. A main goal is to promote intercultural understanding between participants and the local community.

**Status:** Registered charity and company limited by guarantee.

**Timing & Length of Projects:** Most placements short term (between two and four weeks), although there is the possibility for longer-term placements of one to 12 months. The majority of placements are between June and September but can take place year-round.

**Destinations:** 80 countries including France, Germany, Iceland, Italy, Kenya, Ghana, Mozambique, Peru, Mexico, Argentina, Palestine, Turkey, Russia, Vietnam, India, Indonesia, Japan and Philippines.

**Costs:** Short-term workcamps cost £210, in most cases including food and accommodation. Medium- and long-term projects cost £230 plus a registration and monthly hosting fee. All travel and personal expenses are borne by the volunteer.

**Eligibility:** The minimum age is 18 on most projects; there are a few projects open to 15 to 17 year olds. No skills or experience are required. Criminal record checks are required for projects involving children.

**Groups or Individuals:** Volunteers are placed in workcamps of five to 25 participants. It's preferable that participants are individuals, although for larger projects, partners and friends can apply together. In such cases, these participants must make every effort to integrate into the group. There is also the possibility for sending groups.

**Annual no. of Volunteers:** 100 plus.

**Annual Projects:** 1600.

**Partner Programmes:** 120 plus.

**Selection & Interview Process:** All participants must complete an online application form. Participants are invited to attend an orientation weekend or an interview in case they can not attend the weekend.

**In-country Support:** The in country host organisation takes responsibility for volunteers. The infrastructure is usually basic but safe.

# BUILDING & CONSTRUCTION
## AidCamps International
London, UK
📞 +44 (0)84 5651 5412
info@aidcamps.org
www.aidcamps.org

AidCamps works in developing countries, assisting local communities in finding solutions to problems they've identified. Volunteers work alongside locals. In short-term Group AidCamps, volunteers help erect community buildings. With longer-term Independent AidCamps, volunteers are matched to suitable placements within partner organisations.

**Status:** Registered charity.

**Timing & Length of Projects:** Group AidCamps run for between two and three weeks on set dates; Independent AidCamps can be organised for one week to three or more months at any time.

**Destinations:** Cameroon, Ethiopia, India, Malawi, Nepal and Sri Lanka.

**Costs:** AidCamps have a registration fee of between £250 and £350 plus a minimum donation of between £750 and £1,000, which covers accommodation, food at the project site, ground transport and excursions. Independent AidCamps have a £95 registration fee plus a £500 minimum donation for placements up to five weeks. After five weeks, each additional week costs £50.

**Eligibility:** The minimum age is 18 for Group AidCamps. Children can accompany adults on Independent AidCamps. No specific skills are required. Criminal checks are required for volunteers who will be working with children or vulnerable adults. They are not required for the Group construction work.

**Groups or Individuals:** For Group AidCamps, volunteers travel and work as a group of 15 to 20, and you can apply to volunteer with your partner or friend. For Independent AidCamps, volunteers travel and work individually, although you can also do them with friends, partners or families.

**Annual no. of Volunteers:** 50.

**Annual Projects:** 3 to 5.

Partner Programmes: 6.

**Selection & Interview Process:** Acceptance for Group AidCamps is on a first-come, first-served basis. For Independent AidCamps, interviews are in person in London where possible or by phone or email if not.

**In-country Support:** Group AidCamps are led by a UK member of the organisation who remains with the group at all times. Volunteers on Independent AidCamps are overseen by a member of the local partner organisation who provides logistical and personal support.

A spot of artwork by a volunteer with AidCamps International

Photo: © AidCamps International

# COMMUNITY DEVELOPMENT

## Development in Action

London, UK

☎ +44 (0)7813 395957

www.developmentinaction.org

Since the 1990s, DiA has promoted sustainable and responsible overseas development experiences by supporting locally based NGOs in India by providing them with volunteers and interns. Placements are very hands-on and can include teaching, research, fundraising, environmental conservation and working with children with disabilities. The aim is for volunteers to learn from and with the local community, and while in India, participants are encouraged to produce resources for development education in the UK.

**Status:** Registered charity.

**Timing & Length of Projects:** Placements are flexible, but are usually for two months in July and August, or for six months from September to February.

**Destinations:** India.

**Costs:** The fee for a two-month placement is £880; for six months it's £1600. This includes a pre-departure training weekend, in-country orientation and accommodation.

**Eligibility:** The minimum age is 18. There are no specific skills or experience required for most placements, but applicants must show an interest in learning about global issues. Background checks are required for those working with children.

**Groups or Individuals:** All volunteers live in groups of two to four. They also usually work in groups of two to four, although individual placements are possible.

**Annual no. of Volunteers:** Up to 28.

**Annual Projects:** Up to eight.

**Partner Programmes:** Up to six.

**Selection & Interview Process:** Apply online. Those initially selected are invited to attend a further 'selection day' (usually in London) for group activities, workshops and individual interviews.

**In-country Support:** Volunteers are supported by the partner NGO they are working with. There are also two DiA coordinators based in India who are contactable by telephone at all times and able to travel to placements to deal with emergencies.

## Epiphany Trust

Merseyside, Warrington, UK

☎ +44 (0)1925 220999

sharon@epiphany.org.uk

www.epiphany.org.uk

From its initial involvement in supporting the Lugoj orphanage in Romania over 25 years ago, Epiphany Trust's work to help disadvantaged children and young people now spans the globe, with long-term, sustainable initiatives taking place in Asia, Central American and Africa. The charity works closely with partner charities and organisations in each of these regions, as it believes that this is the most effective way of establishing lasting change and self-sufficiency. Volunteering opportunities range from working with children in a Sri Lankan street centre in Kandy to supporting independent living for adults with disabilities in Romania or

supporting learning in Burmese schools..
Status: Registered charity.
Timing & Length of Projects: From four
weeks to up to a year for all projects.
Destinations: Bangladesh, Hong Kong,
Myanmar (Burma), Romania, Sri Lanka,
Thailand and Zimbabwe.
Costs: Volunteers pay local costs for
accommodation, placement and food.
An example one-month placement in Sri
Lanka would cost £500. Transfers, training
and orientation meetings are included,
though airfares, visas and travel insurance
are not. Volunteers are also asked to
fundraise to provide a charitable minimum
donation of £400, which goes directly to
supporting the charity's work.
Eligibility: The minimum volunteer age is
18 years. There is no upper age restriction.
Volunteers need to have good interpersonal
skills and a willingness to learn some
conversational language. They must be
enthusiastic and committed, with an ability
to empathise with young people. Applicants
with disabilities are welcome. CRB or
equivalent background check essential.
Groups or Individuals: Volunteers usually
travel individually but often work in groups.
Annual no. of Volunteers: Up to 60.
Annual Projects: 5
Partner Programmes: 8
Selection & Interview Process: Volunteers
can apply by post or online by application
form. References are taken up, and an
informal interviews are conducted either in
the northwest of England or at a mutually
convenient location in the UK.

In-country Support: Partner charities provide
volunteers with access to 24-hour emergency
contact numbers and support as required.

## Experiment in International Living
Malvern, Worcester, UK
☎ +44 (0)1684 562577
info@eiluk.org
www.eiluk.org

EIL is an educational charity specialising
in cultural-awareness programmes.
Founded over 70 years ago, it tailors group
programmes and individual placements
that give volunteers the chance to work in
rural development, health clinics, children's
groups and conservation. Most placements
include homestays with local families.
Status: Registered charity.
Timing & Length of Projects: For European
destinations, placements are for two to 12
months. For most worldwide destinations,
placements are six weeks to one year.
Destinations: Argentina, Chile, Brazil,
Ecuador, Guatemala, Ghana, Morocco,
South Africa, India, Thailand and the
European Union member countries.
Costs: European volunteering is completely
funded by the European Union. For
placements outside Europe, room and
board is provided but volunteers must be
self-funding.
Eligibility: The minimum age for most
projects is 18. For European placements,
disabled volunteers receive extra financial
assistance and sometimes another volunteer
to provide support. DBS checks are done on
applicants who'll work with children.

Groups or Individuals: Volunteers travel individually but often work within a group. Applicants interested in volunteering with a friend, partner or family should contact EIL about possibilities.
Annual no. of Volunteers: 50
Annual Projects: 40
Partner Programmes: Many, especially in Europe.
Selection & Interview Process: EIL prefers to interview in person in Malvern, however, interviews can also be arranged in other parts of the UK.
In-country Support: EIL has partners in all countries where volunteers are placed. Volunteers are given a 24-hour emergency number and support.

Eligibility: Minimum age is 21. Volunteers need to have a driving licence and empathise with the organisation's aims.
Groups or Individuals: Volunteers work individually but live communally.
Annual no. of Volunteers: 50, with about 90% coming from overseas.
Annual Projects: 10
Selection & Interview Process: Complete an application form; this will be followed up with a reference check and telephone or Skype interview.
In-country Support: Volunteers have access to the office and emergency support at all times. They also receive training on arrival which includes emergency policies and procedures.

## Independent Living Alternatives
London, UK
☎ +44 (0)20 8906 9265
paservices@ilanet.co.uk
www.ilanet.co.uk
ILA promotes the rights of disabled people to live independently by providing them with full-time personal assistance in their own homes in London. Volunteers work full-time, four days per week, supporting clients in day-to-day activities and necessities.
Status: Registered charity.
Timing & Length of Projects: Placements are for four months and occur throughout the year.
Destinations: UK.
Costs: Living expenses and accommodation are provided.

## MondoChallenge
Northampton, UK
☎ +44 (0)1604 859333
info@mondochallenge.org
www.mondochallenge.org
MondoChallenge provides support to schools families and vulnerable communities in developing countries. Volunteers can teach in primary or secondary schools, support agriculture or infrastructure projects, or help assess their impact on the ground.
Status: UK-registered charity.
Timing & Length of Projects: Typically from three weeks to six months, year-round.
Destinations: India, Nepal and Tanzania.
Costs: Volunteers are asked to fund their own travel and accommodation expenses (living with a local family) and to raise £300 for the project on which they work.

# VOLUNTEERING UNWRAPPED

Eileen Bennicke didn't have the type of skills required by VSO or similar organisations, but wanted to volunteer overseas and have a gap-year experience nonetheless. So, armed with ambition and curiosity, she travelled alone to Ecuador. She had signed up for a three-month volunteering stint through Experiment in International Living (p204), but had little idea what the actual work would be. While this is a risky way of embarking on a volunteering placement, this element of the unknown challenged Eileen and spurred her on.

In many respects, Eileen was probably like most of the other volunteers on the project. It was her first time living away from home, she was filling a gap year, and was keen to do something meaningful with her time. But she was different in one respect: Eileen had just turned 60. This was a retirement present to herself.

Eileen started her adventure by spending a month in Quito, having one-on-one Spanish classes and living with a family who included her in all of their activities, which gave her a window into day-to-day Ecuadorian life. Next, she volunteered with an organisation that helped poverty-stricken children in Quito. For five mornings a week, Eileen would go out onto the streets or into the markets and engage children in games. She also helped out with elementary maths in a classroom and painted school furniture. The experience was not very fulfilling for Eileen, who felt that her interaction with locals was limited, and that she didn't really have a role that she could sink her teeth into.

Eileen then set out for the Ecuadorian cloud forest, where she lived and volunteered on a plantation. Initially, she tended an organic garden in the valley, then another one high in the hills. To finish, she assisted an American student with a research project. She found this part of her trip 'a truly wonderful and all-consuming four weeks in a magical environment with lovely people and some proper work to do'.

Upon her return to the UK, Eileen's friends commented that she must have missed her family. Eileen replied that she hadn't 'because life was so full of new experiences'. Nevertheless, speaking very little Spanish and being a naturally chatty individual, Eileen found the language barrier difficult. She did became very adept at energetic arm waving.

Another challenging, but rewarding, task was getting on with the younger people, particularly the other volunteers, who were all about 35 years her junior. In the end, these interactions were a highlight of her placement: one of her most memorable moments was returning from a fiesta in a neighbouring village at 4am in the back of an open truck, with loads of locals and a few young volunteers.

Looking back, Eileen is adamant that her experience far exceeded her expectations:

*'I really would encourage other people to have a gap experience like this between work and retirement. It really took me outside my comfort zone and I gained a lot of confidence knowing I could cope away from family and friends in a continent I had never visited, in a language I could not speak. Since returning, I have sent money back to the community and I stay in touch regularly with my family in Quito. I feel that my life has been greatly enriched by the experience. Go on – give yourself the pressie of a lifetime!'*

Eileen Bennicke volunteered in Ecuador for three months with Experiment in International Living.

Photo: © Experiment in International Living

Eligibility: The minimum age is 18. Many volunteers are career breakers and early retired. Qualified teachers are particularly welcome, but other skills – particularly enthusiasm – are always needed. Enhanced DBS check required for school placements.

Groups or Individuals: Individuals.

Annual no. of Volunteers: 75.

Annual Projects: 35.

Partner Programmes: 3.

Selection & Interview Process: Application form, interview (by phone or in person) and references are required.

In-country Support: In-country managers and deputies provide support (24 hours in most locations). Local partners manage health and safety issues.

## Pod Volunteer

Cheltenham, Gloucestershire, UK
☎ +44 (0)1242 250901
info@podvolunteer.org
www.podvolunteer.org

Pod Volunteer (formely Personal Overseas Development) is a leading not-for-profit organisation which has been sending volunteers abroad since 2001. It provides worthwhile placements that allow volunteers in Africa, Asia, Central and South America to support sustainable projects in community support, animal care and conservation. Pod Volunteer is an Approved Activity Provider for the Residential section of the DofE (Duke of Edinburgh's) award.

Status: Non-profit organisation with associated charity.

Timing & Length of Projects: Projects run year-round, with placements from one to 12 weeks.

Destinations: Belize, Cambodia, Costa Rica, Ghana, India, Madagascar, Namibia, Nepal, Peru, South Africa and Thailand.

Costs: Volunteer fees start from £475, with a £200 deposit due upon booking.

Eligibility: All child care and teaching volunteers are required to complete a telephone interview, provide a reference and have an enhanced criminal records check, complying with the Pod Volunteer Child and Vulnerable Adult Protection Policy.

Groups or Individuals: Volunteers can join projects as individuals, families or as a group. Trips can be arranged for corporate teams, schools, universities, and general group trips.

Annual no. of Volunteers: 600 to 700.

Annual Projects: 44.

Partner Programmes: 32.

Selection & Interview Process: A detailed online application allows you to detail your skills, medical issues (if any) and the type of project (and destination) you're interested in. Pod Volunteer then responsibly matches you to the right placements. Informal phone interviews may follow before you receive an acceptance letter.

In-country Support: Support from its local team, plus 24-hour emergency phone line and detailed incident management and emergency response plans.

# EDUCATION & TRAINING

## Ecologia Youth Trust

Moray, Scotland, UK

☏ +44 (0)1309 690995

volunteers@ecologia.org.uk

www.ecologia.org.uk

Ecologia Youth Trust is a small Scottish charity offering personalised, meaningful placements for volunteers at Kithoka Amani Community Home in Kenya. Run by its local partner, International Peace Initiatives, this innovative, child-centred, and community-based home provides shelter to around 30 orphaned or vulnerable children, many of whom are living with or affected by HIV/AIDS. As well as caring for, teaching, and enriching the lives of the children, volunteers work to empower young mothers and the wider community, by supporting a range of grassroots activities, from skills-training workshops to eco-farming and social enterprise projects. Ecologia has been placing volunteers abroad for over 20 years.

**Status:** Registered Scottish charity.

**Timing & Length of Projects:** Placements are for two to three months and are available throughout the year.

**Destinations:** Kenya.

**Costs:** Placements cost £1265 for two months, including visa support, in-country transport, accommodation and food. The fee for three months is £1460. Airfares, visa and insurance extra.

**Eligibility:** The minimum age is 18, and while no particular qualifications are required, volunteers need to feel able to teach English. Other useful skills include being able to teach music, arts and crafts and sport. Applicants must provide criminal background checks.

**Groups or Individuals:** There is a maximum of six volunteers at any one time.

**Annual no. of Volunteers:** 24

**Annual Projects:** 4

**Partner Programmes:** Ecologia also runs a volunteering programme in Georgia.

**Selection & Interview Process:** Applicants complete an introductory questionnaire, which is put before the Kenyan partners for approval. After supplying two suitable references, applicants then have an informal telephone/Skype interview and are sent a booking form.

**In-country Support:** Participants live within the community with 24-hour support from a resident volunteers coordinator. Ecologia is available at all times by phone and email.

## Sudan Volunteer Programme

London, UK

☏ +44 (0)20 7485 8619

www.svp-uk.org

SVP organises volunteers to teach English in universities, schools and colleges in Sudan. English is the second official language of Sudan, and while many locals have studied it, most have never had the opportunity to practice with a native speaker. Volunteers work approximately 25 hours per week.

**Status:** Registered charity.

**Timing & Length of Projects:** Placements

begin in January or October for a minimum of six months.

**Destinations:** Sudan.

**Costs:** A fee of £80 covers insurance and accommodation. A modest stipend is paid during the placement.

**Eligibility:** Graduates or undergraduates with English as their native language. A criminal check is also required.

**Groups or Individuals:** Volunteers work individually or sometimes in pairs. Married couples may apply.

**Annual no. of Volunteers:** 20 to 40.

**Annual Projects:** 1.

**Partner Programmes:** 1.

**Selection & Interview Process:** Potential volunteers are interviewed in person or by video call.

**In-country Support:** A local support group is available at all times and organised to respond to emergencies.

**Task Brasil**
London, UK
☎ +44 (0)20 7735 5545
info@taskbrasil.org.uk
www.taskbrasil.org.uk
www.facebook.com/taskbrasiltrust

Task Brasil started caring for street children and young people in 1998 after receiving a donation from Jimmy Page, the rock icon guitarist from the band Led Zeppelin. The generous contribution was the result of him witnessing first hand the deprivation of the children and troubles in the *favelas* whilst he was playing in Rio de Janeiro. Placement volunteers are needed in Rio to help run the charity's socio-educational projects. This involves working alongside its team of staff to teach children attending Casa Jimmy English, reading and writing, music, art, and computer skills.

# DEAR DIARY...

Even extended placements can zip past and morph into hazy recollections. Before you board that plane, consider the words of Tom Wilmot, who volunteered for six months as an engineer in India:

> So many stories spring to mind, and so many come flooding back on re-reading my diary. This, in itself, prompts me to highly recommend keeping a diary. It can become a chore, but approach it with good humour and try to record all those little events as regularly as possible. It really is worth it when you look back. It doesn't have to look beautiful (mine is barely legible), but looking back at it is one of those things MasterCard just can't buy!

**Status:** Registered charity in the UK, USA and Brazil.

**Timing & Length of Projects:** Placements are for a minimum of one month and preferably at least three months, with extended stays up to one year being possible. Placements begin throughout the year.

**Destinations:** Rio de Janeiro, Brazil.

**Costs:** There are no costs to volunteers, and they receive three meals a day, accommodation and a weekly Portuguese lesson for free.

**Eligibility:** Volunteers must be at least 21, have a genuine interest in helping children and possess a volunteering visa. Skills in music, IT, teaching English, crafts, sports or lifesaving are an advantage, as is a working knowledge of Portuguese, Spanish or Italian. Criminal background checks are required.

**Groups or Individuals:** Placements are made for individuals, although volunteers may work in groups of two to four at Casa Jimmy.

**Annual no. of Volunteers:** 4 to 6.

**Annual Projects:** 2.

**Partner Programmes:** Task Brasil has a number of trusts and companies supporting its work.

**Selection & Interview Process:** Applicants apply in writing and interviews are conducted in person (if possible) in London.

**In-country Support:** While on placements, volunteers work with Task Brasil staff.

# CONSERVATION & WILDLIFE PLACEMENTS

In addition to the listings in this section, many of the organisations included in the Development section have an environmental component. For example, see Pod Volunteer (p208).

## INTERNATIONAL ORGANISATIONS

### Earthwatch Institute

Boston, MA, USA

☎ +1 978 461 0081

info@earthwatch.org

www.earthwatch.org

The US branch of this global conservation charity places volunteers on scientific research expeditions in over 50 countries, with the aim of promoting the understanding and action necessary for a sustainable environment. Past volunteer expeditions have included projects as diverse as looking at climate change in the Arctic, researching the habitat of the cheetah in Namibia, studying elephant behaviour and protecting turtle hatchlings.

**Status:** Registered charity.

**Timing & Length of Projects:** Expedition lengths vary from one to two weeks, with departure dates throughout the year.

**Destinations:** Worldwide.

**Costs:** The cost varies from around US$750 to US$5775, depending on the project and duration. This includes briefing, training, food, accommodation, medical insurance and in-country transportation.

**Eligibility:** Depending on the project, volunteers need to be at least 16 or 18.

Skills and experience isn't required on most projects. Earthwatch tries to accommodate all disabilities.

**Groups or Individuals:** Most Earthwatch volunteers travel alone but on an Earthwatch expedition you will be in a group of between four and 20 volunteers, depending on the project.

**Annual no. of Volunteers:** 2000.

**Annual Projects:** 50.

**Partner Programmes:** Earthwatch works with a large number of individuals, NGOs, government organisations, schools and universities worldwide.

**Selection & Interview Process:** Volunteers submit medical history forms to ensure their physical health matches the activity level of the project selected.

**In-country Support:** Volunteers are supported by the Earthwatch research team throughout the project. A risk assessment is carried out for each project and volunteers are given a 24-hour emergency telephone number. Medical and evacuation insurance covers all volunteers.

## Greenpeace

Greenpeace International,
Amsterdam, The Netherlands
☎ +31 2071 82000
supporter.services.int@greenpeace.org
www.greenpeace.org

Started as a small, campaigning organisation in Vancouver, Greenpeace is now an international organisation with offices around the globe. Its mission has remained unchanged: to use non-violent, creative confrontation to expose global environmental problems and force solutions. All offices offer plenty of volunteering opportunities, from stuffing envelopes to public outreach, and from lobbying to Amazon survival training. Many offices also offer intern positions to applicants with appropriate skills. As each office is its own legal entity, you'll need to reach out to your local branch for current openings (see www.greenpeace.org/international/en/about/worldwide to find contact details). Placements on Greenpeace's international ships are run from the Greenpeace International in Amsterdam.

**Status:** Varies between countries.

**Timing & Length of Projects:** There are various opportunities within each country, including short- and long-term placements.

**Destinations:** Worldwide, including aboard Greenpeace ships.

**Costs:** Varies with placements and between countries.

**Eligibility:** Depending on the project, volunteers can be unskilled or may need specific training and expertise. A commitment to the aims of Greenpeace is essential.

**Groups or Individuals:** Varies.

**Annual no. of Volunteers:** Numbers vary depending on each office's current needs.

**Annual Projects:** Each national office undertakes numerous projects.

**Partner Programmes:** Greenpeace works with various grassroots NGOs around

Greenpeace activists on an oil rig near Sicily as part of a climate campaign

the world but does not place volunteers through them.

**Selection & Interview Process:** The selection process varies between countries and depends on what the placement entails.

**In-country Support:** This also varies between countries and on the types of placements concerned.

## World Wide Opportunities on Organic Farms (WWOOF)

Manchester, UK

www.wwoof.net

Well respected and long standing, WWOOF organisations compile lists of organic farms that host volunteers. Placements usually involve helping out on a farm, smallholding or community food growing project. In winter, volunteers can prepare garden beds and orchards, help with composting, planting fallow crops or maintenance. The programme largely appeals to 'townies' looking for a rural experience and those interested in organic practices.

**Status:** Varies between countries, but most often not-for-profit organisations.

**Timing & Length of Projects:** Each placement is unique and the duration and timing depends on the needs of the host. Placements are year-round, although there is less work in winter months. Volunteers generally help for four to six hours per day five days a week.

**Destinations:** WWOOF has organisations in 60 countries, including Togo, Sweden,

Mexico, Italy and Korea. It also has independent hosts in around 50 more countries.

**Costs:** Most WWOOF organisations charge a membership fee of about £15, which gives you access to a host list and a membership card. Other than that, volunteers are entirely self-funding, although room and board are provided for free by the host for the duration of your visit.

**Eligibility:** An interest in conservation, community development or environmental teaching.

**Groups or Individuals:** Volunteers must be over 18 years old.

**Annual no. of Volunteers:** Approximately 110,000.

**Annual Projects:** Approximately 15,000 host farms world wide.

**Partner Programmes:** 0

**Selection & Interview Process:** WWOOF does not select volunteers. Placements are offered at the discretion of the host. To apply, you must first join the WWOOF organisation of the country you'd like to volunteer in (via the website), after which you will be sent a copy of the list of available hosts. It's then up to you to contact the farms and make your own arrangements.

**In-country Support:** WWOOF does not supply any in-country support: it's up to the hosts and the volunteer to arrange this. However in the event of complaints, misunderstandings or disagreements between hosts and volunteers, WWOOF has a complaints ombudsman.

Life on the farm with World Wide Opportunities on Organic Farms (WWOOF)

# UK ORGANISATIONS

## Biosphere Expeditions

Norwich, UK

☎ +44 (0)8704 460801

info@biosphere-expeditions.org

www.biosphere-expeditions.org

This non-profit offers volunteers the chance to be involved in hands-on wildlife and conservation research alongside local scientists in locations around the globe. Promoting sustainable conservation, the organisation runs 'adventures with a purpose'. Past projects have included snow leopard research in the Altai mountains, whale studies on the Azores, human-elephant conflict resolution in Sri Lanka, and chamois, bear and wolf conservation projects in the Tatra mountains.

**Status:** Not-for-profit organisation.

**Timing & Length of Projects:** Project length is usually one or two weeks, but people can join for up to 10 weeks at a time. Start dates for different expeditions vary throughout the year.

**Destinations:** Project locations vary, depending on where there is a need, however, they generally include Oman, the Azores Archipelago, Peru, Slovakia, South Africa, Costa Rica, the UAE, Maldives, Malaysia, Kyrgyzstan and Thailand.

**Costs:** Between £1280 to £1890, including all food, lodging and in-country transportation. At least two-thirds of this contribution goes directly into the conservation project to fund long-term sustainability.

**Eligibility:** Biosphere aims to be inclusive and there are no age or physical restrictions

(the oldest participant so far was 87!). Expeditions vary in the amount of physical ability required and you must be confident that you can cope with the demands. Volunteers under the age of 18 must have parental consent.

**Groups or Individuals:** Volunteers travel in groups of up to 12 and work in smaller research teams of two to four once in the field. You can apply as an individual or with a partner, friend, family or group.

**Annual no. of Volunteers:** 400.

**Annual Projects:** 13.

**Partner Programmes:** 23.

**Selection & Interview Process:** The process is self-selecting with the requirements that you can speak English and you are physically able to undertake the work of the project that you have selected. Two projects require a diving qualification. You can join a project immediately by completing an online form.

**In-country Support:** There is an expedition leader on every project who works and lives with the volunteers, liaises with the local partner organisation and deals with all emergencies.

## Blue Ventures

London, UK

☎ +44 (0)207 697 8598

enquiries@blueventures.org

www.blueventures.org

Blue Ventures runs projects and expeditions to research and conserve global marine life. Its volunteer programme is popular and has won a number of prestigious eco-awards. Volunteers carry out research with scientists and camp staff, which can include diving to collect data, monitoring sites, surveying coral reef habitats and identifying new sites. Onshore, volunteers assist with surveys, community environmental education and other awareness-raising initiatives. Placements can be focused towards volunteers' interests.

**Status:** Not-for-profit organisation.

**Timing & Length of Projects:** Typically six weeks, although there are shorter options from nine days. Projects begin year-round.

**Destinations:** Madagascar, Belize and Timor-Leste.

**Costs:** For nonqualified scuba divers, the cost is between £2750 and £2900 for six weeks, including all food and accommodation, training and diving.

**Eligibility:** The minimum age is 17. There are no skills or experience required. Those with disabilities are accepted whenever possible. All volunteers must pass a medical.

**Groups or Individuals:** You can apply as an individual, with a friend, partner or as a family. Volunteers travel to the site as a group and work as part of a team, with a maximum number of 20.

**Annual no. of Volunteers:** 150.

**Annual Projects:** 1.

**Partner Programmes:** Blue Ventures works with a number of NGOs, private companies, community groups and national institutions like the Wildlife Conservation Society, WWF, ZSL, Marie Stopes and the fisheries departments of Madagascar, Belize and Timor-Leste.

**Selection & Interview Process:** Receipt of an application form is followed by a telephone interview.

**In-country Support:** Each expedition has an expedition manager, dive instructor, field scientists and a number of other supporting staff available at all times. Annual risk assessments are carried out and satellite communications mean emergency services are always contactable.

## National Trust
Swindon, UK
☎ +44 (0)179 381 7400
volunteers@nationaltrust.org.uk
www.nationaltrust.org.uk/volunteering

The National Trust maintains over 248,000 hectares of land, which are home to over 500 historic buildings, coastline, countryside, gardens, houses and farms throughout the UK. It has been accepting volunteers since 1895 and there is plenty of different ways to get involved across a number of locations, from running activities that get families closer to nature, to researching and caring for its precious collections.

**Status:** Registered charity.

**Timing & Length of Projects:** Placements are available year-round and range from very short term (one to seven days) to full-time (meaning up to 30 hours per week for six to 12 months).

**Destinations:** England, Wales and Northern Ireland.

**Costs:** Travel to and from projects is generally covered, and other expenses including subsistence are offered at local

# WAY DOWN DEEP...

**Having gained a degree in zoology, Katie Yewdall packed her bags for a volunteering placement with Blue Ventures (p216) in Madagascar. She found herself doing everything from underwater marine surveys to teaching English and biology and even scrubbing the bottom of a dive boat. She loved it enough to extend the usual six-week placement to 12 weeks. Her experience highlights the freedom possible through structured placements, as well as the motivation and initiative required to turn these sorts of placements into fulfilling adventures.**

My main reason for choosing Blue Ventures was that I wanted to take part in a research and conservation project, not just to travel for its own sake. I wanted to contribute to a project that was set up to really benefit the local community and not to solely recruit paying gap-year volunteers, something many rival organisations appeared to be doing. The country appealed to me as a place I didn't know much about and because few tourists venture there – I liked the sense of adventure. Other attractions were the small size of the organisation and the fact that volunteers seemed to range from gap-year students to career-breakers.

Part of being a volunteer means that you are expected to 'muck in' with the less pleasant tasks, and live a less-than-luxurious lifestyle, including showering from bottles of water that were filled during the rare occasions when the water was running! But these are small hardships compared to those suffered by the villagers just along the beach, and I found it a humbling experience. You are also expected to motivate yourself, work independently and take on difficult tasks.

I was very happy with my experience and I tried to approach it with few expectations, as projects such as these can often be a let-down. I did feel that the research we were doing was worthwhile, but I was disappointed that the level of scientific knowledge involved with it was not as high as I had hoped. However, this is a common problem with volunteer-based research.

It's hard to select one standout experience as there were many. These included passing research tests, meeting research targets and socialising with the locals. The most rewarding parts, however, were the things I accomplished independently in my spare time. One of the best parts of the trip was that we were given plenty of freedom to shape our own experience. We could take part in as little, or as much, of the research and conservation work as we liked and were encouraged to initiate smaller short-term projects. Although a few volunteers complained of being bored and not getting enough diving, it was those who got involved and explored the culture and environment – taking pirogue sailing lessons with the locals, going for walks into the baobab forests, snorkelling, swimming or just hanging out in the village bars – were the ones who got the most out of the experience.

We had a lot of interaction with the local population through the English and nature lessons, the fisherman's-catch and fishing-observation surveys. We were also encouraged to go into the village to buy goods and to socialise and, like much of the experience, we could interact as little or as much as we liked. I felt that interaction with the locals immensely enhanced my experience.

After my time at Blue Ventures, I travelled around the north of the country for a week independently using public transport and the little Malagasy that I had learnt – I would highly recommend it.

I returned from Madagascar over two years ago, but I often think about my time there as it has changed the way I look at the world. It's not something that I would recommend to someone who wants a relaxing diving holiday. There are difficulties and problems, and it's not for everyone, but if you are willing to get involved and don't expect to be handed the experience on a plate then you will find it very rewarding. The beaches are beautiful, the work is fulfilling and the locals are captivating!

**Katie Yewdall**

Katie Yewdall working in the depths of the Indian Ocean off Madagascar with Blue Adventures.

discretion. Full-time volunteers can receive free accommodation but may need to cover other costs such as meals, heating or electricity.

**Eligibility:** Non-EU nationals will need a valid visa, and some short-term programmes (called 'working holidays') are age specific. But volunteers of all ages are welcome to apply for other opportunities.

**Groups or Individuals:** Most conservation tasks are carried out by groups.

**Annual no. of Volunteers:** 61,000.

**Annual Projects:** There are hundreds of different types of volunteering roles available and many different projects.

**Partner Programmes:** The National Trust works in partnership with many organisations, including RSPB, Woodland Trust, National Parks UK and The Prince's Trust.

**Selection & Interview Process:** Ideally, applicants for full-time placements will be interviewed in person at the volunteering location. Interviews for short-term placements tend to be more flexible.

**In-country Support:** Volunteers are given an induction and consistent support.

## Orangutan Foundation

London, UK

☎ +44 (0)20 7724 2912

info@orangutan.org.uk

www.orangutan.org.uk

This well-respected charity actively conserves the orang-utan and its Indonesian rainforest habitat. Volunteer placements are generally construction based, such as building release camps or conservation health centres. While volunteers do not have hands-on contact with orang-utans, they are likely to encounter some of the free ranging, ex-captive orang-utans in the locality and will have the opportunity to accompany resident assistants into the forest to search for wild orang-utans. They're also given the chance to visit the orang-utan care centre.

**Status:** Registered charity.

**Timing & Length of Projects:** Three to six weeks in length between July and August.

**Destinations:** Indonesian Borneo.

**Costs:** The fee can range from £695 to £950 and includes accommodation, food and materials, but not flights.

**Eligibility:** Previous field experience is desirable but not necessary. Volunteers must be at least 18, physically fit, in good health and a member of the Orangutan Foundation. Applications should note that the placements require a great deal of physical exertion. Due to the nature of the work, placements are not open to those with physical disabilities.

**Groups or Individuals:** Volunteers can apply as friends, partners or families. Volunteers live as part of a team of 12 but are sometimes divided into smaller groups for field work.

**Annual no. of Volunteers:** 12.

**Annual Projects:** 1.

**Selection & Interview Process:** Application details are advertised on www.orangutan.org.uk Interviews are held in London or over the phone.

**In-country Support:** English coordinators are on-site, speak the local language, are trained in first aid and provide support and assistance to volunteers. While all health and safety precautions are taken, the project is located in a very remote area. A satellite phone is available for emergencies.

# NORTH AMERICAN ORGANISATIONS

## Caribbean Volunteer Expeditions

Corning, NY, USA

☎ +1 607 962 7846

ahershcve@aol.com

www.cvexp.org

CVE offers working and learning vacations in the Caribbean that focus on historic preservation. Programmes include archaeology, recording and photography, museum development and historic cemetery surveys.

**Status:** Not-for-profit.

**Timing & Length of Projects:** Projects are offered during the winter months and are usually of one- to two-week duration.

**Destinations:** Mainly the English-speaking Caribbean.

**Costs:** Participants arrange and pay for their own travel expenses, accommodation and meals. A small registration fee (which varies with the project) covers insurance, group leader expenses and programme transportation.

**Eligibility:** Participants must be aged 21 and over. Work is often physical, in tropical conditions.

**Groups or Individuals:** Small groups (five to 10 people). Individual or pair programmes

can be arranged.

**Annual no. of Volunteers:** 15 to 20.

**Annual Projects:** 5 to 6.

**Partner Programmes:** CVE provides programmes for Exploritas (formerly Elderhostel) and can organise affinity-group programmes.

**Selection & Interview Process:** Register via the website.

**In-country Support:** CVE has knowledgeable and experienced group leaders as well as local community support and participation.

## Oceanic Society

Ross, CA, USA

☎ +1 800 326 7491

www.oceanic-society.org

Oceanic Society is a non-profit organisation dedicated to conserving marine wildlife and habitats worldwide. Research and conservation projects are sponsored in cooperation with selected universities, researchers, and local projects; volunteers help fund and conduct fieldwork.

**Status:** Non-profit organisation.

**Timing & Length of Projects:** Projects last seven to 10 days. Some projects (such as humpback whale migration research) have seasonal departure dates, but others operate year-round.

**Destinations:** Belize, Costa Rica, Mexico and Palau.

**Costs:** Project fees of US$1500 to US$3000 cover meals and lodging, research activity costs, and in-country transport. Volunteers must provide their own insurance.

**Eligibility:** Minimum age is 16 (except on family volunteer programmes). Some fieldwork may be conducted under challenging conditions; scuba diving programmes require prior certification.

**Groups or Individuals:** Volunteers usually work side-by-side with research scientists in small groups.

**Annual no. of Volunteers:** 200.

**Annual Projects:** 20.

**Partner Programmes:** 7.

**Selection & Interview Process:** The organisation collaborates with field-based partners to conduct its programmes; partners must share a responsible and sincere interest in conservation, education, and research. Volunteer openings for each project are limited.

**In-country Support:** Oceanic Society staff and/or partner programme staff guide participants throughout the project; each project enforces volunteer safety protocols.

# AUSTRALASIAN ORGANISATIONS
## Conservation Volunteers Australia
Ballarat, VIC, Australia
☎+61 (0)3 5330 2600/1800 032 501
info@conservationvolunteers.com.au
www.conservationvolunteers.org
From wildlife surveys to tree planting, Conservation Volunteers Australia's work aims to protect, preserve and restore the unique and beautiful Australian environment. In urban, regional and remote Australia, projects include removing introduced weeds, building and restoring tracks and trails, seed collecting, conservation fencing,

habitat restoration and heritage restoration. In 2006, **Conservation Volunteers New Zealand** (☎+64 (0)9 376 7030; www.conservationvolunteers.co.nz) was launched. offering similar programmes.

**Status:** Not-for-profit organisation.

**Timing & Length of Projects:** These take place year-round in Australia and New Zealand with weekly departure dates; departure dates for programmes in other countries are advertised on www.conservationvolunteers.org (under World Conservation).

**Destinations:** Australia, New Zealand and Turkey (the Gallipoli project).

**Costs:** Programmes in Australia and New Zealand start from A$40 per day, including meals, accommodation and in-country, project-related transport (international airfares and travel insurance not included).

**Eligibility:** Volunteers must be aged 18 to 70 and should be in good health. Volunteers with disabilities are catered for where possible.

**Groups or Individuals:** Volunteers are placed in teams of up to 10, with a team liaison officer who provides on-site training and management.

**Annual no. of Volunteers:** 12,500.

**Annual Projects:** 2500.

**Partner Programmes:** 1000.

**Selection & Interview Process:** A short application form covering pre-existing medical conditions, allergies or injuries which may affect participation must be completed.

**In-country Support:** Teams are managed by team leaders who provide on-site training and management. Volunteers are given comprehensive safety advice and orientation before commencing projects.

# OVERSEAS ORGANISATIONS
## Elephant-Human Relations Aid
Swakopmund, Namibia
☏ +264 64 402 501
rachel@desertelephant.org
www.desertelephant.org
The EHRA works to reduce conflicts between elephants and humans by providing practical and realistic solutions. The first week of each placement involves the construction of elephant-proof walls around desert-dwelling locals' water sources, or alternative drinking points for elephants. In the second week volunteers move away from the base camp to work with EHRA guides to track, identify and monitor the movements of desert-adapted elephant herds. During this second week you sleep under the stars in a different location each evening.
Status: Not-for-gain organisation registered in Namibia.
Timing & Length of Projects: The programme runs two-week rotations, but it's possible to extend up to a maximum of 12 weeks.
Destinations: Namibia.
Costs: The cost for a two-week stint is £850, with each extra two-week block costing slightly less. Airfares are not included and all volunteers must ensure that they have a good quality insurance policy that covers emergency evacuation by air and road and repatriation.

Eligibility: Volunteers must be 17 or over, but there is no upper age limit. Children can take part in the annual family volunteering projects.
Groups or individuals: There are a maximum of 14 volunteers at any one time. It's possible to be placed with partners or friends.
Annual no. of Volunteers: 336.
Annual Projects: 24.
Partner Programmes: The EHRA works in conjunction with the Ministry of Environment and Tourism, Integrated Rural Development and Nature Conservation and Save the Rhino Trust.
Selection & Interview Process: Places can be booked by downloading, completing and emailing an information form to the EHRA.
In-country Support: EHRA organises all in-country transfers and briefing before the placement begins. All project managers have first aid qualifications and years of in-field experience in dealing with medical issues. A satellite phone and GPS are carried by volunteer teams at all times.

## Project Primates
Somoria, Guinea
contact@projectprimates.com
info@projectprimate.org
www.projetprimates.com
Project Primates runs the Centre de Conservation pour Chimpanzés (CCC) in Haut-Niger National Park, Guinea. The sanctuary was established in 1997 on the banks of the River Niger, and it rehabilitates orphaned chimpanzees that have been

rescued from illegal traffickers by the Guinean government. Volunteers, including volunteer veterinarians, come from various backgrounds from all over the world.

They provide assistance to the staff and Guinean animal caretakers at the sanctuary, helping with caring for the chimps, general infrastructure, maintenance and various camp tasks. This includes preparation and distribution of meals to chimpanzees and outings in the bush with various chimpanzee groups. Life in the bush is just that – no electricity, no continuous running water, cooking is done over a wood fire and shelter is provided in huts with beds of straw.

**Status:** Not-for-profit organisation.

**Timing & Length of Projects:** Six months, working every day from 6.30am to 7pm.

**Destinations:** Guinea.

**Costs:** Lodging and food is provided while on placement, but airfares, visa, vaccines and repatriation insurance are not included. A voluntary contribution to the CCC of €50 per month (or US$65) is suggested.

**Eligibility:** The minimum age of volunteers is 22. Other than needing to be fluent in French, there are no other requiremens besides having a strong desire to help and an open mind, and being eco-conscious.

**Groups or Individuals:** Individuals.

**Annual no. of Volunteers:** Approximately 20. There are always a minimum of eight volunteers at each of its two sites.

**Annual Projects:** 2.

**Partner Programmes:** Pan African Sanctuary Alliance, Global Federation of Animal Sanctuaries, Great Ape Trust, US Fish and Wildlife Service, Ecogine, Arcus Foundation and others.

**Selection & Interview Process:** European applicants send CV and cover letter to contact@projectprimates.com, while Americans and others should send their application to info@projectprimate.org. Interviews are conducted on Skype.

**In-country Support:** The two camps are far from villages and communication with the outside world. Each weekend one volunteer goes to town, where they can use a phone and the internet. There's no doctor on site, and the nearest hospital is five hours away by car.

## The Gibbon Rehabilitation Project
Phuket, Thailand
☑ +66 76 260 491
volunteer@gibbonproject.org
www.gibbonproject.org

The Gibbon Rehabilitation Project is managed by the Wild Animal Rescue (WAR) Foundation of Thailand, which as been in operation since 1992. It rescues gibbons from the illegal pet trade and tourist industries, rehabilitates them and then releases them back into the wild. Financed entirely by donations, the project is run by local Thai staff and volunteers.

**Status:** Not-for-profit organisation.

**Timing & Length of Projects:** Placements are for a minimum of three weeks and commence year-round.

**Destinations:** Thailand.

**Costs:** Fees vary according to the duration of the project and the kind of activities involved, but include orientation and accommodation. In-country transport is not included, but pick-up from the local airport and a weekly trip into town is.

**Eligibility:** The minimum age is 18 and fluent English is essential. No other experience is required, although participants need to have a genuine interest in the care of animals, good teamwork skills and must be physically fit. A number of vaccinations are required.

**Groups or Individuals:** Volunteers work in a group of up to 12. It is possible to apply with a friend or partner.

**Annual no. of Volunteers:** Approximately 50.

**Annual Projects:** 1.

**Partner Programmes:** WAR works with a number of local NGOs and governmental organisations like the Royal Forestry Department and Department of National Parks, Wildlife and Plants Conservation.

**Selection & Interview Process:** Send an application form and short letter about your motivation, along with description of related experience or a CV and a recent passport-sized photo.

**In-country Support:** Local staff are available at all times for support and assistance and in case of an emergency.

# SKILLED VOLUNTEERING

In addition to the organisations listed here, many of the projects in the Development (p195) and Conservation & Wildlife (p211) sections are keen to accept volunteers with relevant skills, qualifications or experience and will sometimes tailor a placement for you.

# OVERSEAS ORGANISATIONS
**Ecuador Volunteer Foundation**
Quito, Ecuador
☎ +593 (2) 255-7749
www.ecuadorvolunteer.org

EVF offers international volunteer opportunities in community development, environmental protection and education in South America, Asia and Africa.

**Status:** Non-profit.

**Timing & Length of Projects:** Short-term projects from one week. Projects are available throughout the year.

**Destinations:** Ecuador, Galapagos, Brazil, India and Uganda.

**Costs:** Volunteers are responsible for travel and insurance costs. 'Low-cost projects' involve volunteer house accommodation or homestay with a local family, and a monthly room-and-board fee of approximately US$450. There is a US$250 application fee.

**Eligibility:** Volunteers must be between 14 and 70 years old; no nationality restrictions apply. There is no accommodation available for applicants with disabilities. Criminal record checks are required by all who will be working with children.

**Groups or Individuals:** Individual and group opportunities are available.

**Annual no. of Volunteers:** 250.

**Annual Projects:** 30.

**Partner Programmes:** 11.

**Selection & Interview Process:** Candidates are interviewed by partner programme staff, then selected based on experience.

**In-country Support:** Upon arrival

in-country, volunteers attend a brief orientation at the organization's main office of each destination. Local partner-programme staff support volunteers throughout projects.

# AUSTRALASIAN ORGANISATIONS

## Australian Business Volunteers

Canberra, ACT, Australia
☎ +61 (0)2 6151 9999
fax +61 (0)2 6103 9129
info@abv.org.au
www.abv.org.au

Since 1981 ABV has been delivering development projects across Asia and the Pacific implemented by experienced business-skilled volunteers. ABV's focus is to strengthen the private sector, with a vision of alleviating poverty through inclusive economic growth. Volunteers undertake short-term training and mentoring assignments with micro-businesses and small businesses, local government bodies, NGOs and civil society organisations. ABV collaborates with its partners to create effective development projects which are customised, needs-based, and community driven.

Status: ABV Ltd is a not-for-profit incorporated company, limited by guarantee.

Timing & Length of Assignments: Volunteers are sent on assignments throughout the year, lasting between one and four months.

Destinations: Cambodia, Fiji, Indonesia, Laos, Papua New Guinea, Philippines, Samoa, Solomon Islands, Vanuatu and Vietnam.

Costs: ABV pays all costs (visas, airfares and insurance). Volunteers receive a weekly allowance.

Eligibility: No age restrictions (but ABV is unable to provide insurance coverage for those over 80). The average age of ABV volunteers is about 58. People with disabilities can apply. All volunteers must pass a criminal record check.

Groups or Individuals: Individual volunteers. Some volunteers are accompanied by their partners (who travel at their own expense).

Annual no. of Volunteers: 140.

Annual Projects: Approximately 110.

Partner Programmes: In-country organisations, business councils and chambers of commerce in the Asia-Pacific, and Australian professional organisations.

Selection & Interview Process: A CV with evidence of work skills and experience is required, along with recent work referees. This is followed by an interview which focuses on a set of core competencies.

In-country Support: There's an in-country manager in each country to provide support.

## Engineers Without Borders Australia

North Melbourne, VIC, Australia
☎ +61 (0)3 8582 1866
info@ewb.org.au
www.ewb.org.au

EWB Australia may be the ideal opportunity for engineers with a global conscience. Founded in 2003 with the belief that engineering, along with complimentary skill sets and aligned organisations, can lift people out of poverty, EWB connects, educates and empowers people through humanitarian engineering. Volunteers work to respond to four major humanitarian challenges in the areas of water, sanitation and hygiene, clean energy, appropriate housing and digital access.

**Status:** Not-for-profit limited company.

**Timing & Length of Projects:** EWB believes in creating long-term, sustainable change by building the capacity of its partners. Placements reflect this, varying from 12 to 18 months.

**Destinations:** Vietnam, Cambodia, Timor-Leste, Vanuatu and Australia.

**Costs:** Participants receive a stipend to cover their costs; this payment varies depending on the country of placement.

**Eligibility:** Open to Australian and NZ citizens (and permanent residents), overseas positions are advertised and volunteers are selected based on merit. Applicants must be over 18 years of age and provide a criminal background check.

**Groups or Individuals:** Volunteers are typically sent on their own, although some volunteers may spend time with other field professionals on ongoing projects.

**Annual no. of Volunteers:** Around 12 per year; 140 since 2005.

**Annual Projects:** In 2016 EWB Australia managed 15 projects.

**Partner Programmes:** EWB works with over 30 partner organisations ranging from small grassroots organisations to the UNHCR.

**Selection & Interview Process:** All overseas positions are advertised on the website and are open to all paid EWB members (membership is A$100 for professionals; A$20 for students). You must submit a formal application for a position that outlines your experience and addresses project-selection criteria. Applicants are then interviewed and selected based on merit.

**In-country Support:** Volunteers are supported by EWB partner organisations and their safety is monitored by EWB's internatioanl development team. In addition to financial support, volunteers receive pre-departure training.

# OPTIONS FOR THE UNDER 30S

Many people choose to volunteer soon after leaving school, either as a means of gaining work experience and directing career goals or simply as a way of contributing to the global community before heading into university or the workforce. The organisations listed in this section cater largely to younger volunteers. There are also organisations listed elsewhere in this chapter that aren't geared specifically to those under 30, but are nevertheless popular with younger participants. Check out AidCamps International (p201) and the Orangutan Foundation (p220).

# UK ORGANISATIONS

## Concordia

Brighton, UK

☎+44 (0)1273 422218

info@concordiavolunteers.org.uk

www.concordiavolunteers.org.uk

Concordia offers diverse opportunities, with past volunteers undertaking tasks such as painting orphanages in the Ukraine, organising art activities for kids in Mexico, working with disabled people in France, and constructing a health centre in Uganda. Other activities include restoration, archaeology, construction and conservation.

**Status:** Registered charity.

**Timing & Length of Projects:** Most projects run for two to four weeks, with the majority operating from June to September. There are also some medium term projects lasting between two and six months.

**Destinations:** Worldwide.

**Costs:** Volunteers pay a registration fee to Concordia (£225 to £280) and fund their own travel and insurance. Board and accommodation is free of charge for projects in Europe, North America, Japan and South Korea. For projects in Latin America, Asia, the Middle East and Africa, volunteers pay an extra fee on arrival of between approximately £100 to £250 that covers food and accommodation, as well as funding the programme in the host country.

**Eligibility:** Volunteers must be at least 16. There are no required skills or experience, but volunteers must be motivated, and committed to the project. People with disabilities can apply, however, there is a limited number of suitable projects available. Police checks are required for some projects.

**Groups or Individuals:** A maximum of two volunteers are usually sent to any one project. Once there, they work with a group of 10 to 15 participants from around the world. You can apply to be placed with a friend or partner. Groups are also possible.

**Annual no. of Volunteers:** 150.

**Annual Projects:** Approximately 1500 to 1800.

**Partner Programmes:** 80.

**Selection & Interview Process:** All projects open to individuals and pairs are listed on the website with an application form. For projects in Africa, Asia and Latin America volunteers must attend a preparation training session before departure.

**In-country Support:** During the project, volunteers are supported 24 hours a day by a local co-ordinator. On their return, volunteers give a report of their experience and any issues that arose are followed up.

# NORTH AMERICAN ORGANISATIONS

## Youth Challenge International

Toronto, ON, Canada

☎+1 416 504 3370

www.yci.org

www.eqwiphubs.org

Youth Challenge International (YCI) is a global youth development organisation that believes youth innovation drives positive change. YCI develops creative solutions and programmes to launch young people around the world into a sustainable livelihood through meaningful employment or entrepreneurship. Volunteer opportunities are currently part of a consortium project EQWIP HUBS and its own Pro-Innovator programme.

**Status:** Registered charity.

**Timing & Length of Projects:** Two months to one year.

**Destinations:** Ghana, Tanzania, Senegal, Rwanda, Philippines, Cambodia, Bolivia, Peru and Indonesia.

**Costs:** For EQWIP HUBS, applicants must fundraise between C$2750 (three month placement) and C$3600 (one year placement); these funds contribute to the Youth Innovation Fund that supports young entrepreneurs in a business start up. YCI provides a monthly stipend to cover meals, lodging, and local transportation.

Airfare, medical insurance and visas are also provided. The majority of Pro-Innovator spaces placements are funded and no fundraising is required.

**Eligibility:** Canadians aged 18 to 30. Criminal background checks are required for those working with children.

**Groups or Individuals:** Individuals.

**Annual no. of Volunteers:** 150.

**Selection & Interview Process:** Prospective volunteers can apply online through EQWIP HUBS (http://eqwiphubs.org/opportunities/) or YCI (http://yci.org/solutions/innovators/). Interviews are conducted by phone. Volunteers are selected based on motivation, suitability to the role, experience and attitude.

**In-country Support:** Volunteers are supported in country by local staff and managers in Canada.

Becoming part of a community is one of the greatest rewards of international volunteering.

# 07

# Religious Organisations

Assisting those in need has long been the custom of faith-based and religious organisations. Many of these organisations, particularly from the three monotheist faiths – Christianity, Judaism and Islam – provide aid and relief through overseas missions, and often welcome volunteers to help them achieve their goals. The degree to which religion plays a role in volunteer work varies from organisation to organisation. Some focus mainly on specific hands-on projects and faith is more of an underlying element; others have a strong evangelistic mission, with the promotion of faith being their main aim.

So, although many of these organisations require you to belong to the faith in which they are rooted, the extent to which you need to be practising depends both on the organisation and the specific project. In general, though, you don't need to be devout to obtain a placement through a religious organisation. In some cases you don't even need to be a member of the faith in which the organisation is based. Many Christian organisations are non-denominational or inter-denominational, meaning that as long as you support the Christian basis of faith, it doesn't matter whether you are Catholic, Baptist or whatever. Christian organisations do offer the most opportunities for volunteers. Islamic relief organisations tend to rely on permanent staff, but several Judaist organisations place Jewish volunteers overseas, and there are also some Buddhist groups.

The types of work volunteers become involved in through religious organisations are similar to that offered by other charities and NGOs working in the development sector, taking in everything from medical aid to teaching, construction to running soup kitchens. Volunteering programmes also take various forms: some farm out groups of volunteers on short-term workcamp-style placements, while others send individuals to live and work in communities for extended periods (usually for a minimum of one year).

Why volunteer through a religious organisation? Perhaps you relish the thought of sharing and working through your faith overseas. Or perhaps you never made it past the first page of the Talmud, Bible or Quran but agree with the principles which motivate the work of these organisations. If you have an interest in volunteering and, in addition, are in tune with the beliefs and practices of a religious sending organisation, then combining the two may lead to your ideal placement.

This chapter takes a look at what kinds of volunteer placement are available through religious organisations. As these organisations run both structured and organised placements, it's worth reading the How Do They Work? and Pros & Cons sections of this chapter in conjunction with the equivalent sections in Chapters 5 (p132) and 6 (p185). Though we've pulled together a lot of information here, it's worth keeping in mind that your local faith communities can also be a good source of information, as many have links with overseas communities or NGOs that take on volunteers.

# HOW DO THEY WORK?

## COSTS & LENGTH OF PLACEMENTS

Religious volunteering programmes generally work in the same way as secular programmes. Most religious programmes are well established and many have been running for a long time (one over 200 years!), so they are often exceptionally well organised. Depending on whether they're organised or structured, the cost and duration of placements vary. Many require you to fundraise a substantial chunk of the cost and then they make up the shortfall, providing anything from your airfare to a roof over your head. Others are totally self-funding – you're responsible for all costs. None of the religious organisations listed in this chapter is profit based; all money raised goes towards the cost of your placement, or is invested in the overseas community or the aims of the religious group itself.

While there are a few short-term placements, in general religious organisations are looking for an extended time commitment from their volunteers.

## SELECTION & ELIGIBILITY

The eligibility criteria and selection processes for volunteers also vary greatly between organisations. However, almost all require you to have an understanding of the faith in which the organisation is rooted, and some may require a demonstrated devotion to it. Many of these organisations send only a handful of volunteers overseas each year and so competition for placements can be stiff. Interviews are generally conducted in person and references are required (sometimes these are from your local faith community). Depending on the type of work you'll be doing, qualifications or relevant experience may also be required. And if the placement involves working with children or vulnerable adults, you'll also need to pass a criminal background check.

The main qualities that religious organisations are looking for in a volunteer are: an understanding of the fundamental tenets of their religion; an ability to empathise; a capacity to live in basic conditions; and a willingness to take on various (sometimes not-so-pleasant) tasks as the need arises.

*"Everyone has the power for greatness, not for fame, but for greatness, because greatness is determined by service."*

*Martin Luther King Junior*

## WHAT TO LOOK FOR

In choosing a religious organisation to volunteer through, there are a number of things to keep in mind. A fundamental point to consider is the level of evangelism required of you in your placement, or the extent to which religion will play a role in the work. It's vital that you are clear about this in advance and feel comfortable with what's expected of you. Many placements are based in affiliated churches or organisations overseas and so you'll also need to consider the way in which religion is followed in the community you're going to. For instance, a not particularly conservative religious organisation in the UK might place you in a very orthodox community abroad, which could make for difficulties. It might also pay to find out whether or not the religion of your sending organisation is accepted or practised in the wider community you'll be placed in; you may find yourself working within a community of a different faith. Robin Dawson, for example, managed a community development programme in Afghanistan through the Church Mission Society (p245):

*Afghanistan is an Islamic state and I was working for a Christian organisation. I knew that there would be tensions and limitations… and this proved to be the case. However, I was also aware of the rich exchanges that can be experienced as part of an international community… We are required by the protocols our organisations sign with the government not to proselytise. However, in a faith-dominated society such as Afghanistan, this does not prevent Afghans from asking questions about our religion (which they see as essentially corrupt and containing doctrines which are clearly both incorrect and illogical). It is most interesting trying to answer these questions. In many ways, I have felt more comfortable discussing matters of faith in Afghanistan than I have in secular Western society. God is not called upon to justify his actions in Afghanistan. Where I have felt uncomfortable is with the tensions that arise between those, like me, who see our protocols not to proselytise as a discipline to be adhered to, and others who feel that there should be more proclamation of the Christian message. The way these issues are dealt with can be a matter of life and death to Afghanis who may become involved.*

It's also important to be clear about your expectations and goals and whether or not these are a good fit with the organisation's programmes. If you're hoping for very hands-on work and the chance to accomplish something tangible, you need to make sure that the programme has the kind of project-focused approach to enable this. On the other hand, if your main goal is to develop your faith through volunteering, be sure that there is adequate provision for you to practise it. Liz Bodner found this more difficult than she expected when volunteering with the Missionaries of Charity in India:

*When I went to Kolkata, I thought that I would have a very spiritual experience and would grow in my faith. This wasn't the case, however. It was very easy to get into the routine of work without being spiritually aware. The Missionaries of Charity are service oriented and are focused on sharing God's love through acts rather than words… I had to make the decision to go to mass in the mornings and adoration in the afternoons in order to keep myself connected to my faith.*

## PROS & CONS

Volunteering with a religious organisation is not for everyone. However, if you're considering going down this path, the pros and cons in this section zero in on some of the defining features of these placements.

# SUPPORT

A strong characteristic of most religious organisations, and one which is a drawcard for prospective volunteers, is the level of support they offer. This extends to many aspects of the placement. Firstly, there is the shared faith, which provides the foundation for the project as well as, in most cases, a corresponding community of faith into which volunteers are welcomed. Ben Martin worked with a renewable energies empowerment project in India with a Buddhist charity, as well as fundraising for the organisation in London. While he is not Buddhist, he found the faith-based support impressive and constructive:

> I have to admit that the fact that the organisation was Buddhist had little bearing on my decision to volunteer with them... Having said that, however, I cannot stress enough the benefits I gained from working with a group of people sharing a common bond of Buddhist faith. The atmosphere in the office is one of mutual respect and friendliness; office 'politics' simply don't come into play. Frank conversations about motivations, goals and personal contributions really helped me think more about myself, and also ensured that I did as much as I could to help the organisation.

Your faith can also act as a sort of security blanket, as it offers an element of the 'known' within a culture and country that may well be unfamiliar to you. If you are religious, you can also feel comfortable knowing that your beliefs and practices will be accepted in your placement. Ele Ramsey found this to be the case when she volunteered in the UK and Nicaragua:

> My placement working in 'new' evangelical and charismatic churches meant that I didn't feel, at any point, that I had to suppress my own interpretation of Christianity. All the congregations I worked with held the same set of beliefs as I did.

Perhaps due to their community-minded focus, religious organisations tend to offer a huge amount of support in non-religious areas as well. Volunteers placed together are generally very team oriented, and even those working as partners or individually often maintain close contact with other volunteers and the organisation's base through emails, blogs and newsletters. Sue Towler, the programme manager of Tearfund's volunteer programme (p249), describes the support given to a volunteer in an emergency situation:

*We had a six-week Transform team in western Uganda, volunteering at a rural hospital and local school… During the trip, one girl developed suspected acute appendicitis. In close contact with Tearfund, the team immediately contacted the British High Commission and ACE Rescue (a 24-hour travel insurance company for business travellers that Tearfund uses for all Transform teams). We were in very close contact with the girl's parents throughout, as well as the doctor at the hospital the girl was volunteering at. Because she was a diabetic, her condition was too serious to be treated at the local hospital, so [we] arranged for her to be evacuated by helicopter to Kampala to receive treatment. We also arranged for her mother to fly out to Kampala to be with her. We were concerned that the incident had an impact on the team, so arranged for them all to have a full debrief on their return.*

## FAITH PROPAGATION

If you choose to volunteer through a religious organisation, you can feel fairly confident that the aspirations and views of the organisation will be similar to your own. It's encouraging to know that the aims underpinning a project you're volunteering on are things you believe in. This was one of the main reasons why Ele Ramsey chose to volunteer with a Christian charity in the UK and Nicaragua:

*I wanted an opportunity to put my faith into action. I agreed with the organisation's policy of being a Christian-motivated organisation without being explicitly evangelical in its work. I had been heavily involved with the Christian Union at university and was desperate to get away from insular, theological debates and into the real world!… It was also great to act as a peer educator and inspire young people to take action in the name of their faith.*

It is always important to ascertain to what extent, and under what conditions, you will be expected to propagate your faith. Does the organisation attempt to convert the local population? Many religious projects are run and managed by a local contingent of the same faith and so such issues don't arise. It's also important to be aware of how the project is perceived by the wider community in which it runs. Is it well received by the community and accepting of their culture? Find out the level of involvement of the local population and to what extent the project works and interacts with the community.

# BUILDING BRIDGES

**Matt and Polly Freer chose to devote three years to working with a community in Zambia, through the Church Mission Society (p245).**

Before we met, we had both spent a year volunteering in rural Africa supporting the work of the local church. So, coupled with a joint background in community development, it was no surprise to anyone that we wanted to return to Africa after we married. Having both worked for Tearfund, we were not short of contacts with local organisations. However, we wanted to go through an organisation that specialised in building long-term links by encouraging the sharing of cross-cultural experiences.

We soon chose to volunteer with the Church Mission Society for a variety of reasons. We are both Christians and wanted to work with the church, which is generally seen as a local network ideal for bringing about long-term sustainable development. CMS has over a hundred years' experience in building links with churches around the world – but we were probably attracted more by the fact that it's not afraid of change.

Having left our jobs and packed, we were ready to leave the UK for Zambia, but ended up waiting three months for visas. Even when we did arrive we were seconded to work for a different organisation in another part of the country – but that's all part of the adventure! We were supporting a national organisation in Zambia that fights poverty through empowering poor communities to stand up and speak out against the injustice of poverty, training leaders and building global partnerships. It was really important to us that we were not coming into a country and just imposing something, we were working for an organisation that was run and governed by Zambians, and which existed without a foreign organisation telling it what to do.

Through such a set-up we are able to share some of our skills and experience, as well as learn new skills from Zambian friends and colleagues. That helped us to question our own culture. The fact that we had experience of working for donor organisations and had come through CMS with support from churches and individuals in the UK meant we could help build the links between the work here and there. Deepening these relationships builds the worldwide church community and prevents the donor–recipient imbalance that has often plagued such relationships.

It isn't always straightforward but that is the beauty of cross-cultural exchange. We have the privilege of standing with, and speaking up for, those that are suffering in the world. Being part of a wider long-term movement enables us to share that experience, both the joys and suffering, with other people from our own culture.

# DEVELOPMENT PLACEMENTS

One of the overall aims of projects run by religious organisations is to help people in need, so it's no surprise that their programmes are almost all in the development arena. While few of these programmes require volunteers to have specific skills, most organisations welcome applicants with training or skills in relevant fields.

## INTERNATIONAL ORGANISATIONS

**Habitat for Humanity International**
Europe, Middle East and Africa Regional Office: Bratislava, Slovakia
☎+421 2 3366 9000
emea@habitat.org
www.habitatemea.org
UK Office: Slough, Berkshire, UK
☎+44 (0)1753 313611
www.habitatforhumanity.org.uk
Australia Office: Sydney, NSW, Australia
☎1 800 88 55 99/+61(0)2 9919 7000
www.habitat.org.au
US Office: Americus, GA, USA
☎1 800 422 4828
www.habitat.org
This non-denominational Christian housing charity is dedicated to eliminating poverty housing around the globe and works in around 100 countries. Volunteers are sent overseas to work in teams alongside the local community to build improved accommodation. The family for whom the house is built invests their own labour, fostering community development, dignity and pride of ownership.

**Status:** Registered charity and company limited by guarantee.

**Timing & Length of Projects:** Placements are for one or two weeks, with set departure dates throughout the year.

**Destinations:** The organisation sends volunteers to over 40 countries in Asia and Pacific, Europe, Africa and the Middle East, Latin America and Caribbean, and America and Canada. Recently, projects have been in Ghana, Tanzania, India, Kenya, Romania, Armenia, Chile and South Africa.

**Costs:** Costs vary depending on the sending and hosting country programme. However volunteers are required to raise a donation starting from US$500 to cover the costs of building. In addition, they must be entirely self-funding.

**Eligibility:** Applicants must be 16 years or over, and acceptance of those over 71 is dependent on obtaining insurance cover. Every attempt is made to accommodate applicants with disabilities and acceptance is decided on a case-by-case basis. No building skills are required and all faiths are welcome.

**Groups or Individuals:** Volunteers travel and work in teams of approximately a dozen. You can join a team as an individual or with a friend or partner. Groups can also be accommodated, with projects designed specifically for them.

**Annual no. of Volunteers:** Internationally, thousands of volunteers are mobilised throughout the world.

**Annual Projects:** 150.

Habitat for Humanity International volunteers work to end poverty housing

**Partner Programmes:** The organisation works with other Habitat for Humanity national organisations, located in the countries where they send teams.

**Selection & Interview Process:** An application form is used to determine if the applicant is insurable on the building site and whether their particular needs can be accommodated. Interviews are occasionally conducted.

**In-country Support:** Habitat has an established network in all countries hosting volunteers, and teams are supported by a team leader through the planning process, on the ground and after the trip. The team leader remains in close contact with the hosting country staff through the planning stages and for the duration of the project.

## Reach Beyond

Bradford, West Yorkshire, UK

☎ +44 (0)1274 721810

info@reachbeyond.org.uk

www.reachbeyond.org.uk

This Protestant organisation is strongly rooted in the Christian faith. It has offices in several countries and projects world-wide, often working with partners. Its aim is to show the love of God through its work. Professional volunteers interested in sharing its vision can work in media, IT, health care, clear water projects, community development, training and education.

**Status:** Charitable company limited by guarantee.

**Timing & Length of Projects:** Placements

are from four weeks to two years, with departures possible year-round.

**Destinations:** Latin America, Europe, Asia and Africa.

**Costs:** Volunteers must be self-funding. Costs vary depending on the destination and duration of placement.

**Eligibility:** Volunteers must have a strong Christian commitment and be willing to complete a statement of faith. Professional skills are also required. You must apply in your country of residence if it has a Reach Beyond office (see the website for links to worldwide contact details). Applicants must be at least 18 years of age for some projects, 20 for others. Spanish is required for healthcare placements in Ecuador. Applications from those with disabilities are welcome.

**Groups or Individuals:** Placements are usually for individuals. Partners and friends can sometimes be placed together if an appropriate placement can be found.

**Annual no. of Volunteers:** 2 to 5.

**Annual Projects:** 1 to 3.

**Partner Programmes:** Reach Beyond works with many local organisations and programmes.

**Selection & Interview Process:** Applicants need to complete a form and supply references prior to an interview. Medical clearance and criminal checks are required, and language study and theological preparation may be needed.

**In-country Support:** Reach Beyond staff or local partners will give orientation, arrange accommodation and other local details.

## International China Concern

Morpeth, Northumberland, UK

📞 +44 (0)1670 505622

www.chinaconcern.org

This Christian organisation works with up to 350 abandoned, disabled children in China. Its aim is to provide them with love, hope and opportunities through practical ministry. Volunteers receive an orientation in Hong Kong or Beijing and then work with children in Hunan and Henan Provinces. Placements can include various elements of the children's care, development and integration into society.

**Status:** Registered charity.

**Timing & Length of Projects:** Two-week team placements depart eight times per year. Long-term placements are available at a minimum of three months.

**Destinations:** China.

**Costs:** There is a £60 registration fee for all placements. In addition, two-week team placements cost £890 for food, accommodation and in-country transport. International airfares and visa requirements are not included. Long-term volunteers must be self-funding.

**Eligibility:** Applications are welcome from anyone aged 18 or over but minors accompanied by an adult may be accepted. No skills are required for two-week team placements, other than a genuine desire to make a difference in the lives of the children. All applicants must have a favourable police check or clearance to work with children.

**Groups or Individuals:** Two-week teams work as a group of up to 25. Family and friends can apply together. Long-term volunteers work as part of an expatriate team.

Annual no. of Volunteers: Up to 150.

Annual Projects: 3.

Partner Programmes: 5.

Selection & Interview Process: For a two-week placement, an application form and two references are required. For long-term placements, an application form, references, a CV and an interview are required.

In-country Support: ICC staff travel, work and live with volunteer teams during two-week placements. Long-term volunteers are based with an expat team who offer support. Many full-time staff members have medical, therapy or educational backgrounds.

## Sarvodaya

Sri Lanka office: Moratuwa, Sri Lanka

☎ +94 11 264 7159

sarvishva@itmin.net

www.sarvodaya.org

US office: Madison, WI, USA

☎ +1 608 442 5945

info@sarvodayausa.org

www.sarvodayausa.org

Rooted in Gandhian and Buddhist principles, the Sarvodaya Shramadana Societies operate a grassroots network in 15,000 Sri Lankan villages, with the aim of development through self-governance. Thousands of projects focus on social empowerment, disaster management, IT education and development, community health, rural construction and women's issues.

Status: Non-profit organisation.

Timing & Length of Projects: Several weeks to a year; departures year-round.

Destinations: Sri Lanka and Nepal.

Costs: Volunteers bear all expenses, including travel, insurance and in-country living costs.

Eligibility: No age or nationality restrictions apply. Volunteers must be in good physical condition and pass strict selection criteria if working with children.

Groups or Individuals: Within every project, individual, pair and group work is available.

Annual no. of Volunteers: 140.

Annual Projects: Hundreds.

Partner programs: Hundreds.

Selection & Interview Process: Volunteers are matched to projects in their field of interest.

In-country Support: Projects are conducted only in regions deemed safe by programme staffers. The organisation's headquarters is gated, with security guards on the premises at all hours.

## International Federation of L'Arche Communities

Paris, France

☎ +33 (0)1 5368 0800

international@larche.org

www.larche.org

L'Arche is a federation of 149 communities which provide a family-style living environment for people with intellectual disabilities. Volunteers work as assistants in a home, workshop or day programme and most often live within the community, accompanying people with disabilities in their daily routines.

Status: Not-for-profit organisation.

Timing & Length of Projects: These differ from one community to another but most

L'Arche volunteers provide support for people with intellectual disabilities during daily life

volunteers stay ideally for one year. Shorter stays are also possible.

**Destinations:** There are L'Arche communities in 37 countries on all continents.

**Costs:** This also varies. Volunteers are usually provided with accommodation and meals and sometimes pocket money. Airfares are covered by the volunteer.

**Eligibility:** While L'Arche communities are usually of a particular religious denomination, every community accepts people of all faiths or no faith. Age restrictions apply to volunteers in some countries. Applicants should be prepared to engage in close relationships with others – both those with and without intellectual disabilities. People with physical disabilities are invited to apply. Criminal background

checks are required where relevant.

**Groups or Individuals:** Volunteers are usually accepted as individuals. Where possible, couples or friends are admitted to the same community.

**Annual no. of Volunteers:** L'Arche's 149 communities are always in need of volunteers, especially around August and September.

**Annual Projects:** There are 131 L'Arche communities worldwide.

**Partner Programmes:** France: Intercordia, La Guilde and La DCC; Germany: Bez e.V., I.C.E e.V., EIRENE, VIA, InVia; USA: Brethren Volunteers, among others.

**Selection & Interview Process:** Communities usually select applicants via telephone or email. In some cases, it is the regional or national office which carries out the selection process and then dispatches volunteers to different communities. Volunteers can also apply through one of the partner organisations mentioned above

In-country Support: Volunteers usually work under the supervision of a leader. All volunteers are mentored by an experienced member of the community, who helps to deal with difficult situations. L'Arche communities comply with the health and safety procedures of the country in which they are based.

## UK ORGANISATIONS

## BUILDING, CONSTRUCTION & CONSERVATION

### Quaker Voluntary Action

Manchester, UK

☎+44 (0)1484 687139

mail@gva.org.uk

www.qva.org.uk

QVA offers opportunities for volunteering that combine practical engagement with learning and reflection. Its Working Retreat programme encourages an active witness to find sustainability, peace and friendship. Each volunteer's varied tasks will be matched to their skills and capabilities.

Status: Registered charity and limited company.

Timing & Length of Projects: From a weekend to two weeks, April to October.

Destinations: UK, France, Poland, Sweden, Netherlands, Germany, Hungary, Spain, Slovenia, Israel and Palestine.

Costs: From £50 to £490 depending on length of project. This includes accommodation and food, but not travel.

Eligibility: Volunteers need to be sympathetic to Quaker values.

Groups or Individuals: Placements are in groups of six to 12. During the project volunteers cook and eat together.

Annual no. of Volunteers: 30 to 60.

Annual Projects: 5 to 10.

Partner Programmes: QVA has links with many national and international organisations.

Selection & Interview Process: Following receipt of an application form, project places are allocated.

In-country Support: Provided by the QVA coordinator and a Link Truste.

## COMMUNITY DEVELOPMENT

### Assumption Volunteer Programme

London, UK

☎+44 (0)20 7361 4752

vc@assumptionvolunteers.org.uk

www.assumptionvolunteers.org.uk

An initiative of the Sisters of the Assumption, an international Catholic religious order, AV enables people to share their skills in a poor and cross-cultural context overseas and in the UK. Projects are broadly in education in primary and secondary schools and in informal education and social outreach.

Status: Registered charity.

Timing & Length of Projects: Placements are for one academic year. Departures are in August/September.

Destinations: The Philippines, India, Lithuania and the UK.

**Costs:** Volunteers raise £750 if going abroad and pay for any vaccinations.

**Eligibility:** The minimum age is 20. Volunteers with a Catholic or other Christian faith may feel more comfortable in this programme, but it also accepts those with no faith who are open to and respectful of the religious dimension. Some placements prefer a teaching qualifications. Whether applicants with disabilities can be placed depends on the ability of the overseas projects to accommodate them. DBS record checks are standard.

**Groups or Individuals:** Volunteers may be sent individually or in pairs. Applications are welcome from single or married people. It doesn't accept families with children.

**Annual no. of Volunteers:** Up to 10.

**Annual Projects:** 5.

**Partner Programmes:** 4.

**Selection & Interview Process:** Interviews are held in person in London and there is a residential training week in London in July.

**In-country Support:** Volunteers work with Assumption Sisters overseas who offer in-country support and the co-ordinator keeps in touch from London by Skype/phone.

## BMS World Mission

Didcot, Oxfordshire, UK

📞 +44 (0)1235 517700

www.bmsworldmission.org

This Christian organisation aims to improve the quality of life in impoverished communities through a large range of programmes. Placements can include working with street children, teaching basic English or helping to run church programmes. Medics and lawyers are also placed in a professional capacity. One of BMS's explicit aims is to enable the local communities to know Christ and volunteers must be committed to Jesus.

**Status:** Registered charity.

**Timing & Length of Projects:** Placements range from just a few weeks to years. Departure dates vary but are throughout the year.

**Destinations:** Countries throughout Africa, Asia, Europe and Latin America.

**Costs:** Fees vary between programmes and destinations. Two weeks as part of a medical team costs about £1200, while six weeks on a legal team is £2100 and 10 months on an unskilled project is around £4475. Fees include insurance, food, health clearance, accommodation and training, but not flights or visas (apart from the gap year programme). Individual placements are entirely self-funding.

**Eligibility:** Applicants must be practising Christians. Age restrictions vary with projects but there are placements for those between 18 and 74. Background checks are required for those working with children.

**Groups or Individuals:** There are opportunities for individuals, couples and families. There are also team programmes.

**Annual no. of Volunteers:** 50.

**Annual Projects:** Approximately 40 projects and partners worldwide.

**Selection & Interview Process:** BMS holds group selection events and interviews either in Didcot or Birmingham.

**In-country Support:** Volunteers have 24-hour

emergency contacts in the country they're working in, and in the UK. Volunteers are always placed alongside BMS long-term personnel or partner organisations.

## Christians Abroad
Witham, Essex, UK
☎ +44 (0)3000 121201
recruit@cabroad.org.uk
www.cabroad.org.uk

This organisation works with projects of all denominations and mainly with projects that have no other connection with the UK. Most placements are in schools, orphanages, health centres or community projects. Volunteers can work in a wide range of capacities, from teaching English or a range of subjects, to working in healthcare (including medical electives) or administration. All placements are with people and places known to CA and it tries to match the needs and religious leanings of the projects with appropriate volunteers. There is no evangelistic aspect to the placements, although some can have a religious component (for instance, teaching theology or assisting with church programmes).

**Status:** A project of the charity Churches Together in Britain and Ireland.

**Timing & Length of Projects:** Placements are year round with a one- to three-month period for most places.

**Destinations:** Mainly Africa, in Cameroon, Kenya, Ghana, Tanzania, South Africa and Zambia. There are also placements in India, Sri Lanka and Nepal and also in Peru and Bolivia.

**Costs:** There is a £750 deposit payable upon the success of your application. There is a 50% discount for students. All other costs are covered by the volunteer.

**Eligibility:** The minimum age is 18, however, CA prefers volunteers to be at least 21. There are no specific denominational requirements. Specific skills may be required for some placements. People with disabilities can apply; acceptance is dependent on the circumstances of the placement. CRB/DBS criminal checks are required.

**Groups or Individuals:** Usually volunteers are placed as individuals, however, couples and friends can sometimes be accommodated.

**Annual no. of Volunteers:** 20.

**Annual Projects:** 15.

**Partner Programmes:** 21.

**Selection & Interview Process:** Christians Abroad requires a detailed application form, face-to-face interviews in London, a reference check and agreement to a code of practice. The final decision then rests with the project managers, who receive an interview report.

**In-country Support:** All volunteers are given UK staff emergency contacts and details of local healthcare. Day-to-day care is the responsibility of the in-country project.

## Church Mission Society
Oxford, UK
☎ +44 (0)1865 787415
info@churchmissionsociety.org
www.churchmissionsociety.org

CMS dates back to 1799 and works in over 60 countries around the globe. Placements are in church-run projects and can include administration, nursing, work as

# KIBBUTZIM

Big on community? Got that team spirit? Feel like you missed out on the communal living of the '70s? Then think 'kibbutz'.

The kibbutz movement began in Israel in 1910 and was organised by European-Jewish pioneers in pursuit of a communal ideal, where all members would work together, own everything in common and act as an all-inclusive assembly to make the governing rules. The first Israeli kibbutz had only 10 members – by 1940, there were 82 communities with over 26,500 inhabitants. Today there are more than 270 kibbutzim (the plural of 'kibbutz') spread across the country. They are all pluralistic and nonreligious (with the exception of the 17 HaKibbutz HaDati which are Orthodox Zionist).

Kibbutzim are an extremely popular means of combining travel with volunteering, although in recent years the movement has lost some of its lustre, amid the ongoing political and civil unrest in Israel. Nevertheless, the kibbutz movement still chugs along and welcomes volunteers from countries that have diplomatic relations with Israel. In fact, these days you may get an even warmer welcome for making the effort to bridge the growing gap between Israel and the rest of the world.

Each kibbutz is made up of approximately 600 people. As a volunteer, you will be expected to pitch in with the rest of the community, taking on tasks assigned to you and working eight hours a day, six days a week (with an extra two days of breathing space allotted per month) not including Saturdays. You might find yourself picking avocados, maintaining irrigation systems, collecting eggs or farming fish. You might also find yourself working in the kitchens, doing the laundry or helping out in the kibbutz's income-generating venture, if it has one – perhaps a guesthouse, restaurant or shop.

To volunteer, you need to be between the ages of 18 and 35, be in good mental and physical health, be able to commit to a minimum of two months and willing to leave after 12, speak a reasonable amount of English and be willing to undergo an AIDS test on arrival. You'll also need to shell out US$180 for a registration fee and US$130 for the kibbutz volunteer health insurance policy (valid for three months). These fees cover nearly everything for your stay on the kibbutz: communal meals, laundry, shared accommodation (two to three people per room), and even some monthly pocket dosh. It is possible to volunteer alongside your friends or partner but families are not welcome.

To apply, you can register online at www.kibbutzvolunteers.org.il or contact the representative in your home country via contact details listed at www.kibbutz.org.il/volunteers/repres.htm

Kibbutzim are an extremely popular means of combining travel with volunteering.

a hostel warden or care-work in children's homes. CMS tries to match volunteers' skills to openings.

Status: Company limited by guarantee, with charitable status.

Timing & Length of Projects: Placements are year-round, short term (four months to two years) or long term (four years plus).

Destinations: Sub-Saharan Africa, North Africa, Middle East, Central Asia, South and Southeast Asia, Latin America and Europe.

Costs: Costs depend on location and length of placement. CMS does not charge any administration fees; all money is raised and held by the individual. CMS provides 12-day residential training programme and debriefing.

Eligibility: Applicants need to be committed Christians who are actively involved in their local church, with a minimum age of 18. Criminal record checks are required.

Groups or Individuals: Volunteers can be single, married, and with children. CMS looks for an opportunity that suits the whole family.

Annual no. of Volunteers: 30 to 40.

Annual Projects: CMS has long-term relationships with partner churches and is involved in on-going community work rather than a number of individual projects.

Partner Programmes: Many.

Selection & Interview Process: Applicants are given a number of interviews and are subject to medical checks plus a weekend residential selection conference.

In-country Support: Volunteers are matched with an in-country partner church and have a nominated line manager. They also have regular contact with CMS and procedures are in place in case of emergency.

## Latin Link
Reading, Berkshire, UK
☎ +44 (0)1189 577100
www.latinlink.org

Latin Link offers two separate volunteering programmes: 'Step' and 'Stride'. Step gives participants a practical introduction to mission work in Latin America, with team placements working alongside a local church community and undertaking work such as construction or running children's holiday camps. 'Stride' is for individuals, couples or families who are teamed up with a Christian-run project; placements can include project management, publishing, engineering, music, arts, teaching or urban outreach. Projects for both placements are designed to help volunteers develop their faith and explore their Christian calling.

Status: Registered charity.

Timing & Length of Projects: Step teams leave in early March for four months, and in July and August for three to seven weeks. Stride placements run from six months to two years and usually start in February.

Destinations: Argentina, Bolivia, Brazil, Ecuador, Guatemala, Mexico, Peru, Chile, Colombia, Costa Rica and Nicaragua.

Costs: The Spring Step projects cost £2900; Summer Step costs between £950 and £1450 depending on the length of the placement. Prices include everything except personal spending money. Stride has an initial cost of £2500 for singles and

£3300 for couples (both for one year), which covers placement set-up, orientation, DBS criminal background checks, medical clearance, and language school. Added to the Stride cost is £400 to £600 per month for food, accommodation and supervision (this varies by destination).

**Eligibility:** Applicants must have a personal faith in Jesus and be over the age of 17 for Step and 18 for Stride. Skills required depend on the placement. People with disabilities are welcome to apply.

**Groups or Individuals:** Step volunteers are placed in teams of eight to 12 . Ready made church, mixed age, or university teams welcome to apply. Stride is for individuals, couples or families.

**Annual no. of Volunteers:** 70 to 150.

**Annual Projects:** 30.

**Partner Programmes:** Over 50.

**Selection & Interview Process:** Interviews are conducted in person at the Reading office or in Ireland and Scotland. References are required.

**In-country Support:** Each Strider has an approved mentor, work supervisor and the services of a Latin Link co-ordinator.

## Tearfund

Teddington, Middlesex, UK

☎ +44 (0)845 355 8355

enquiry@tearfund.org

www.tearfund.org

Tearfund is a Christian-based organisation that places volunteer teams in developing countries on projects that have been initiated by local communities. These include healthcare projects, literacy classes, implementing systems for clean water and sanitation, HIV/AIDS education, and drug-rehabilitation or food-security programmes. Volunteers work through local churches and Christian agencies. Tearfund hopes that the programmes will act as catalysts for returned volunteers to continue working towards its Christian mission.

**Status:** Registered charity.

**Timing & Length of Projects:** Family and youth groups trips last one to two weeks. Short-term placements are two to four weeks and UK government-funded options are 12 weeks. There are also six-month gap year options.

**Destinations:** Latin America, Africa and Asia.

**Costs:** Trips range from being entirely funded by the UK government to costing £4000.

**Eligibility:** The minimum age is 18, though seven-year-olds can take part in family trips. While specific skills aren't requested, useful training or talents are welcome. Volunteers must agree with, and sign, a basis-of-faith statement. Applicants with specific medical needs or disabilities, or who are over the age of 65, must sign additional forms and have additional insurance. All volunteers are required to complete a DBS check.

**Groups or Individuals:** Volunteers travel, live and work together in teams of six to 12. Tearfund prefers not to place friends together.

**Annual no. of Volunteers:** 450 to 500.

**Annual Projects:** 40 to 50.

**Partner Programmes:** Tearfund has hundreds of overseas partners.

Selection & Interview Process: Interviews are given at special information events or at the orientation which applicants attend before volunteering.

In-country Support: In-country support is provided by the local partners. Tearfund also has an emergency telephone system and a 24-hour international medical support service.

## USPG (United Society Partners in the Gospel)

London, UK
☎ +44 (0)207 921 2200
enquiries@uspg.org.uk
www.uspg.org.uk

The 'Journey With US' programme, formerly known as the 'Experience Exchange' programme, has been run for over 60 years by USPG. The self-funding volunteer scheme offers unique opportunities to volunteers resident in Britain and Ireland to experience and share in the culture, life and mission of church and communities overseas. Placements are arranged to suit volunteers' skills, background and preferences and can include teaching, working on agricultural, health or building projects, and helping in vocational and rehabilitation institutions and/or children and youth projects.

Status: Registered charity.

Timing & Length of Projects: Placements are for three months to a year, with departure dates dependent on the individual.

Destinations: Africa and the Indian Ocean, Asia and Oceania, Latin America and the Caribbean, the Middle East and Europe.

Costs: The cost depends on the placement, destination and timing, but all placements are entirely self-funding. USPG provides a provisional budget for each placement, along with fundraising guidance.

Eligibility: Participants must be at least 18. Acceptance is dependent on a medical clearance. While volunteers from all backgrounds can apply, Christian values and teaching are explored on weekends and during preparation training. Background CRB/DBS checks are required.

Groups or Individuals: Placements are generally for individuals as they are suited to the volunteer's skills and preferences. However, the programme is flexible enough to cater for individuals, couples or friends.

Annual no. of Volunteers: 40.

Annual Projects: Countless projects and activities of USPG partner churches around the world.

Partner Programmes: USPG has partner churches in over 60 countries.

Selection & Interview Process: USPG offers a 'Discernment and Exploration Weekend' in Birmingham for those interested in volunteering. This is followed by an interview day in London. All volunteers are required to take part in a week-long residential training and preparation course run in January and July before travelling overseas.

In-country Support: Volunteers are provided with travel and health advice, and country and cross-cultural orientation prior to travel. Partner churches offer pastoral support in the placement along with UK-based programme manager and staff.

A medical volunteer with
Hope Force International
responding to an
earthquake in Nepal

# NORTH AMERICAN ORGANISATIONS

## Hope Force International

Brentwood, TN, USA

☎ +1 615 371 1271

info@hopeforce.org

www.hopeforce.org

Hope Force International (HFI), founded in 2003, works to ease human suffering caused by natural disasters or persistent human need. The Christian organisation aims to mobilise and equip groups of inspired volunteers, with varied backgrounds and skills, to help anywhere in the world in times of crisis.

**Status:** Non-profit organisation.

**Timing & Length of Projects:** One to two weeks at various times of the year.

**Destinations:** Worldwide, including the USA. Recently working in Nepal and Haiti.

**Costs:** Volunteers must cover airfare and visa costs, as well as varying fees for meals and lodging.

**Eligibility:** The minimum age is 18; no nationality restrictions apply. Some positions require specific professional qualifications and volunteers must be in good physical condition. All applicants are required to complete a medical evaluation; some pre-existing conditions may disqualify service at certain locations. Background checks are required for those working with children.

**Groups or Individuals:** Volunteers engage individually or as members of a pre-existing team, and then live and work in groups.

**Annual no. of Volunteers:** 300.

**Annual Projects:** Varies.

Ongoing programmes in Haiti focusing on reconstruction, education and healthcare. Disaster rebuilding opportunities exist within the USA.

**Selection & Interview Process:** Due to the stressful demands often associated with disaster response a personal reference is required. Volunteers skills, experience and interests are considered in an effort to match applicants to projects.

**In-country Support:** Support: Hope Force International Staff supervise and direct volunteers throughout their service.

## Mercy Ships

PO Box 2020,

Garden Valley, TX, USA

☎ +1 903 939 7000

info@mercyships.org

www.mercyships.org

Mercy Ships is a global charity that has operated hospital ships in developing nations since 1978. Mercy Ships brings hope and healing to the forgotten poor by mobilising people and resources worldwide, and serving all people without regard for race, gender, or religion.

**Status:** Registered charity.

**Timing & Length of Projects:** Two weeks to a year; departures year-round.

**Destinations:** West Africa.

**Costs:** Volunteers must cover airfare and visa costs, as well as varying fees for meals and lodging.

**Eligibility:** The minimum age is 18; no

nationality restrictions apply. Many positions require specific professional qualifications, and volunteers must be in good physical condition. All applicants are required to complete a medical evaluation; some pre-existing conditions may disqualify service at certain locations. All those dealing with children must have a clear criminal record.

**Groups or Individuals:** Volunteers live and work in groups.

**Annual no. of Volunteers:** 1000.

**Annual Projects:** There are current programmes focusing on clean water and sanitation, agriculture, construction, and training of local healthcare professionals.

**Partner Programmes:** Local churches and educators participate in the organisation's work in each country. Volunteers can work alongside the state-of-the-art hospital ship, the Africa Mercy, or with one of its ministry partners.

**Selection & Interview Process:** Volunteers' medical needs, skills and interests are considered when matching applicants to projects.

**In-country Support:** Professional on-board personnel supervise and direct volunteers throughout their service.

# AUSTRALASIAN ORGANISATIONS
## Interserve Australia
Bayswater, VIC, Australia

☎ +61 (0)3 9729 9611; 1800 067 100

info@interserve.org.au

www.interserve.org.au

Mercy Ships provided free surgeries to this girl to correct orthopedic deformities in her legs

Photo: © Ruben Plomp / Mercy Ships

Interserve is an international mission agency offering Christians the chance to use their faith, training and skills in a unique form of service.

**Status:** Not-for-profit incorporated association.

**Timing & Length of Projects:** Six-month to two-year projects are classified as short term (On Track programme); two-year plus programmes are considered long term and volunteers are called Partners. Partners usually return to Australia for six months every three-year term. Occasionally team trips of about two weeks are run, as are six-week medical elective placements for final year medical students.

**Destinations:** Some 30 countries in Asia and the Middle East.

**Costs:** Volunteers raise their own support with the assistance of Interserve. Volunteers will require around A$27,000 per year if single, or around A$48,000 if a couple with children.

**Eligibility:** Christians aged 18 to 70 years. Families with children can apply. All applicants are required to have an Australian Federal Police check that includes a working with children check.

**Groups or Individuals:** Individuals, couples and families.

**Annual no. of Volunteers:** 30 on six-month to one-year projects; eight volunteers departing on long-term programmes.

**Annual Projects:** Interserve seconds skilled volunteers to partner projects.

**Partner Programmes:** 30 partner agencies and projects.

**Selection & Interview Process:** Interserve conducts face-to-face interviews in state offices (Victoria, New South Wales, ACT, Queensland, South Australia and Western Australia), along with a medical assessment and psychological testing. References must accompany applications (one reference must be from the applicant's church pastor or minister).

**In-country Support:** Partner agencies and country teams provide in-country support. Country leaders are situated in all countries.

# OPTIONS FOR THE UNDER 30S

## UK ORGANISATIONS

### Time for God

Harrogate, North Yorkshire, UK

☎ +44 (0)142 353 6248

office@timeforgod.org

www.timeforgod.org

For over 50 years, Time for God has been placing gap-year volunteers in the UK and abroad. Its diverse projects include volunteering in outdoor activity centres, churches, theatrical companies, homeless projects, residential care homes and schools, community development projects and drug rehabilitation projects. Some placements have a specific Christian element and focus, while others are less overtly faith-based. While volunteers are required to demonstrate a level of devotion, the organisation is aimed at giving volunteers the space and support to explore their relationship with the Christian faith.

**Status:** Registered charity and limited company.

**Timing & Length of Projects:** The UK and overseas placements run for 10 to 12 months, staring each September. There's an additional hosting cohort in the UK each January.

**Destinations:** UK, South Korea, Hong Kong, Ireland, Hungary, France, Madeira, Germany and the Netherlands.

**Costs/Pay:** Some of the European Voluntary Service (EVS, see p139) placements for volunteers are free, while the non-EVS placements range from £1200 to £2000 depending on the destination and length of stay. All placements include full board, accommodation and a monthly stipend (£160). Flights, visa costs and insurance are not included.

**Eligibility:** Applicants must be between 18 and 30 for EVS placements. Non-EVS hosting options are for anyone over 18. For overseas placements, the minimum age is 20. No qualifications or experience are required. Police checks from your country of origin are required.

**Groups or Individuals:** Depending on the project, volunteers work either as a team or individually.

**Annual no. of Volunteers:** 125.

**Annual Projects:** 80.

**Partner Programmes:** 25.

**Selection & Interview Process:** Interviews are done in person, or by telephone or Skype.

**In-country Support:** Each volunteer is allocated a trained trained field officer for support and training throughout the year, and has access to 24-hour support in emergencies.

Not all of Time for God's volunteer placements are overtly faith-based

# 08

# Do-It-Yourself Placements

If you've read this far, you're probably seriously considering volunteering as part of your travels, or even as the sole purpose of an overseas trip. Previous chapters may have given you an idea of the type of work you'd like to do (see p11), and which continent or country you'd like to volunteer in. What you may be weighing up at this point, however, is the benefits and risks involved in teeing something up yourself versus paying an intermediary to arrange it all for you.

You may have arrived at this point by doing some online research and have been overwhelmed by the hundreds of agencies offering their services and charging a fee for it. But you may not feel comfortable paying a sending organisation – it may not fit with your image of what volunteering should be about. Simon Roberts, who taught English to underprivileged children in Bolivia, shared this sentiment:

*After initial research we decided we didn't want to volunteer for an organisation where we had to pay for the experience, as we felt this was contrary to our idea of volunteering. The institution we went for was very small and had a grassroots feel to it.*

How, then, do you follow in Simon's footsteps and find volunteering opportunities independently of a middle man? And what are the issues to consider when volunteering independently? For instance, would it be better to arrange the placement before you leave home, or once you arrive at your destination? And how can you ensure that you make a worthwhile contribution as a volunteer and have a good time while doing it? This chapter will give some answers to these questions.

# IS DO-IT-YOURSELF VOLUNTEERING RIGHT FOR YOU?

In many cases the decision to do-it-yourself stems from the frustrations caused by the high costs and time restrictions associated with volunteer placement organisations. However, many prospective volunteers make a hasty decision to go it alone without properly thinking through the demands and challenges. Reflecting upfront on your strengths and weaknesses, your preferred ways of working and your skills and values will help you decided whether a do-it-yourself placement is right for you.

Kirsi Korhonen, who took on a few volunteering roles in Bolivia, including one at the animal refuge Inti Wara Yassi (p274), and a position at the boy's home Amanecer, made an informed decision to volunteer independently:

*We chose to find our own opportunities, to make sure the money went where it was needed and to give ourselves more freedom. Plus, my friend and I are both very experienced in travelling and in all things travel-related.*

All volunteers must possess certain core qualities if they are to make a worthwhile contribution (see p55). However, going it alone places special demands on the volunteer. No matter how much research you've done, there'll be an element of the unknown. You will have to assume complete responsibility for yourself and your actions, as you will have no support network to fall back on. In addition, you will often be out of your comfort zone.

Elizabeth France, who performed a variety of roles with United Action for Children in Cameroon (p277), suggests that self-motivation and persistence are vital for a successful DIY experience:

*From my experience, the most valuable people are those who have a 'stick-to-it' attitude, as they won't give up when the going gets tough.*

Other key attributes which help in facing the kind of unpredictable situations that can crop up when you're volunteering independently include self-reliance, maturity, patience, communication and interpersonal skills, sensitivity to cross-cultural issues and a good sense of humour. In working out whether do-it-yourself volunteering is for you, you need to ask yourself honestly whether you can consistently demonstrate such qualities amid the inevitable challenges of a placement.

# PROS & CONS OF GOING IT ALONE

## PROS

### Lower costs, and payments usually goes directly to the project

With some grassroots organisations you may not need to pay any placement fee; for others you will be expected to make a donation or fundraise. Jason Rogers, who volunteered at schools in Thailand and Laos, paid a donation for his Thailand placement:

*There was a pretty strict volunteer fee for Thailand, which included buying presents for the kids. Some of the money went directly to the centre and some went towards the Christmas presents. I think it was about US$350 total.*

Elizabeth France, who volunteered in Cameroon, wanted to ensure that any fees she paid would go directly to the project:

*An important factor in my decision was that the costs were to be paid directly to the NGO, without a cut taken by any intermediary organisation.*

Also, a large proportion of agency fees goes towards practical arrangements for volunteer placements such as board and lodging – if you're going it alone you can save money by making these arrangements yourself.

### Greater ability to tailor the role to suit you

Most local charities and grassroots NGOs are small scale and do not have structured volunteer programmes, and this means you can often define your own role, matching your aptitudes and objectives to a project's needs.

The lack of structure on her Bolivian placement was a positive for Amanda Guest-Collins, who volunteered as an English teacher:

*The set-up was very informal, so our roles and work weren't particularly structured. This meant, however, that we had the flexibility to make the roles our own.*

Joan Hodkinson, a language teacher, chose to look after orphans at a day school in Kolkata (Calcutta), India, because she was confident the pupils would benefit from her skills:

*I knew that we would be teaching English as part of the work, which was something I could be successful at.*

### Being able to fit placements in with your plans

Choosing the agency-free route allows travellers who want the freedom of not being tied to an itinerary to arrange placements at short notice. The ability to extend your placement once you are there is another benefit, as Kristine Randall found when she volunteered on various projects with United Action for Children (p277) in Cameroon:

*I had originally intended to volunteer for two months. After a few weeks I decided to extend my stay for a third month, for a number of reasons, the biggest one being that I felt like I was finally settling in and didn't feel ready to leave.*

### You will be supporting small grassroots organisations with limited access to external resources and volunteers

Jo Shuttleworth volunteered independently in two African countries; one of her placements was as a teacher in Ghana. She comments on the rewards of working with a small-scale charity:

*It is nice to find small charities that don't get much attention from the West and who genuinely appreciate your work, rather than you being yet another nameless face.*

Simon Roberts, who volunteered in Bolivia, was keen to help support the work of unrecognised charities:

*We wanted to volunteer in a country where the need for volunteers was the greatest and where government support for small scale projects was in short supply.*

### You have direct ontact with people running local organisations or projects

Many volunteers prefer the more personal experience of dealing directly with the grassroots organisation. In this way, they can inform themselves about the project's mission and iron out any problems in-country rather than relying on a third party – who may or may not have first-hand knowledge – to dispense information or direct matters from afar.

### Deeper interaction with the local community

Volunteering independently means that you'll probably have to organise your own accommodation and entertainment, and you may be the only volunteer in an entire community. As a result, you'll generally be more motivated to mix with people from the local community – Benjamin Blakey, who helped on a construction site for Casas de la Esperanza in Nicaragua, found:

> For the majority of the time I was the only foreign volunteer on the project site. This allowed me to practice my Spanish and forced me to integrate with the locals with whom I was working.

Speaking the local lingo obviously facilitates the immersion process – Kirsi Korhonen, who volunteered in Bolivia, emphasises:

> In Bolivia not many people speak English, so knowing Spanish is almost a must, especially if you want to work with the locals. Otherwise you will just find yourself hanging out with the other volunteers and you won't learn anything about the country and its culture.

# CONS

### Hard work

There's no denying it, organising your own placement can be time-consuming. Benjamin Blakey, who volunteered in Nicaragua, spent many hours researching opportunities:

> Conducting my own research and contacting organisations directly allowed me to find an NGO that did not charge a fee for volunteer placements. The difficulty was that the process required hours of internet searches, emails and dead ends before I contacted an organisation that matched my criteria and which had volunteer opportunities.

Kirsi Korhonen admits that going through an agency can be a much easier route to take:

> Using an agency provides safety and support and is often hassle free compared to finding a placement independently.

## No guarantees

However much advice you're given by people who have volunteered previously, to a certain extent you will be dealing with the unknown when you arrange your own placement. Local organisations or projects will not be vetted by a third party, so you may end up with something that doesn't match your expectations. As Rachel Oxberry, who volunteered in an Ecuadorian home for street children, recalls:

> I was appalled at how the home was run. The bishop who ran the home beat the children and used a lot of the donations to fund his own family's education. The bishop's family ate a balanced diet, whereas the street children ate rice and beans.

Brenda Carter's placement in Ghana didn't turn out as expected either:

> On my arrival, despite all the information I received that led me to believe I'd be working with a local women's group, I was taken to an expensive private school, where I was expected to teach. Not exactly the grassroots community approach I had been hoping for! To top it off, my accommodation was a room where a lady had recently died and no-one had even taken the time to remove her belongings.

If you organise a placement yourself, you'll only really find out how the local project is run, whether it is meeting genuine needs, what you'll be doing and whether you can make a valuable contribution once you are in situ.

## Roles may not be clearly defined

Although some local charities and NGOs are used to taking on volunteers and can offer detailed job descriptions, it's more likely that you'll have to carve out your own role once you start the placement. Mary Sears' experience in Bolivia is typical of many DIY placements:

> It was up to me to make lesson plans and evaluations, to decide what I wanted to teach and how to go about it. I was the first foreign volunteer, so there was nothing in place.

## There's little pre-departure and in-country support

Relying on a small grassroots organisation to give you significant pre-departure or in-country support, with little or no payment, is unfair and a real burden on your hosts. Nor should you expect an organisation to repay you for your help with free accommodation, food, in-country inductions, extracurricular activities etc. Jordan Jones, who volunteered at the Casa Guatemala orphanage (p199), admits that he expected otherwise:

*I hadn't done any research into it, but I assumed that volunteers would be provided with at least free accommodation, if not board.*

Other key things that you will not receive support for are medical emergencies, securing visas and language tuition. Nor will you have an established safety net back home or in-country support with logistical or emotional problems.

### You may feel isolated, volunteering alone

You may be working alongside other volunteers, but equally, you may be on your own, and in that case you have to deal with your experiences alone. Elizabeth France, who volunteered in Cameroon, really valued the support she received from her fellow volunteers:

*For me, the greatest advantage to volunteering with another person is that you have the support of someone you trust and who can relate to you and your new experiences.*

### Under-supply or over-supply of volunteers can be detrimental to a project

Well-established sending agencies will carefully plan the supply of volunteers in conjunction with the local project director, to ensure that placements result in a significant and sustainable contribution. The danger of volunteers organising their own placements is that there is little continuity for the organisation, and previous work may be repeated or even undone.

### Volunteers can become a burden on their host if they can't deal with uncertainty

If the going gets tough and you've paid an agency to arrange your placement, then you've usually got back-up to resolve problems. On the other hand, if you don't have a third party that you are accountable to; if the arrangement is pretty flexible; if you have paid little or no donation; and if you're the type who gives up easily, then you may simply decide to quit. But it's important to remember that you are accountable – both to the organisation that you have agreed to help and to yourself – and you do have a responsibility to honour your commitment. Should you quit, you could be disappointing the organisation, draining their resources and damaging the image of international volunteers.

# THE SEARCH BEGINS

*There are thousands of organisations around the world desperate for volunteers. Having travelled for many years and volunteered in several places, I know that it's a unique way to get to know local people and the way they live.*

If this assertion from Mary Sears, who volunteered in Bolivia, is to be believed, then surely it can't be too difficult to find the right DIY volunteering opportunity? But which approach will produce the best results: arranging your placement before leaving home, while you're en route or once you reach your destination?

## ARRANGING THE PLACEMENT FROM HOME OR IN SITU

Whether you choose to make arrangements for your placement before you leave home or in situ may depend upon your personal decision-making style; and specifically whether you prefer to be spontaneous or to be organised in advance. It may also depend upon the time limitations of your travel plans.

Jenny Smith chose to sort out her sea-turtle placement once she arrived in Costa Rica:

*I had found out about it and contacted the organisation beforehand but it wasn't finalised until I got there.*

In contrast, Jason Rogers, a volunteer in Thailand and Laos, chose to arrange all the details prior to leaving home:

*Each volunteer trip was the main reason for my travels and was set up ahead of time.*

Of course, there is one type of independent volunteering that doesn't involve a decision about whether to be organised in advance or not – emergency relief following a disaster. In Eoin Canny's case, volunteering post-tsunami on Koh Phi Phi with the NGO HI Phi Phi was an on-the-spot decision when he arrived on the Thai island and saw a sign requesting volunteers:

*Giving help at the place of need, directly to the people that need it, regardless of the time, effort or work involved, can be an immensely satisfying experience.*

The boxed text below is a first-hand account of one man's experience of impromptu emergency relief following a disaster.

## RESEARCH SOURCES

Regardless of which approach to planning you adopt, matching your skills and philosophies with an appropriate organisation requires time and effort. You may be lucky and chance upon an opening when chatting to a contact at home or a local once abroad; however, a word-of-mouth lead should not be taken as a guarantee of an approriate placement.

## UNEXPECTED VOLUNTEERING

Guatemala was hit by a tropical storm and in a few days hundreds of people were killed in landslides and floods. I was studying Spanish in Antigua when the call went out for volunteers to help in Jocotenango, a suburb of Antigua which had been engulfed by mud when the local river burst its banks. I bought a pair of Wellington boots and took the bus to Jocotenango, which was a very sad sight, as the streets had been filled a metre deep with mud, and the people's ruined possessions were piled outside their houses. I joined the (mainly German and British) volunteers from Antigua's language schools in digging trenches to allow the dirty water to drain away. There seemed to be little organisation, but one afternoon it was decided we should build a dam to divert the water away from the houses. The dam was made of fertiliser bags filled with earth – each weighing about 30 kilos – and hundreds were needed, so it was very hard work. What was really impressive was how we organised ourselves into a team to build a substantial structure in a short space of time, and the next day I was pleased to see that our dam still stood. By then the army had arrived in force and were using machinery to clear the streets, so the volunteers helped clean out houses. On Monday it was back to school, with sore hands but with a sense of satisfaction in having done something to help.

**Graham Williams**

Most people who set up their placement before arriving in-country use a variety of information channels, including personal networking, websites, online directories and forums, guidebooks and volunteering fairs. Amanda Guest-Collins, who volunteered in Bolivia, browsed the internet and guidebooks for ideas:

*I found the site www.volunteersouthamerica.net very useful, plus postings on Lonely Planet's ThornTree. I also looked at several entries in their GAP Year Book and South America on a Shoestring guidebook.*

Clodagh Mullen, who volunteered with Safe Passage/Camino Seguro in Guatemala (p276), surfed the web and used her contacts:

*After an exhaustive internet search, I met a girl at my college who had been volunteering in Guatemala for six years.*

## YOUR PERSONAL NETWORK

Who do you know that may be able to suggest organisations to volunteer with? What other contacts do you have that may know of opportunities? Don't just limit this to your immediate circle of friends, family and colleagues. Ask them to spread the word among their social and work networks too. Victoria Jaberi found her role in administration and translation work in Peru through networking:

*A friend of mine worked for Hope. So I contacted him and the president of Hope. Both told me they didn't have any research placements at that time, but their friends introduced me to other people who had projects as well.*

It is likely that organisations in your home country working in areas that interest you will have foreign connections. If you are keen to volunteer in a school or contribute to community projects, it's worth talking to schools at home that may have links with foreign communities. This method worked for Joan Hodkinson, who volunteered in India:

*I spoke to people who had worked in schools across India to get contacts and more ideas.*

## Surfing the Web

Although the internet seems like the obvious place to look for inspiration, it is only in the last few years that independent volunteering opportunities have really become visible, thanks to the creation of several online directories dedicated to listing local charities and grassroots NGOs which accept volunteers directly (see the list of directories on p273).

The advantage of these online directories is that you can search for organisations by continent, country or type of work in just a few clicks. Some of the directories rely solely on recommendations from travellers, whereas others will check out the credentials of each listed organisation, either by visiting or by sending an in-depth questionnaire about how they work with volunteers. All directories will suggest that you use them as a starting point for your research but that you should seek other opinions, and contact organisations and past volunteers directly.

For a small fee, some directories offer a matching service, whereby you submit your interests and skills and are sent a list of appropriate DIY vacancies. Another great way to learn about opportunities is to review forum postings, which not only tell you about organisations and how to approach them but also discuss the benefits and pitfalls of volunteering without an intermediary organisation.

If you've already narrowed down your country preferences, national tourism websites can provide information and useful links for a good range of volunteering vacancies. Another avenue is to type 'NGOs in country x' into a search engine – this will bring up NGOs that may accept volunteers directly. For example, a search for 'NGOs in Cambodia' will bring up www.ccc-cambodia.org, an NGO member organisation which promotes information exchange and NGO co-ordination in Cambodia.

Being proficient in the language of your chosen country will enable you to widen your search much further, as Kirsi Korhonen, who volunteered in Bolivia with the boys' home Amanecer, discovered:

*I just started searching the net with all kinds of keywords and, after having decided on Bolivia, concentrated on finding opportunities there. We found Amanecer with the keyword combination* trabajo voluntario, niños de la calle *(voluntary work, street kids).*

Just keep in mind that, more often than not, typing 'volunteering in country x' into a search engine will produce lists of sending agencies rather than local charities, as only a few of the latter have the resources to exploit the web effectively.

## Guidebooks & Career or Travel Fairs

Elizabeth France used a variety of channels in her research, and found her university helpful:

> *I went to a number of career fairs and information sessions at my university and found out about different NGOs and their projects. I took information sheets from these sessions and then checked out the projects online.*

With the growing popularity of international volunteering, some guidebooks also list the contact details of grassroots organisations.

## Researching Opportunities In-country

Karla Gergen, who volunteered for a child care foundation in Ghana, opted to find a placement once she reached her destination:

> *I was with some friends on a planned trip that was to include touring and volunteering for two weeks each. My plan was just to keep my ears and eyes open during the two touring weeks to find an opportunity.*

Karla was able to adopt this approach in Ghana, as she spoke English, which is widely understood there. However, without a basic knowledge of your chosen country's language you may struggle to find a suitable placement. Even if you are accepted, the language barrier could limit your contribution, as Jo Shuttleworth, who volunteered in Burkina Faso, admits:

> *My French isn't amazing so it was limited in what I could do, but I could mark work and correct spelling.*

It is useful to have at least one lead to get you started on your in-country research. Generally, in popular tourist destinations, facilities used by travellers (such as hostels, internet cafes, laundrettes, language schools and tour offices), will have noticeboards displaying ads for jobs and volunteering vacancies.

Talking to other travellers and locals connected with the travel industry, such as tour guides or hostel owners, can often point you in the right direction. Jordan Jones, who volunteered in Guatemala, tuned in to the local community to find leads:

*From the day I landed and began travelling I just kept my eyes and ears open for volunteer projects. I checked bulletin boards in hostels and asked all the other travellers I met if they had heard of any projects on their travels. I would even directly ask projects and national park employees if they wanted a volunteer, even if I had no indication that they had a volunteer programme.*

Another source of ideas and contacts is local newspapers – news items will cover issues affecting the local community and environment.

If you're clear about the type of volunteering activity you wish to undertake, then it makes sense to focus your search. Visit some local orphanages and schools in the area if you're passionate about working with orphans or in education (although do take school holidays into account in the latter case). Local churches or religious organisations can also be a valuable source of information for volunteering in community organisations.

Equally, if you are qualified in a particular field such as medicine or IT, then approach organisations that could most benefit from your skills: medical centres, community technical centres or local businesses, for instance.

## SOME FINAL ADVICE

Getting in touch with a couple of past volunteers who have worked with the organisations on your shortlist could mean the difference between a life-changing experience and total disillusionment. Of course, seeking endorsement may not be possible if you are the organisation's first volunteer or, indeed, if you are *in situ*.

Kristine Randall, who volunteered in Cameroon, emphasises the importance of seeking advice from past volunteers:

*As pessimistic as it may sound, many organisations in developing countries are not managed or run to the high standards that we expect, coming from a developed country. Their answers to your queries may not always reflect the reality of the situation. I would strongly suggest contacting a previous volunteer and asking them all the same questions that you would put to the project director. You may be truly surprised by just how different the answers can be!*

## CHOOSING A MUTUALLY BENEFICIAL PLACEMENT

It's all too easy to make a snap decision when selecting a placement for yourself. You might be so keen to slot volunteering into your travel plans that you focus on practicalities such as costs and time frames and meeting your own objectives. You might not take enough time to reflect upon whether you believe in the ethos of the organisation, whether there's a clear need for you, or whether you have the necessary skills. Elizabeth France, who volunteered in Cameroon, advises:

> *I think it's important to remember that, although you want do to something that you'll find interesting and rewarding, you also want to do something you feel could be useful to the organisation and which will truly benefit them.*

A hypothetical scenario will help illustrate this point. Imagine yourself in the situation of an orphanage with no government support, run by a single devoted individual who wants to improve the lives of people in his or her community. A foreigner turns up on your doorstep offering to lend support. You've never met an international volunteer before and you don't really know whether this stranger has the appropriate skills or attitude, but in your eyes all foreigners are wealthy and any interest and help is appreciated. Not wishing to appear ungrateful, or to refuse them hospitality, you take them in. As it turns out the volunteer ends up being a drain on your resources rather than a help. They don't speak your language, have never cared for children before and require constant supervision. They complain all the time and leave after only a few days, not having paid for their board.

Nobody wants to be a party to that kind of scenario. The last thing you want is to be a burden or a drain on an organisation's resources – it's totally at odds with the concept of ethical volunteering. So bear in mind that as an independent volunteer the onus is on you to ask the right questions and ensure that offering your skills leads to a mutually beneficial outcome. (See p32 for a comprehensive list of appropriate questions to ask an organisation to ensure this).

## FURTHER PREPARATION

If you're arranging the placement before you leave home, then you'll have a hundred and one things to sort out before you leave (for more on this, see Chapter 3). Even if you decide to chance it and find a placement once you arrive

# MINIMISING THE RISKS OF INDEPENDENT VOLUNTEERING

Kristine Randall, who volunteered with United Action for Children (p277) in Cameroon, was aware of the pitfalls involved with undertaking a volunteering role without a large organisation behind her, and took some steps to minimise her worries and the potential risks:

*I chose Cameroon, because I wanted to go to a French-speaking country, but also because I recognised that, organising this trip independently, I wouldn't have a strong support network available if something were to go wrong. I wanted to go to a country that has been relatively stable in the past, and where I would feel relatively safe on my own.*

*I ensured that I registered with my embassy. In preparation, I spoke with previous volunteers and communicated as much as possible with the project director. It truly was my own initiative, my own project, my own time, effort and money and in the end I feel that these factors made for a much more satisfying experience.*

in the country, you will still need to sort out board and lodging and check that you have the appropriate visa.

Without a support network back home and with little, if any, support in country, you need to be aware of the potential risks to your health and safety and general wellbeing, and put together a back-up plan for dealing with emergencies. Critical questions to consider include:

- Is the area politically stable or unstable?
- Are the transport links adequate if I need to get out quickly?
- Where are the nearest medical facilities if I become sick?
- What access do I have to telecommunications?
- Do I have basic knowledge of the local language?

## MAXIMISING YOUR CONTRIBUTION

Wow, that was a lot of effort fixing up an independent placement! Things should run smoothly from here on, as you've asked all the right questions. You can relax now – or can you?

Finding the placement is one thing – actually seeing it through independently requires even more effort and commitment. Here are some wise words from Kirsi Korhonen, who volunteered in Bolivia:

*You need to understand that sometimes things are done differently and not get all worked up about the little things. Living abroad can be hard and you just have to take things as they come. Your attitude is the most important thing. If you think positive, things will go positively. If you let the unknown and the unexpected get you down, you're in trouble. Because the one sure thing about volunteering abroad is that there is always something unexpected, and it's not always good…*

This is the advice of Karla Gergen, who volunteered in Ghana:

*You need to really listen to the people you are working with, to suspend judgement and learn from them. In that process, and through the work that you do, you may be of some use. If you fall into the trap of thinking you can save the world (or this group of people or this place), you will fail. You cannot do that. In order to be of any help, you need to recognise the limits of what you can do.*

The last word on independent volunteering goes to Mary Sears, who volunteered in Bolivia:

*Don't listen when people tell you it's too hard. Every little bit can help in ways grander than you could ever imagine.*

Boarding the Safe Passage/Camino Seguro bus after a day of volunteering in Guatemala.

## DIRECTORIES & USEFUL ORGANISATIONS

These organisations provide the contact details of grassroots organisations and projects that accept volunteers directly.

## INTERNATIONAL ORGANISATIONS

### True Travellers Society

www.truetravellers.org

This Canadian-based website lists worldwide independent volunteering opportunities, which you can search as a non-member by destination or project type. With free membership, you can access the forum and a personal blog, and add your comments to any content on the site.

### VolunteerSouthAmerica.net

www.volunteersouthamerica.net

This online directory lists free and low-cost volunteering opportunities in Central and South America. The lists are driven by user recommendations, so it's advisable to contact returned volunteers and the organisation as well.

## UK ORGANISATIONS

### Volunteer Latin America

www.volunteerlatinamerica.com

Volunteer Latin America provides volunteer opportunities throughout Central and South America. It connects prospective volunteers with grassroots organisations and projects that offer complimentary accommodation, food

and other benefits, with little or no fees. To register a £9 fee applies for a two-year basic membership.

### Worldwide Volunteering

www.worldwidevolunteering.org.uk

This organisation has a database of 3000 volunteer organisations and 1.2 million volunteer opportunities throughout the UK and in 214 countries worldwide. It's possible to search by location, cause (conservation, education etc) and volunteering role.

## NORTH AMERICAN ORGANISATIONS

### Idealist

www.idealist.org

An online initiative of the non-profit Action Without Borders, Idealist. org is perhaps the largest and most comprehensive database of non-profit and community organisations in the world. The website lists over 11,000 volunteering opportunities around the world. Individuals can search the database for domestic and international volunteer and paid opportunities by name, location and area of focus (community development, poverty, civic engagement etc). On the website you can also receive organisation updates, create a customised search profile and participate in online discussions – all free. The site includes a separate section devoted to international volunteering, with informational resources, links and networking tools.

### International Volunteer Programs Association

www.volunteerinternational.org

The International Volunteer Programs Association (IVPA) is is a non-profit accrediting body dedicated to promoting awareness and access to quality volunteer aboard programs. The alliance currently has eight NGO members based in the USA. All member and prospective member organisations are required to adhere to 35 best principles and practices in order to ensure programme quality. IVPA's website has a searchable catalogue of international volunteer positions with these organisations, as well as general advice on volunteering abroad and links to related sites.

## AUSTRALASIAN ORGANISATIONS

### Friends of the Earth

Collingwood, VIC, Australia

☏ +61 3 9419 8700 (ext 20)

www.foe.org.au

FoE is an international network of environmental organisations campaigning on ecological and social justice issues, including climate change, forests, energy and genetic modification. Popular with the greenie set, FoE has a reputation in Australia as a caring and practical environmental organisation. FoE Australia doesn't have a formal volunteer program, but encourages people to liaise with the Collingwood branch to discuss volunteer options in the country.

FoE is active in more than 70 countries and there are volunteer opportunities with some groups. However, many of the international offices are under-resourced and may not have English speakers. For a full listing of FoE member groups worldwide, refer tohttp://www.foei.org/member-groups

### Volunteering Australia Inc

www.volunteeringaustralia.org

This national peak body works to advance volunteering in the Australian community. Volunteering Australia provides information on a wide variety of topics related to volunteering in Australia including the National Standards for Volunteer Involvement. One of its initiatives is the GoVolunteer website (www.govolunteer.com.au), which matches willing volunteers with appropriate opportunities. A GoVolunteer app is now available (visit www.govolunteer.com.au/app for more information).

## GRASSROOTS CHARITIES & NON-PROFITS

These grassroots charities and non-profit organisations all accept volunteers directly.

## OVERSEAS ORGANISATIONS

### Inti Wara Yassi

Cochabamba, Bolivia

☏ +591 44 136572

info@intiwarayassi.org

www.intiwarayassi.org

# FROM MONGOLIA TO LAOS ON A VOLUNTEERING ADVENTURE

I was between jobs and planned to travel, but I wanted it to be a productive time for me and I wanted to contribute to the communities that I was visiting. When I tried to locate volunteer opportunities before I left, I could only find programmes where I had to pay a considerable fee. For this reason, I located places to volunteer through word of mouth while travelling.

I wanted to work with children, since my background is teaching and I have a Master of Education. On the train from Siberia to Mongolia I was fortunate enough to meet an American living in Ulaanbaatar, and I asked him if he knew of an orphanage where I might be of help. He gave me the name of a woman who ran a children's centre there. Before I left Mongolia I asked her if she knew of any programmes in Laos where I could continue volunteering, and she suggested a school in Vientiane.

Once in Laos I was able to secure a position at that school for two months, assisting the English teacher in the classroom and developing curriculum. As part of the latter, I researched and added games and interactive activities to the English programme. Despite finishing the project, I was sad to leave as it wasn't enough time to really become part of the community and to learn the language.

I felt safe when volunteering and I asked for support when needed. Often these schools and organisations are operating on small budgets or with few staff and they need volunteers who can be independent and who don't need much hand-holding. On the other hand, I think volunteers should make sure that they communicate with those in charge when confused or not comfortable with their tasks. This ensures that you are doing what they want and also that you have a good experience.

One piece of advice I'd give is that before you end your time volunteering, try to tie up loose ends and leave clear notes on what you did. Many organisations get so many volunteers coming and going that improvements or suggestions can easily get lost in the shuffle.

Volunteering abroad is an experience that changes you forever. You grow as a person and you meet people who are kind and generous. It was a shame that I was at each of these places for such a short time, but I see fundraising as a way of continuing to make these children's lives better. I think that there is a risk that, as volunteers, we drop into people's lives and have this great, rewarding experience and then we just jet back to our world and simply resume our lives with barely a thought for those we've left behind. For me, it is important to maintain the relationships that I made, in order to honour the kindness and generosity my hosts showed me.

**Sally Armbrecht**

Three wildlife refuge Centres (WCC) in Bolivia that house over 500 animals including monkeys, jaguars, pumas, ocelotes, dozens of birds, tortoises, coatis and other species. All were illegally poached and the refuge aims to offer these animals a second chance of life, and if possible rehabilitate them for re-release into the wild. Volunteers work hard during the day to clean the cages, tend sick animals, maintain the areas and in the evenings enjoy the quiet jungle life with friends from all over the world.

**Status:** Grassroots NGO.

**Timing & Length of Projects:** A minimum 15-day stay. To be able to work with the cats or the bear, a stay of at least 30 days is required. No maximum length of stay.

**Destinations:** Parque Machia in Villa Tunari, WCC Ambue Ari and WCC Jacj Cuisi, all in Bolivia.

**Costs:** US$260 to US$300 for the first 15 nights, US$450 to US$550 for 30 nights, then US$10 to US$12 for each night thereafter. Prices vary according to the park in which you are volunteering.

**Eligibility:** Minimum age is 18. Families are welcome. Volunteers must be willing to work hard to save the animals.

**Annual no. of Volunteers:** 1500.

**Annual Projects:** 3.

**Selection & Interview Process:** Volunteers do not need to apply in advance, as permanent staff believe that the experience of the volunteer is as important as the work they do, and everyone can help.

**In-country Support:** Support is provided at the refuge.

## Safe Passage/Camino Seguro

La Antigua, Guatemala

☎ +502 7832 8428

volunteers@safepassage.org

www.safepassage.org

This organisation provides educational and social support services to children and families living and working in the community surrounding the Guatemala City garbage dump. Volunteers serve in a variety of capacities with students, including providing classroom assistance, one-on-one tutoring and English teaching. They also help with programme management and administrative support.

**Status:** Safe Passage is a registered 501(c) fundraising charity in the USA. In Guatemala, Camino Seguro is the operational part of the organisation and is a registered NGO.

**Timing & Length of Projects:** Projects operate 11 months out of the year (closed in December); the minimum stay is five weeks.

**Destinations:** Guatemala City, although volunteers live in La Antigua.

**Costs:** Volunteers are responsible for a nomimal application fee and for covering the cost of their transport and living expenses while in country. There is a limited number of long-term housing stipends available for key positions. Visit www.safepassage.org/get-involved/volunteer for more details.

**Eligibility:** The minimum age is 18, and you must pass the criminal background test.

**Annual no. of Volunteers:** 200.

Safe Passage provides support services to children and families living in Guatemala City

Photo: © Safe Passage/Comino Seguro

Selection & Interview Process: Volunteers must complete an application form and submit references.

In-country Support: The volunteer department provides help with transportation from the airport, Spanish school, accomodation with local families, orientation, placement, general support and management.

## United Action for Children

Muyuka, Cameroon

✆ +237 7772 0418/+237 9785 8394

unitedactionforc@yahoo.com

www.unitedactionforchildren.org

This organisation, which is committed to developing a caring society for children and young people, offers volunteering roles in education, vocational training, economic and agricultural development, IT, accounting, fundraising and general HIV/AIDS awareness.

Status: Registered grassroots NGO.

Timing & Length of Projects: Projects are available all year round; the minimum placement is three weeks; the maximum is six months.

Destinations: Cameroon.

Costs: Two weeks costs US$165, one month US$305, a second month is an extra US$165, and any subsequent months cost US$165.

Eligibility: The minimum age is 18 years. Clean criminal records are required for all volunteers.

Annual no. of Volunteers: 60.

Annual Projects: 5.

Partner Programmes: 4.

Selection & Interview Process: Applicants must submit their CV in advance.

In-country Support: United Action for Children provides transport for volunteers from the airport to project.

# 09

## Coming Home

As the saying goes, 'All good things must come to an end.' But how will you feel once your volunteering stint is over, and what long-term impact will volunteering have on your life back home?

# LEAVING

When you're volunteering, you throw yourself heart and soul into a project. As Michelle Hawkins, who volunteered in Ghana and Costa Rica with Raleigh International (p151), says:

*You end up putting a lot more energy into work overseas as the need is so much greater.*

This often means you make strong bonds with the people you work with which can make it hard when the time comes to leave your volunteer programme. Kate Sturgeon, who volunteered in Zimbabwe with MSF (p181), remembers:

*It was quite hard to leave. After 16 months I'd become very attached to all my patients, the staff and the work I'd put into the clinic. The clinic put on a wonderful send-off party where all the staff said a few words and we had a special lunch (take-away pizza, which is a real treat in the clinic!) and they gave me some leaving presents. Then a friend of mine also organised a farewell party at the MSF house where we were living and a surprise band, which was fantastic. They had to drag me to the airport the next day, I really didn't want to leave.*

Jacqueline Hill volunteered for a year with VSO (p175) in Bangladesh and felt the same way:

*There is a strong tradition of celebration at Dipshikha. I not only had more than one 'leaving do' with speeches and gifts, but they also put on a party with cake, balloons and a photographer for my 40th birthday. Leaving was quite an emotional time, as I realised that I might never see these people who I had spent one of the most significant years of my life with again.*

If you have volunteered with children, become part of their lives and started to care about them, leaving can be heartbreaking. Poonam Sattee who worked with street kids in Guatemala, recalls:

*I was incredibly upset leaving. I felt like I was abandoning the children – particularly as they equated 'needing to leave' with 'wanting to leave' and they couldn't understand the difference. Before I left, I organised a thank-you party for the children to say thanks for everything they shared with me: the fun times, their patience with me and for accepting me like a friend. I was given lots of handmade cards with messages that were incredibly beautiful and meant a lot – my emotions were really running high that day.*

And it is not that much easier if you have volunteered as a team member on an environmental rather than development project. Robin Glegg, who has volunteered on three separate expeditions in the Altai, Namibia and Oman with Biosphere Expeditions (p216), says:

*On all three expeditions there was a sense of deflation and disappointment that they were coming to an end. Everybody bonds, enjoys the work and the time just goes too quickly.*

## REVERSE CULTURE SHOCK

It is hard to know which is greater: the cultural unease that you can feel when you start your placement, or the shock of life back in your home country when you return. Reverse culture shock is a perfectly natural thing to experience on coming home.

Poonam Sattee found it very hard to adjust after one year in Guatemala:

*I hated being home! I think the biggest culture shock was when I was sent into the supermarket by my mum to buy some tinned tomatoes. I was used to buying plain fresh tomatoes from the market! I went into the aisle for tinned veg and saw tinned tomatoes, chopped tomatoes, tomatoes with peppers, tomatoes in juice, brined tomatoes, tomatoes in salsa etc, and I pretty much had a breakdown in the aisle (tears and everything). I couldn't understand the consumer society we live in where we sell about 25 different varieties of tomatoes. It was ridiculous.*

After 12 months in Bangladesh, it was mayonnaise that did it to Jacqueline Hill:

*I felt quite numb for a few months. I put off seeing people for the first couple of weeks because it was enough just to absorb being with family and in a modern, Western house again. I went to the supermarket one day and was paralysed by the choices available. 'Mayonnaise' said the list. There were two rows of different types. How to decide? In Bangladesh there was only ever one of anything, if it was available at all! I regret having everything available all the time. I loved the seasonality of food in Bangladesh. I miss the excitement of the run-up to the very short lychee season and the gloriously long mango season. My first trip on the London Underground felt like I was in some kind of nightmare, futuristic movie. No-one smiled and they were all wearing black and grey.*

It's not just the abundance and waste of commodities that returned volunteers find hard to accept, but the values and attitudes of people back home. Kate Sturgeon remembers:

*I found everyone incredibly superficial and preoccupied with how they looked and what people thought about them and all those neuroses everyone has. Compared to how I had been living, it all seemed grossly out of proportion. I found it very hard working back at the hospital, as I was overwhelmed with the amount of drugs, resources and equipment; I was so sad and angry thinking about how little we had in Zimbabwe where the real need is. I also hated the way patients expect so much here and are forever complaining. They just don't realise how much they have. Everything is taken for granted.*

Elaine Massie and Richard Lawson, who have volunteered on some 15 wildlife projects, agree wholeheartedly:

*It has made us realise how lucky we are and how much we as a society take for granted. In Mexico very little is thrown away, even old nails are taken out of wood to be reused, yet we live in a throwaway society where just about everything is disposable.*

These experiences certainly make you stop and think which society is 'developing' one. But what about friends and family; do they help you get back into the swing of things back home? It's hard to generalise, but Poonam Sattee says:

*Talking to friends and family was hard as my life there, the culture, my living conditions etc were so different. They just couldn't comprehend why I found it so difficult to adjust.*

However, coming home is a much more positive experience for some volunteers. Ann Noon, who volunteered in Peru for 10 months, recalls:

*At first it was almost as if I hadn't been away. I'd expected to have trouble settling back in, but really I just slipped right into my old ways – probably because it was just so great to see people again and be back in my flat. It was probably three months down the line when I realised that I was restless and missing the beauty of the Sacred Valley around Cusco.*

And, even for Jacqueline Hill, who had trouble readjusting after a year in Bangladesh, there were compensations for being home in the UK. As well as creature comforts, there was the reassuring thought that she'd left certain creatures behind:

*I had to get used to not reacting to flying insects which were unlikely to bite me and creepy crawlies which were likely to be nothing more alarming than small spiders. I could also leave a glass of juice on the table without finding it full of ants! I found sleeping without a mosquito net quite unnerving at first, but gloried in being able to leave the washing-up knowing that it would survive without becoming overrun by cockroaches!*

# SETTLING BACK IN

Resuming your life back home after a placement requires practical planning. For many people, it also means establishing links that will help them to integrate their volunteering experience into their life in a meaningful and rewarding way for the long term.

## DEBRIEFING

Many organisations have a formal process of following-up with returned volunteers. For medium- and long-term volunteers who have worked in development, a face-to-face debrief interview is often arranged. Kate Sturgeon explains:

*I had one debriefing session in Barcelona with Médecins Sans Frontières Spain, who I had gone out to Zimbabwe with, and I had another session in the MSF UK office, talking to different people: human resources; communications; managers etc. I felt like I had a lot of support. Some people asked to see a counsellor if they'd seen a lot of trauma, but I felt OK just talking to MSF and friends and family.*

A debrief is an excellent opportunity to talk about what you did, what it was like and how you feel at the end of it. It is also a chance to offer constructive feedback on the organisation's procedures and systems and suggest improvements. Poonam Sattee, who worked with street children for one year, says:

*I went to the office and talked the experience through, which really helped put perspective on the year. I gave recommendations on how certain things could be improved or changed. Debriefing helped me begin to build positively on the experience and go forward, as opposed to just missing being there.*

Some organisations make a whole day or weekend out of the debriefing experience. Kerry Davies, who volunteered in Cambodia for two and a half years, remembers:

*At first I buried my head in the sand, but then I attended a VSO Returned Volunteer Weekend and realised I was feeling the same as everyone else. I felt much better afterwards.*

Sometimes a debrief may simply take the form of a questionnaire sent out to all returned volunteers, possibly followed up by a telephone call. Other organisations email out debrief information, as Martyn Roberts, who has volunteered on six environmental expeditions, explains:

*Biosphere Expeditions has an email debrief package that every volunteer is sent immediately after each 'slot'. The page includes information on when the expedition report will be out, details of their website where photos can be shared, and information on the alumni network and the Friends of Biosphere organisation.*

Of course, if you choose to find a volunteer placement yourself, you will forgo any support when you return to your home country. Also, post-placement 'after care' is not a feature of all sending agencies; so if you think this service will be important to you, ask about follow-up procedures.

## MEDICAL CHECKS

As well as debriefing, it is wise to arrange a thorough medical examination once you arrive home. Try to have this done with a specialist organisation that knows what to look for in returned volunteers. In the UK your best option is **InterHealth** (☎ +44 (0)20 7902 9000; info@interhealth.org.uk; www.interhealthworldwide.org; 63-67 Newington Causeway, London, SE1 6BD), a charity that specialises in healthcare for humanitarian, development and mission workers.

**The International Society of Travel Medicine** (☎ +1 404 373 8282; istm@ istm.org; www.istm.org; 315W Ponce de Leon Ave, Suite 245, Decatur GA 30030, USA) offers an extensive online directory of travel medicine practitioners specialising in immunisations and post-trip consultations throughout the world. In Australia, the **Travel Doctor** (www.tmvc.com.au) offers medical reviews for returned volunteers who may have been ill while away or who may be symptomatic upon return.

## RETURNED VOLUNTEER NETWORKS

If you volunteer for a short while only, it is likely you'll pick up your life where you left off. Even so, your experience might set you apart from those closest to you, which is hard when you want to talk in-depth about what happened, how you feel, and what you want to do with your experience. As Jacqueline Hill says:

*I developed a very short response to the question 'How was it?' as most people had very short attention spans.*

If you volunteer medium- or long-term, the sense of 'otherness' at having done something that most people don't fully comprehend is 10 times greater. Your debrief will help process these feelings, but often you'll crave some longer-term mechanism for continued support and involvement with volunteering.

Many sending agencies recognise this and actively encourage you to stay in touch, not only with themselves, but with other returned volunteers as well. Some have a magazine or email newsletter that you can sign up to – there also may be opportunities for you to contribute to these publications. Others may have a more formal network for returned volunteers. Martyn Roberts, who has volunteered in Namibia, the Azores, Slovakia, Sri Lanka and Brazil, explains:

*I have stayed in touch with Biosphere Expeditions ever since my first volunteering expedition with them. They have an alumni network comprised of people who have been on two or more expeditions, and who offer to be points of contact for potential volunteers and to stay in email contact with other returned volunteers. They also provide journalists and others with information on what it is like to be on an expedition. The organisation also encourages you to join Friends of Biosphere Expeditions, which is a support network of people who want to become or stay actively involved.*

Once you come home, you'll realise that there are hundreds of different ways you can still be part of the world you left behind. For Oliver Walker, who volunteered in Sri Lanka, it worked this way:

*MondoChallenge asked me to interview potential volunteers in the light of my experiences.*

And, Kate Sturgeon explains:

*I often go to MSF meetings, scientific days or nights out and I've done interviews for them and talks at universities. They keep in touch with me via email or phone.*

Many North American international volunteer organisations have strong alumni networks to support returned volunteers. Perhaps the largest is the **National Peace Corps Association** (www.rpcv.org), which has affiliate branches throughout the USA. Even if your organisation doesn't formally sponsor a returned volunteer network, alumni frequently run internet-, app- or social media-based groups and local social chapters on their own.

Most organised volunteer programmes in Australia and New Zealand offer some form of debriefing or networking. Programmes like Australian Volunteers for International Development (AVID, see Scope Global, p155; and AVI p164) and and Volunteer Service Abroad (VSA, p165) have excellent post-volunteering options.

If you did not volunteer through an organisation in your home country, you may miss not being part of any formal returned volunteer network in your part of the world. If this is the case, contact an umbrella organisation that represents the views of international aid and development agencies in your country. There is a list of these with contact details on p291.

## MONEY

If you are a short-term volunteer, chances are you didn't give up your job or accommodation before going overseas. However, if you volunteered for longer and didn't manage to negotiate extended time out from your employer, settling back in at home may involve a degree of financial planning.

Some of the larger sending agencies that dispatch skilled volunteers overseas long term offer a resettlement grant to returned volunteers. If you don't volunteer with one of these, you might have to budget (see p69) for your return home. Depending on your personal and professional circumstances, money is often required to untie all those 'loose ends' covered in Chapter 4, like finding a job or somewhere to live.

Sian Davies, who volunteered in Tanzania for two years, makes this point succinctly:

*If you're away for some time, you have no credit rating so you have to pay upfront for rent etc. Make sure you have a few thousand saved up for when you return.*

## JOB-HUNTING

If you are returning home from a longish volunteering stint, one of your primary considerations is likely to be finding yourself a job. The good news is that in most cases international volunteering is an asset on your CV and should

# VIRTUAL VOLUNTEERING

Writer Isaac Asimov said 'I do not fear computers – I fear the lack of them', and certainly in this age of technology haves and have-nots, access to information is at the cutting edge of raising living standards worldwide. It was predicted that the entire human race would be online by 2016, and while this did not happen, it's conceivable that it won't be long off. This digital shift continues to change the face of sustainable development. It's no surprise then that a new space for 'virtual volunteering' has emerged on the information superhighway. Virtual volunteering refers to volunteer tasks completed, in whole or in part, via the internet. It's for people searching for volunteer opportunities they can complete via computer because of time constraints, personal preference, a disability or a home-based obligation that prevents them from volunteering on-site. Virtual volunteering allows anyone to contribute time and expertise to organisations that utilise volunteer services, without leaving home.

But how do you get involved in virtual volunteering? The **United Nations** has set up a website promoting an online volunteer service (www.onlinevolunteering. org) to bring development organisations together with people who can contribute their skills and expertise online, from administrative staff to translators to web designers. You can register on the website and then browse through a database of projects. You can also search for virtual volunteering opportunities worldwide on the **Volunteermatch** website (www.volunteermatch.org/search).

And you can always keep an eye out for your own virtual volunteering opportunities. Spotted a small-scale weaving operation in Southeast Asia that could benefit from having a website designed for it, for instance? Travelling is a great way to spot grassroots organisations that could do with an extra set of hands.

be highlighted as opposed to buried. Many volunteers choose to list it as one of their achievements, showing fully what skills they learnt and developed while away. It is also a subject that often comes up in job interviews – employers can be genuinely interested in what you did, what it was like and how you think it was of benefit.

John Lees, career coach and best-selling author of *Take Control of your Career* and *How To Get a Job You'll Love*, says:

*International volunteering is great for your CV because it shows resourcefulness and imagination (choosing and planning to do it), and also gives you a broader perspective on the world. The danger is that the experience says little to a recruiter. Communicate why you did it, what you learned and achieved, and how this experience makes you a smarter/sharper/wiser employee!*

If possible, you should also try to obtain a reference from a key person on your volunteer programme. If you have difficulties arranging this, a reference from the sending agency or charity you volunteered with will be just as good.

## CHANGING CAREERS

Karen Hedges is very clear about what nine months of volunteering did for her life, career (and hair):

*Volunteering literally changed my life. It enabled me to change careers and I am now doing something I truly love (working in the press office of an international development charity). It also taught me that I CAN live without a hairdryer (if I have to).*

When you volunteer overseas you step out of your usual environment and step back from your current life and your profession. This gives you an unusual degree of objectivity, which can lead to reassessing your career and life choices.

A significant percentage of international volunteers come home and decide to change their career paths, go freelance or start their own businesses. For example, Jacqueline Hill returned to consultancy work when she came back to England from Bangladesh, but only for four days a week. On the fifth day she volunteered for the charity **WaterAid** (✆+44 (0)20 7793 4500; wateraid@wateraid.org; www.wateraid.org; London, UK) and **Hope and Homes for Children** (✆+44 (0)1722 790111; info@hopeandhomes.org; www.hopeandhomes.org; Salisbury, Wiltshire, UK). Six months later she set up as a sole trader offering management consultancy services to the charity sector at substantially reduced rates. Similarly, Katherine Tubb worked in tourism, but after she volunteered with VSO (p175) she returned home and set up her own not-for-profit volunteering sending organisation.

Interestingly, some returned volunteers end up working for the sending agency they volunteered with. After doing a masters degree in marine biology, Jan-Willem van Bochove worked as a postman before volunteering with Coral Cay Conservation (p170):

*I was a Project Scientist and Expedition Leader on two Coral Cay Conservation projects in Southern Leyte in the Philippines and Marsa Alam in Egypt. I was working voluntarily to oversee the science programme, give scientific training to volunteers, set up Marine Protected Areas and do community work to increase awareness of the issue and help local people to develop their coral reefs in a sustainable manner. When I was in Egypt, the founder and Managing Director of Coral Cay Conservation called me and asked if I would be interested in a paid position as the Chief Technical Adviser on the Southern Leyte project. I said 'yes' immediately and am now responsible for writing up the final reports, analysing the data and overseeing the scientific work.*

Of course, not only can volunteering enhance your CV, it can also give you valuable work experience so you can change your career in a more strategic way when you come home. This is what Michelle Hawkins, who volunteered in Costa Rica and Ghana, did:

*I consciously chose to use my career break as a springboard into the charity and aid sector. Job ads frequently state that you need experience in the sector. How can you get the experience unless you already have a job in that sector? It's a Catch-22. My solution was to pay to be a volunteer staff member on two Raleigh International expeditions. This made my transition into the competitive charity sector easier. I also got the Raleigh International Expedition leaders to write me two references that I attached to my CV when applying for jobs. It took me a year of applying, but I did it! I now work for the international aid organisation Médecins du Monde as the communications and fundraising officer.*

## NEXT STEPS

Depending on what you did and how long you were away for, it can take between six and 12 months for you to settle back in properly, sometimes longer. In many cases, a volunteer experience is not something you can, or want to, forget. Often you will wish to integrate it into your life in some way. Some returned volunteers do this by changing careers, others by becoming more involved with their charity or sending agency in their own country. Others do it by volunteering locally or even internationally again.

# LONGER-TERM LINKS

It is often possible to maintain ongoing links with volunteer sending agencies once you return home. After two and a half years of volunteering in Cambodia, Kerry Davies says:

*I am now on the VSO steering committee. I am also an email and telephone contact person for prospective volunteers either in the health sector or in Cambodia.*

Poonam Sattee has gone one step further:

*I stay in contact with the kids. I regularly send them cards, some are in email contact with me and at Christmas I send out presents. I am also a newly appointed trustee for the charity in the UK and that has helped me to still feel part of the organisation and to still be part of the lives of the kids in an indirect way. I also fundraise for them.*

And, Karen Hedges, who travelled to the Indian Ocean with SEED Madagascar (p168), has also become involved with the charity at this higher level. She explains:

*When I came home I was keen to stay involved. After spending nine months living and working in Madagascar I felt I could not just come home and forget about the projects and the people. The managing director saw that I was keen to stay involved and approached me about becoming a trustee. We have four or five trustee meetings per year, which usually happen on a Sunday and take up most of the day. We discuss how the charity is run by analysing income and expenditure, fundraising ideas, web content, strategic planning and the volunteer scheme. What I like about being a trustee is that you get involved in all aspects of the charity. All trustees have different backgrounds so that helps us to bring different expertise to the charity.*

Sarah Turton volunteered as an art, photography and English teacher in Ghana after she'd finished her Postgraduate Certificate in Education (PGCE). When she came home she started her first proper teaching job in her home country. Ten months later she explains:

*I am developing the link between the school in Ghana and the one I am now teaching in. A Year 7 group has done the same photography project and next month we are exhibiting both sets of work and raising money through sales and donations for both the school and the organisation. In the longer term, we are hoping to take a team of teachers out on a research trip with a view to getting an exchange programme up and running, plus enhancing all areas of both curricula.*

You might also establish longer-term links on a more personal level. When Jacqueline Hill left Bangladesh she thought she might never see the people she worked with again, but as she says:

*As it turned out, I went back to visit in 2005 and hope to host a visit by two of my former colleagues to the UK this year.*

## VOLUNTEER LOCALLY

As the old saying goes, 'Charity starts at home.' If you've travelled to the ends of the earth to volunteer and are now hooked, there are plenty of volunteering opportunities in your home country.

In the UK one of the best places to start researching the options is at your local volunteer centre. Otherwise, there are a number of useful websites that have comprehensive databases of volunteering opportunities in your area:

## UK WEBSITES

• **Do-it.org.uk** (www.do-it.org.uk) Lists over 1.5 million volunteering opportunities in the UK. It is free to register.

• **Timebank** (www.timebank.org.uk) Register your details and receive a list of organisations in your area that need volunteers.

• **vinspired** (http://vinspired.com) Aimed at 16- to 24-year-olds, this site encourages young people to devote a period of time to volunteering. Certificates are awarded for 50 and 150 hours volunteering.

• **Volunteer Development Scotland** (www.vds.org.uk) National volunteer development organisation for Scotland.

• **Volunteer Now** (www.volunteernow.co.uk) Promotes, develops and supports volunteering across Northern Ireland.

• **Volunteering England** (www.volunteering.org.uk) National volunteer development organisation for England.

• **Volunteering Matters** (www.volunteeringmatters.org.uk) It engages 30,000 volunteers every year to focus on the needs of young people, disabled people, families and senior citizens.

• **Wales Council for Voluntary Action** (www.wcva.org.uk) The voice of the voluntary sector in Wales.

## NORTH AMERICAN WEBSITES

• **AmeriCorps** (www.americorps.gov) Often dubbed 'the domestic Peace Corps,' AmeriCorps offers community service opportunities lasting 10 months to a year throughout the USA.

• **CoolWorks** (www.coolworks.com/volunteer) This database lists volunteer jobs in great places in the US, many in national parks.

• **Mercy Volunteer Corps** (www.mercyvolunteers.org) In partnership with the Sisters of Mercy, MVC promotes social change by placing and supporting volunteers for one year of service with people who are poor and marginalised in the USA and South America. Volunteers work in education, healthcare, and social services while living together in community and growing spiritually.

• **Serve.gov** (www.serve.gov) Established by President Bush in 2002, USA Freedom Corps links individuals to local service opportunities.

• **Teach for America** (www.teachforamerica.org) A vehicle for recent college grads to teach in underprivileged schools across the US.

• **Volunteer Canada** (www.volunteer.ca) With Volunteer Centres offering local service positions throughout Canada, Volunteer Canada is one of the nation's most prominent forums on volunteering.

• **VolunteerMatch** (www.volunteermatch.org) Over 40,000 American non-profit organisations recruit through this site.

## AUSTRALASIAN WEBSITES

• **Volunteering Australia** (www.volunteeringaustralia.org) This is the peak body promoting volunteering in Australia.

• **Volunteering New Zealand** (www.volunteeringnz.org.nz) Promotes and supports volunteering in that country.

## VOLUNTEER INTERNATIONALLY...AGAIN

For some, volunteering abroad just once is not enough. Whether you want or are able to commit to another placement depends very much on your personal circumstances.

Deborah Jordan and David Spinney, who volunteered in Ethiopia with VSO (p175), are both retired, so they have a little more time:

*We are in contact with other returned volunteers and VSO in London, and have friends in many parts of the world. We have recently been to a meeting to discuss strategies for recruiting more 'mature' volunteers. And, yes, we have just re-volunteered ourselves and are looking forward to discussing options with our placement officer!*

Catherine Baroun, who has volunteered on a number of wildlife programmes with Earthwatch (p211), says:

*I can't stop myself now. This year I am heading to Kenya with Earthwatch to do a Forest Monkey Survey. Next year I am hoping to find a longer volunteering project to celebrate my 40th birthday.*

And as she explains, her volunteering doesn't interfere with her full-time job:

*Projects I have participated in have ranged from five to 13 days, so I have just booked the time off work.*

Martyn Roberts, who works full time but spends his holidays volunteering, is in a similar boat:

*Having done one I knew as soon as I got back home that it was something I would do again. I think I've become something of a volunteering addict. Since my first expedition in November 2002, I have always had the next one planned.*

However, a short-term conservation or wildlife programme that you can easily fit into a busy professional life is very different to a long-term development placement. Kate Sturgeon admits:

*Yes, I'd definitely like to do another volunteer placement but I needed to have a substantial rest when I came back. I felt quite exhausted by the whole process, however positive it was, and I really felt I needed to recharge my batteries before going again. I also have commitments in my current job and have to give two months' notice before leaving, so I think I will go again but not until next year.*

# 10

## Start Your Own Charitable Project

You may not fancy yourself as a budding Mother Teresa or Princess Di – but chances are that if you're reading this chapter, you've been overseas, have seen a need and want to do something substantial to alleviate it. Perhaps you identified this need as an international volunteer; maybe it presented itself to you while you were travelling, or perhaps you've spent years doing business in a region and feel that it's time to give something back. Whatever your motivations are, starting up your own aid organisation can be fulfilling and exciting. It can also be hard work and a lifelong commitment.

What you aim to do could take many forms. The organisation you set up might turn out to be a volunteer-sending agency, a fundraising charity, or it might simply involve you raising money at home and returning to a particular place to make tangible improvements. While these all sound like noble aims, it is important to remember that even the most well-intentioned efforts can create more problems than they solve by inappropriately injecting funds, volunteers or projects into an area on the basis of a presumed 'need'. To avoid such a negative outcome, it's crucial that your project is based on local participation and that it aims for sustainability. You need to be sure that the local community is fundamentally supportive of what you're proposing and that you're in it for the long haul. With these things in mind, the rest of this chapter will give some starting points from which to embark upon the adventure of a lifetime.

# THE IDEA

This may seem obvious, but first and foremost you need to have an idea. In many cases, this is sparked by something you've experienced and a desire to 'do something' about it. Alex Tarrant, co-founder of Pod Volunteer (p208), describes the dawning of the idea that gave rise to his organisation:

> *It all started in the summer of 2001 when Mike, Rach and I (old friends and now business partners) spent time in Tanzania, volunteering our time to help set up a small British charity. It was an amazing trip that turned out to be career changing for all of us. One of the ideas that came out of the work was to recruit volunteers from the UK to go and work with the charity in Tanzania, and this led to us starting Pod Volunteer.*

The fact is, you may have hundreds of ideas, but trimming them down to the core aims of an organisation is essential. To arrive at this point, some of the searching questions you might need to ask yourself are: What is it that I want to achieve? How do I plan to go about it? Has it been done before? Is there a genuine community need for the services I envisage? Whose experiences can I learn from? A good way to kick off the process is to get out there and talk to as many people as possible, to find out how others got started, the obstacles they encountered on the way, and soak up any advice they're willing to dole out. Details of NGOs worth approaching can be found on the websites listed in the Getting Help section on p304.

## AIM FOR A PARTICIPATORY PROJECT

The crux of a successful project is that it's participatory. This means more than simply talking to the local people where you plan to initiate your project. It means that the idea for the project should essentially come from them. It also means including them at every step: discussing the project with them; taking their views and ideas on board; and giving them as much hands-on involvement as possible – including involving them in the day-to-day running of the project. In essence, it means working *with* the local community towards a common goal.

It is important to stay in regular contact with the local community to ensure that the community remains supportive of the project and that it's continuing to meet their needs. It also helps if your project has the capacity to evolve

# MORE HARM THAN GOOD

The Teach Ghana Trust was a UK-based charity established to advance the education of children in Ghana. The founders' motivation for setting up the Trust was a frustration with many volunteer-sending agencies who didn't appear to be prioritising the needs of the overseas communities in which they were operating. In reaction to this, the Trust aimed to arrange volunteer teaching placements in schools in Ghana with the needs of the children being the absolute priority. However, as the trustees developed their programme and began to interview for volunteer placements, they began to seriously question the consequences of their volunteer placements and whether or not they had chosen an appropriate means of achieving their initial goals. After three years the Trust voted not to pursue any further volunteer placements.

While this may seem like an odd move, it is worth considering some of the reasons that prompted the Trust to end its volunteering programme:

• It knew that, as an organisation, it was in a good position to arrange placements in schools in Ghana. However, it wanted to make sure that any volunteering scheme it implemented was offering real, long-term and sustainable solutions to the issues it was seeking to resolve.

• The Trust did not want to make schools in Ghana reliant on volunteers. There was a danger that a reliance on volunteers would lead to schools not recruiting Ghanaians to teach, which would not be good for employment levels and the domestic economy.

• Equally, the Teach Ghana Trust had no guarantee that it would be able to send out volunteers consistently – in fact numbers would fluctuate throughout the year. As such, it would not be able to guarantee a consistent service to schools, making it difficult for them to plan effectively.

• The majority of the applicants were unqualified. The Trust was anxious that it could not be sure that it was arranging a placement for somebody who would make an able teacher and who would be of real benefit to the children they taught.

• There were already a number of organisations which offered excellent volunteering schemes and the Trust did not want to duplicate their work, or increase competition for volunteers and funding that are so badly needed elsewhere.

Ultimately, the goal for the Teach Ghana Trust would be for schools in Ghana to no longer require volunteers, but to be able to teach pupils with a staff of trained, salaried Ghanaian teachers. The trustees believe that a better way to ensure this would be to act as a charity that supports a greater number of able locals being trained as teachers.

along with the community's needs. Key ways to ensure that a project remains participatory and well connected to the community include employing locals as project managers and staff and basing the organisation in the overseas community, rather than as a satellite in your own country. Alex Tarrant talks about embracing participatory elements when implementing Pod Volunteer projects (note the strong presence of the word 'local' in his description):

*Most of our projects are 'local' projects, driven and managed by the local community. In other cases, the local community is always involved and all our projects are evaluated on their benefit to the local community... We either respond to local requests to provide volunteers or we approach local projects and ask if they would like volunteers. We feel [spending time in the overseas communities] is important, and that is why we either have our own staff in each country, or we work with an organisation or charity that is based there. It is very important to keep in touch with the local communities and we feel it is also essential to have strong local support for volunteers. From the UK, we make visits each year to our overseas projects.*

Anthony Lunch founded the MondoChallenge Foundation on the back of MondoChallenge (p205), a volunteer-sending agency he'd previously initiated. When asked how much the local communities participate in the charity's projects, he provides great examples of the extent to which an organisation's work can be driven by the community:

*In every conceivable way! They often provide the on-site work, with materials funded by the Foundation. Sometimes they are teachers at the school we support with desks, books and sports equipment. When we fund the 'seeds projects', whereby kids are encouraged to learn about growing plants they can then eat to supplement their diet, the teachers are the local organisers and we merely provide the small grants needed to set the project up. Our HIV Small Grants Programme in Tanzania and Gambia is totally run by local volunteers, backed up by MondoChallenge. We only work with organisations who have demonstrated their commitment over a period of time.*

While participation may seem like an obvious component of any aid initiative, in reality constant vigilance and an ongoing commitment are required to ensure that it endures for the life of the project.

## AIM FOR SUSTAINABILITY

Working towards sustainability is one of the biggest challenges faced by volunteering organisations. Organisations and their projects (or programmes) should aim for a long lifespan, and come to an end only when the original goal is achieved or the instigating needs are alleviated. What they should not be about is the knee-jerk dumping of resources, money or volunteers into a community on projects that will rapidly peter out. To build the trust of a community and to see the effects of your work, you will need to be both committed and patient. The aims of most aid projects are ongoing – things like counteracting environmental degradation or decreasing poverty are obviously not issues that are solved overnight. One of the fundamental aspects of programmes based on sustainable action is that they're underpinned by empowerment rather than charity. They're about helping people to help themselves and to achieve their own goals, rather than simply ladling out aid.

Examples of ways projects can be sustainable include:
• Training members of the local community in a needed occupation such as teaching, medicine, IT or anything else identified by the community.
• Providing practical knowledge in things like nutrition or first aid.
• Helping to establish local, income-generating enterprises.
• Assisting in improving people's living conditions as a means of improving health and increasing confidence.
• Helping to set up ecotourism projects.

Even a project that initially appears sustainable can play out differently in reality; for an example of this, see the box More Harm Than Good (p297). It's therefore crucial to constantly re-evaluate the work of your organisation to ensure it's continuing to foster sustainable outcomes.

## COMMUNICATING ACROSS CULTURES

You think you've got your idea all sorted out. You've discussed it at length with the local community, they've given their consent and you've shaken on it. But can you be sure that nodding actually means 'yes' in the local body language? It might just mean 'maybe'. Or it could even mean a flat 'no'. And do handshakes mean anything at all in the local culture?

# GETTING FUNDING

Good news. There are thousands of charitable foundations, many of which exist for the sole purpose of giving grants. However, the size and form these foundations can take varies enormously. Some give nationally and others internationally, while others only give to organisations in a particular region. Some give to a variety of causes, others to organisations pursuing specific goals such as work with children or healthcare. Some give millions every year, others give only a few hundred here and there. But the bottom line is: they all give.

Foundations tend to fund projects that offer aid to disadvantaged groups. Of the more than £2 billion given by foundations annually in the UK, for example, by far the largest chunk goes towards health and social-welfare initiatives. A decent-sized portion of the pie goes towards arts and recreation and a smaller slice goes to faith-based projects. As foundations' funds come from private endowments and the like, their funding is not geared towards what's trendy in mainstream society or a particular government; instead they give to whatever takes their fancy.

Some foundations are very well known for their generous giving – for instance the Wellcome Trust, the Joseph Rowntree Foundation and the Diana, Princess of Wales Memorial Trust. Nevertheless, if you're looking to apply for funds, don't just go for the big fish. Filling out funding applications is a mammoth task, taking up lots of time and energy, and so the first, fundamental step is to wade through the various options and select those most likely to look favourably upon your cause. The next step is filling out the application, making sure it's tailored to the foundation's criteria, and that it's clear about your goals and gives specifics as to how you will spend the funds.

See the Association of Charitable Foundations (p304), Foundation Center (p305) or Philanthropy Australia (p306) for help and resources. UK residents should also check out the Directory of Social Change (www.dsc.org.uk) for guides to UK trusts.

Open and mutually understood communication is essential to establishing a participatory and sustainable project. And while you may be adept at communicating at home, throw a foreign culture into the mix and you might just be left wondering which way is up – or worse, believing that you've got a deal sewn up when the local community is actually completely opposed to your proposal.

Cross-cultural misunderstandings can stem from issues with spoken language, body language and etiquette. In some cultures, for instance, there are 20 ways of saying 'yes' but half of these actually mean 'no'. In other cultures, women are unable to speak openly or express their views in the presence of men. Some cultures equate being direct with being rude and pushy. In other cultures, spitting is not considered bad mannered but blowing your nose into a hanky and stuffing it into your pocket is truly rude. Even seemingly trivial things such as the colour of the ink that you choose to write in can cause offence. Showing the soles of your feet can be taken as an insult, and touching (or not touching) the person you're speaking to can be taken amiss. You must also be aware that within any one country subcultures exist based on factors such as gender, ethnicity and social status and that differing communication strategies might be required within these.

Kalene Caffarella, International Partnership Manager at the Australian Red Cross, was previously at intercultural consultant for 11 years and offers some great starting points for successful exchanges:

> Showing respect for the local community in which you are volunteering is the first step in avoiding cross-cultural miscommunication. It is crucial not only to see things from the local point of view, but to be able to respect that point of view as valid and logical. Ask yourself how a local person would go about accomplishing the task that you want to accomplish. Would they communicate in a direct manner, or would they use indirect communication to get their message across? Would people need to build trust with others before they begin working together, or would they focus on the task alone?
>
> For example, you may want to go into a meeting with local community members to brainstorm ideas or give feedback on project progress. If locals see the purpose of a meeting as simply getting information from the local head, then chances are you may not get any input. Think, instead, of how locals would gather suggestions. Be aware of the strategies they use and adapt to doing things their way.

While communicating across cultures is likely to lead to at least a few misunderstandings, there are ways to minimise them. Many adult educational institutions offer cross-cultural introductory courses and, depending on where you are planning to work, you may find that a cultural centre exists in your home country where you can discuss possible barriers or differences. Also check out chapters on culture and etiquette in guidebooks, and visit the country's official tourism website. Arm yourself with as much knowledge and awareness as possible and remember to keep an open mind.

# GETTING IT ROLLING

## COMMITTING YOUR TIME & MONEY

How long it takes to set up an aid organisation, the amount of money you'll need, and the number of hours you'll need to commit, depends greatly on the size and breadth of the project you're setting up and whether or not there's already an infrastructure in place upon which to build. It may require five hours per month, or 50 depending on circumstances. For instance, Katherine Tubb spent a year researching, developing and planning a new volunteer sending agency and had this to say about her experience of setting up a larger organisation:

*The actual registration of the organisation and starting trading was really easy – it was building the foundations that took time… People used to say to me that it would be a slow process setting up an organisation and that it would take time to build. I never believed them and thought I would be up to speed in a few months. The reality is that it took two to three years to get to a stage where I felt we were placing a good number of volunteers and that the organisation was running in a way that I was happy with. I see it like a wine maturing: it takes time and actually, the slower you take things, the better they often are in the end.*

Even with the organisation up and running, Katherine was required to work 40 to 50 hours per week to make enough to fund the organisation's immediate overheads. Such long hours are common among people running aid organisations. Anthony Lunch, founder of MondoChallenge, works 'never less than 50 hours' per week and describes his biggest challenge as, 'The time it takes to do things the way they need to be done, when staffing is minimal and the activities are full on!'. Despite the hours he commits, he assures us that it's a labour of love rather than a road to wealth:

*I do not make a living from the charity. In fact nobody does, as there are no employees! However, I do earn my living from the MondoChallenge volunteer organisation (a not-for-profit company)… But the expression 'earn one's living' is somewhat of an exaggeration! Everybody employed at MondoChallenge is earning substantially less than the market rate and thereby making their own personal contribution to the work we do…*

# GOING INTO BUSINESS

With thousands of charities in existence, it is a sound idea to ask whether it's worthwhile establishing yet another one, as the need you're proposing to address may already be met by an existing organisation. A better alternative may be to plunge in solo with some hands-on action or an environmentally sustainable business.

Former youth ambassador under the Australian Volunteers for International Development (AVID) programme, Amber Rowe worked as a research development officer with the Centre for Environmental Awareness and Education (CEAE) in the Philippines, where she spent 12 months researching and writing an environmental education module with a local counterpart. The work she began greatly influenced her work practices and future direction. Amber created an environmental education portal with the assistance of a development internship, and also established the fair-trade business Trash Bags, offering an attractive range of environmentally friendly and ethical products made from recycled materials by livelihood and community organisations in the Asia-Pacific region. Amber says:

> Our collection of bags and homewares are made by community-managed and operated organisations who, by the creation and selling of these wonderful products, are securing a better future for their communities and our shared environment.

Consider at the outset how much time you have and how much you're willing to devote to your organisation. If you're planning to dedicate your 'free time' to it and work it in around your present job, think seriously about what you'll have to give up and whether you'd be willing to do this for an extended period of time. If you are placing volunteers overseas, it is not at all unusual for it become a seven-day-a-week job. As Alex Tarrant explains:

> When we are in England, it's usually about 40 to 50 hours a week, but there is a need to be flexible as we have volunteers overseas at all times of the year and need to be available at any time to provide assistance if required.

The amount of money you'll initially need varies immensely; the type of equipment you'll require, whether you'll need to pay rent or have administrative overheads all play a role. Initial set-up costs are almost always one of the biggest hurdles you'll have, with marketing and running costs quickly adding up. You might consider fundraising to cover the initial set-up cost, getting a bank loan or applying for a grant. See Getting Help (below) and Getting Funding (p300) for more on this. You may also want to pay an accountant to crunch your budget: a good accountant can set you up with a bank that is sympathetic to the needs of a fledgling non-profit organisation. Keep in mind that the not-for-profit scene is just as competitive as any industry, so being realistic about fundraising potential is crucial.

Penelope Worsley reflects on how she overcame the financial hurdles involved in setting up her organisation in Thailand and gives some invaluable advice:

*The only tip I would give is to suggest that you look around to see where support can be found… search out groups of people (expat groups or community groups in the UK, for instance) and talk about your work. Be very focused about what you need money for and make sure you know how the money will be spent. Tell the story! If the story is right, the money will come.*

# GETTING HELP

There is lots of help available out there – and there are organisations established for the very purpose of supporting, assisting and funding aid organisations and new businesses. Here are just a few options listed by region:

## UK Organisations

• **Association of Charitable Foundations** (☎+44 (0)20 7255 4499; www.acf.org. uk; London, UK) The ACF is the membership association for foundations and grant-making charities in the UK. For 25 years it has provided its more than 330 members with information and learning opportunities, as well as advocating for an enabling policy environment in which foundations and grant-makers can thrive.

• **Bond** (☎+44 (0)20 7837 8344; www.bond.org.uk; London, UK) Bond is a network of voluntary organisations that promotes the exchange of experience, ideas and information among its members both in the UK and internationally.

• **Business West** (☎+44 (0)1275 373373; www.businesswest.co.uk; Bristol, UK) Offers advice and support with all aspects of setting up, such as writing a business plan, recruiting staff, management and website design. It also hosts networking events and hooks you up with marketing opportunities.

• **Charity Commission** (www.gov.uk/government/organisations/charity-commission) The regulator and registrar for charities in England and Wales, this body also supports and supervises charities and offers sound advice to those starting up new organisations.

• **Companies House** (☏+44 (0)303 1234 500; www.gov.uk/government/organisations/companies-house; Cardiff, UK) The UK's regulator for registered companies, this organisation has a good selection of online booklets on company formation, regulations, administration, management and legislation. It also organises seminars to fill you in on your obligations for filing taxes.

• **Friends of the Earth England, Wales & Northern Ireland** (☏+ 44 207 490 1555; www.foe.co.uk; London, UK) A grassroots environmental network which unites dozens of diverse national member groups and thousands of local activist groups around the world to campaign jointly on environmental and social issues. Joining a group like this can add legitimacy to your organisation and give you some much-needed support.

• **Prince's Trust** (☏+44 (0)800 842 842; www.princes-trust.org.uk, London, UK) The Prince's Trust Enterprise programme provides support for young people under 30 interested in setting up a business. This includes workshops and guidance, a low interest loan and the support of an experienced business mentor.

## North American Organisations

• **Canada Revenue Agency** (www.cra-arc.gc.ca/chrts-gvng/menu-eng.html) This is the tax information site for charities in Canada.

• **Charity Village** (https://charityvillage.com) In Canada, check out this site for tips and links to relevant government authorities, helpful outfits and discussion forums.

• **Friends of the Earth USA** (☏+1 877 843 8687; www.foe.org; Washington DC and Berkeley, CA, USA). The American branches of this worldwide network of organisations can offer plenty of advice. There's also a Canadian group (see www.foecanada.org).

• **Foundation Center** (http://foundationcenter.org) Information on grant-seeking and a directory of foundations, as well as useful statistical information, publications and training courses.

• **Internal Revenue Service** (www.irs.gov/charities-non-profits) The IRS has all the details of tax exemptions for US non-profits online.

• **National Council of Nonprofit Associations** (www.councilofnonprofits.org) This group offers a wide range of assistance to up-and-coming organisations.

• **Starting a Nonprofit Organization** (http://managementhelp.org/startingorganizations/start-nonprofit.htm) Browse Carter McNamara's excellent online guide to starting a charity in the US for many useful resources.

### Australasian Organisations

• **Australian Aid** (http://dfat.gov.au/aid/pages/australias-aid-program.aspx) The latest information about Australian government's development policy.

• **Australian Council for International Development** (ACFID; www.acfid.asn. au) Some practical information under 'Facts and Figures' on how to start your own NGO, including accreditation procedures and the ACFID Code of Conduct.

• **Australian Taxation Office** (ATO; www.ato.gov.au/non-profit) The tax office's non-profit area is the place to learn more about charity tax concessions in Australia.

• **Friends of the Earth Australia** (☎+61 (0)3 9419 8700; www.foe.org. au; Collingwood, VIC, Australia) A useful resource, FoE supports various environmental and social campaigns. There is also an FoE New Zealand (☎+64 9 360 9149; foenz@kcbbs.gen.nz; Auckland, New Zealand).

• **Inland Revenue New Zealand** (http://www.ird.govt.nz/notforprofits) Tax information for New Zealanders.

• **Pathways Australia** (www.pathwaysaustralia.com.au) This group offers information, management and marketing services to not-for-profit organisations.

• **Philanthropy Australia** (www.philanthropy.org.au) The information hub for all things giving-related Down Under including the annual Giving Australia report.

# STATUS

Should you go for registered charity status, limited company status, or not-for-profit status? How about registering as a non-government organisation (NGO)? Deciding which form your organisation is going to take can be difficult. To legally register, and refer to yourself, as any particular breed of organisation you'll need to closely consider the requirements of each. There can be benefits to some; for instance, registering as a charity can give you favourable tax treatment and allow you to apply for funds not available to non-charities. Depending on tax laws in your country and/or state, having charitable status can also mean that donors can deduct their donations from their tax liabilities, and this can make a massive difference to the amount of money people are willing to give.

It's a good idea to seek professional advice on which status to apply for. Often, the best route is not the most obvious one. Catheryn Goodyer who helped established a clinic in the Himalayas explains her company's reasoning for not registering as a charity:

*We did not apply for charitable status. We enquired right at the beginning with the Charities Commission. Reading between the lines, we discovered that if your application is turned down, you, as an individual, are not allowed to apply again. The Charity Office also recommended that we run the clinic for at least a couple of years so that we had accounts to show. In addition, they recommended that we take on a charity lawyer to reduce the risk of having our application turned down, which is quite an expensive thing to do. The only reasons we could see for registering were for fundraising and tax purposes. As we have had no problems raising funds unregistered and most of our purchasing was carried out in India (where costs are very low and no VAT applies) and the clinic only needed a small amount of funding, we decided it wasn't worth spending the money on a lawyer.*

However, one reason for wanting to register as a charity is for the credibility that comes with it. For instance, a sending agency may be concerned that potential volunteers would prefer to sign up with a charity, as they're less likely to fear that profit motives might come before the desire to help overseas. If charitable status isn't quite on your horizon yet, an alternative is to become a company limited by guarantee, also known as a not-for-profit organisation. This means that the organisation's earnings must be directed towards defined, non-profit aims.

For some guided assistance in making your way through the status minefield, check out some of the organisations under Getting Help on p304. If necessary, consider enlisting the help of a lawyer familiar with non-profit law to assist with incorporation and tax matters.

## REWARDS

You may well ask yourself, 'What makes it all worthwhile?' The answer lies in that 'feel-good' factor. Alex Tarrant describes his most rewarding experiences in running a volunteering organisation:

*It's definitely two things: dealing with people who have chosen to volunteer their time; and working with small overseas projects and charities. Seeing the contribution that volunteers make, and the enjoyment and personal development they gain in the process, is fantastic. It's also wonderful to see how we have helped small projects and charities to grow and become stronger and, as a result, have enabled them to provide greater help to the communities they work in.*

# Acknowledgements
# & Indexes

This book was originally commissioned and managed by Bridget Blair and Will Gourlay in Lonely Planet's Melbourne office. This edition was overseen by Robin Barton and edited and updated by Matt Phillips in the company's London office.

## THANKS FROM THE AUTHORS

### FROM CHARLOTTE

I would like to thank my commissioning editor, Bridget Blair, for being so collaborative about the nature of this book and for being so lovely to work with. I'd also like to thank: all the returned volunteers whose words I have poured over endlessly (I even feel I know the ones I haven't met); our Special Advisors who gave up their time to meet me, help with the brief and who I'd call day or night with some thorny volunteering question that needed answering straight away; Jez Sweetland who offered invaluable advice about the charitable sector; David Orkin who checked the travel information in Chapter Three; John Masterson of Trailfinders who checked the visa section; and my husband, Simon, who took the girls to school as frequently as he could so I could get on and write.

### FROM NATE

I'd like to dedicate my work to my love Florence Chien, and thank her for bottomless reserves of patience, a ruthless eye for unnecessary verbiage, and the ability to bring me back to normal after a long day of being cooped up in my office. I'd also have been completely awash without the help of co-authors

Korina Miller and Charlotte Hindle and commissioning editor Bridget Blair. For the advice I'd like to thank John Ruiz, Matt Cavalieri and Matt Meuller. For the support, I'd like to thank Rob Harvilla, Garrett Kamps, Tommy Craggs, Matt Palmquist, Joe Hayes, Vanessa Kong, Cory Mescon, Ben Baumer and last but hardly least, Danny Palmerlee, who inspired me to work for Lonely Planet with his excellent Baja guide and kind advice.

## FROM RACHEL

My big thank you goes to all the independent volunteers who have shared their stories with me and to the grassroots charities and online directories for answering my questions. I am delighted that the book has received such a positive response. I am also very grateful to Charlotte Hindle for her support and advice.

## FROM KORINA

A big thank-you to Bridget Blair for including me in this challenging but very rewarding project. Also thanks to my co-authors and the publishing and production crews at LP. Special thanks to the countless organisations and volunteers who gave me their time, shared their insight and answered my unending questions; extra thanks to Anna Demant, Katherine Tubb, Alex Tarrant, Penelope Worsley, Catheryn Goodyer, Lennox McNeely, Kalene Caffarella, Anthony Lunch, the Teach Ghana Trust, Seattle University's Calcutta Club (particularly Lucas McIntyre), Matt & Polly Freer, Peggy Fussell, Katie Yewdall, Eileen Bennicke and Clare Wearden.

## FROM MIKE

Thanks go to my long-time friends for their encouragement, my Peace Corps colleagues for their inspiring example, and my parents and family for their constant support. You know who you are.

## FROM SARAH

A heartfelt thank you to commissioning editor and fellow yogi, Bridget Blair, and coordinating author, Charlotte Hindle, for being such a pleasure to work with. I am also grateful to the following people who aided my research: Andrew Criss; Andrew Jack; Belinda Williams; Brad Atwal; Cam Walker; Christine Crosby; Colin Salisbury; Danny McDowell; Erin Cassidy; Erin Green; Irene Bukhshtaber; James Nichols; John Webber; Marita Lofts; Rhodri

Wynn-Pope; Shona Jennings; Steve Bradbury; Tim Burns; Tim Prohasky; Terry Hoey and Veronica Culjak. Peter Hodge's Volunteer Work Overseas for Australians and New Zealanders was a helpful resource. Thanks to fellow RAYADs, Amanda Allen-Toland, Jacqui Pringle and Amber Rowe for sharing their thoughts, and a salute to the Intake 14 volunteers – a cool crew. Cheers to my extraordinary friends (what sànùk we did have) in Bangkok. And special thanks to Mum and Dad for letting me work from the holiday house (an oxymoron indeed) and making my transition from volunteering overseas that little bit smoother. As the late Audrey Hepburn wrote, we have two hands: one is for helping ourselves and the other is for helping others. Volunteers around the world are living proof of this.

## THANKS FROM LONELY PLANET

Special thanks to the following volunteers and organisation staff members who gave their time and enthusiasm to contributing to this book.
Amanda Allen-Tolland, Ryan Andersen, Sally Armbrecht, Catherine Baroun, Sharon Baxter, Peter Bennett, Eileen Bennicke, Michael Best, Benjamin Blakey, Liz Bodner, Jackie Bowles, Kalene Caffarella, Emma Campbell, Eoin Canny, Brenda Carter, Vikki Cole, Tabitha Cook, David Daniels, Kerry Davies, Sian Davies, Robin Dawson, Ben Donaldson, Robert Driver, Louise Ellerton, Samantha Elson, Ian Flood, Elizabeth France, Matt Freer, Polly Freer, Claire Fulton, Laurence Gale, Karla Gergen, Robin Glegg, Catheryn Goodyer, John Gordon, Gerrard Graf, Heather Graham, David Grassham, Amanda Guest-Collins, Rachel Guise, Michelle Hawkins, Karen Hedges, Jacqueline Hill, Katie Hill, Joan Hodkinson, Victoria Jaberi, Jordan Jones, Julie Jones, Deborah Jordan, Ben Keedwell, Kirsi Korhonen, Mike Laird, Richard Lawson, Claire Loseby, Anthony Lunch, Eoghan Mackie, Ben Martin, Elaine Massie, Peggy Melmoth, Oliver Middlemiss, Michele Moody, Jo Morgan, Clodagh Mullen, Gemma Niebieszczanski, Ann Noon, Clodagh O'Brien, Rachel Oxberry, Ele Ramsey, Kristine Randall, Martyn Roberts, Simon Roberts, Jason Rogers, Amber Rowe, Andrew Sansom, Poonam Sattee, Jo Shuttleworth, Sandra Sinclair, Jenny Smith, Dave Spinney, Judith Stephen, Antonia Stokes, Kate Sturgeon, Phil Sydor, Matthew Sykes, Alex Tarrant, Sue Towler, Michael Tuckwell, Diane Turner, Sarah Turton, Jan-Willem van Bochove, Oliver Walker, Linda Walsh, Clare Wearden, Maggie Wild, Tom Wilmot, Graham Williams, Nayna Wood, Penelope Worsley, Katie Yewdall

# INDEX

# Destinations Index

# Organisations Index

# DISCARD

## VOLUNTEER
### A traveller's guide to making a difference around the world

Published in August 2017 by Lonely Planet Global Limited
CRN 554153
www.lonelyplanet.com
ISBN 978 1 7865 7867 9
© Lonely Planet 2017
Printed in Singapore
10 9 8 7 6 5 4 3 2 1

**Managing Director, Publishing** Piers Pickard
**Associate Publisher** Robin Barton
**Editor** Matt Phillips
**Commissioning Editor** Bridget Blair
**Art Direction** Daniel Di Paolo
**Cover Design** Hayley Warnham
**Layout** Mariana Sameiro
**Indexing** Nick Mee
**Proofing** Tasmin Waby
**Print Production** Larissa Frost, Nigel Longuet

**STAY IN TOUCH** lonelyplanet.com/contact

**AUSTRALIA**
The Malt Store, Level 3, 551 Swanston St,
Carlton, Victoria 3053   ☏03 8379 8000

**USA**
124 Linden St, Oakland, CA 94607
☏510 250 6400

**IRELAND**
Unit E, Digital Court, The Digital Hub,
Rainsford St, Dublin 8

**UNITED KINGDOM**
240 Blackfriars Road, London SE1 8NW
☏020 3771 5100

Although the authors and Lonely Planet have taken all reasonable care in preparing this book, we make no warranty about the accuracy or completeness of its content and, to the maximum extent permitted, disclaim all liability from its use.

Paper in this book is certified against the Forest Stewardship Council™ standards. FSC™ promotes environmentally responsible, socially beneficial and economically viable management of the world's forests.